A Joseph Smith Chronology

J. Christopher Conkling

Prepared for BEI Productions, Inc., Los Angeles, California

Deseret Book Company
Salt Lake City, Utah
1979

Library of Congress Cataloging in Publication Data

Conkling, J. Christopher, 1949-
  A Joseph Smith chronology.

  Bibliography: p.
  Includes index.
  1. Smith, Joseph, 1805-1844—Chronology.
2. Mormons and Mormonism in the United States—
Biography. I. Title.
BX8695.S6C64   289.3'092'4 [B]   79-896
ISBN 0-87747-734-5

Contents

Introduction

This book began because of a personal need. Having heard the hundreds of inspirational and fascinating stories about Joseph Smith throughout our lives, it one day occurred to us that we knew almost nothing about him historically. We had no historical framework within which to place the many incidents of Joseph's amazing life. We did not understand how the events were connected with each other, or what other events were transpiring simultaneously. We thought that it would be useful for students, teachers, and researchers of the life of Joseph Smith to have a historical outline within which they could place these events. However, with the exception of the rather brief chronology printed in the annual *Church Almanac*, we could not find anything published since Andrew Jenson's chronology of 1914. We began to compile our own list, beginning with a few key dates per year.

Then the list grew.

After going through Joseph Smith's six volumes of personal history three times (plus the seventh by his successors), reading all the current biographies about Joseph Smith side by side, and studying dozens of other books and articles about him, we were able to put this chronology in its present form.

We were surprised to learn that most authors seem to agree on the basic facts. It was not where or when a certain revelation was given or decision made that was debated, but why it was given, what effect it had on the early Saints, and what outside influences might have affected Joseph's thoughts at that time. Each author seemed to have taken the known facts, surrounded them with historical and national environment, given more or less credence to earlier pro- or anti-Mormon claims, and then added his or her own interpretation and explanation of the motivations and effects of a certain event.

It therefore seemed that—in contrast—a chronological listing of those known facts, with as little personal interpretation as possible, might be a useful aid in the study of Church history.

We realize that in the case of a person as controversial as Joseph Smith, even the mere printing of "nothing but facts" is a highly subjective undertaking. Since it is impossible to print every fact, the mere selection of which facts to print will betray the bias of the compiler. We have included every date of major importance in Joseph's dealings as a religious leader (and numerous dates of minor importance). Such items as "sold a cow" or "sliding on ice" with the children, are included as random samples of the other kinds of activities that Joseph was involved in.

Of course the information included here is intended to be only a sketch. For details the reader will have to go to the many biographies available. (We have included an extensive bibliography in the back of this volume.) Probably most helpful in finding details on day-to-day events is the *History of the Church of Jesus Christ of Latter-day Saints,* by Joseph Smith himself. (Salt Lake City: Deseret Book, 1978.)

Key to Abbreviations

A&L James B. Allen and Glen M. Leonard, *The Story of the Latter-day Saints.*

BAPM Joseph Fielding Smith, *Blood Atonement and the Origin of Plural Marriage.*

BYS *Brigham Young University Studies* (various issues).

CEM Cecil E. McGavin, *Mormonism and Masonry.*

CHC Brigham H. Roberts, *A Comprehensive History of the Church* (6 volumes).

DCC Hyrum M. Smith and Janne Sjodahl, *The Doctrine and Covenants Commentary.*

DH Donna Hill, *Joseph Smith: The First Mormon.*

DLG *Dialogue: A Journal of Mormon Thought* (various issues).

DM David E. and Della S. Miller, *Nauvoo: The City of Joseph.*

EE Hugh Nibley, *The Message of the Joseph Smith Papyri: An Egyptian Endowment.*

ENS *Ensign* (various issues).

FMG Francis M. Gibbons, *Joseph Smith: Martyr, Prophet of God.*

FMM F. Mark McKiernan, *The Voice of One Crying in the Wilderness: Sidney Rigdon. Religious Reformer 1793-1876.*

FWK Francis W. Kirkham, *A New Witness for Christ in America* (2 volumes).

HA Hyrum L. and Helen Mae Andrus, *They Knew the Prophet.*

HC	*History of the Church of Jesus Christ of Latter-day Saints* (7 volumes).
HHB	Howard H. Barron, *Orson Hyde: Missionary—Apostle—Colonizer.*
HS	Harold Schindler, *Orrin Porter Rockwell: Man of God, Son of Thunder.*
IE	*Improvement Era* (various issues).
IJB	Ivan J. Barrett, *Joseph Smith and the Restoration.*
JD	*Journal of Discourses* (26 volumes).
JFS	Joseph Fielding Smith, *Essentials in Church History.*
JSMS	Hyrum L. Andrus, *Joseph Smith: The Man and the Seer.*
KJH	Klaus J. Hansen, *Quest for Empire.*
KWG	Kenneth W. Godfrey, *Causes of Mormon Non-Mormon Conflict in Hancock, Illinois 1839-1846.*
LJA	Leonard J. Arrington, *Great Basin Kingdom: An Economic History of the Latter-day Saints.*
LMS	Lucy Mack Smith, *History of Joseph Smith by His Mother.*
NC	Jerry Burnett and Charles Pope, *Nauvoo Classics.*
NE	*New Era.*
OFW	Orson F. Whitney, *Life of Heber C. Kimball.*
OPJ	Elden J. Watson, comp., *The Orson Pratt Journals.*
PC	Paul R. Cheesman, *The Keystone of Mormonism.*
PHC	Pearson H. Corbett, *Hyrum Smith: Patriarch.*
PN	Preston Nibley, comp., *The Witnesses of the Book of Mormon.*
PPP	Parley Parker Pratt, *Autobiography of Parley Parker Pratt.*
RSG	Rodger S. Gunn, *Mormonism: Challenge and Defense.*
TFO	Thomas F. O'Dea, *The Mormons.*
TPJS	Joseph Fielding Smith, *Teachings of the Prophet Joseph Smith.*

ULR   *Utah Law Review* 9:4 (Winter 1965).

WC   James B. Allen and Thomas G. Alexander, *Man-chester Mormons: The Journal of William Clayton 1840-42.*

WEB   William E. Berrett, *The Restored Church.*

WMRM   William Mulder and A. Russell Mortensen, eds., *Among the Mormons.*

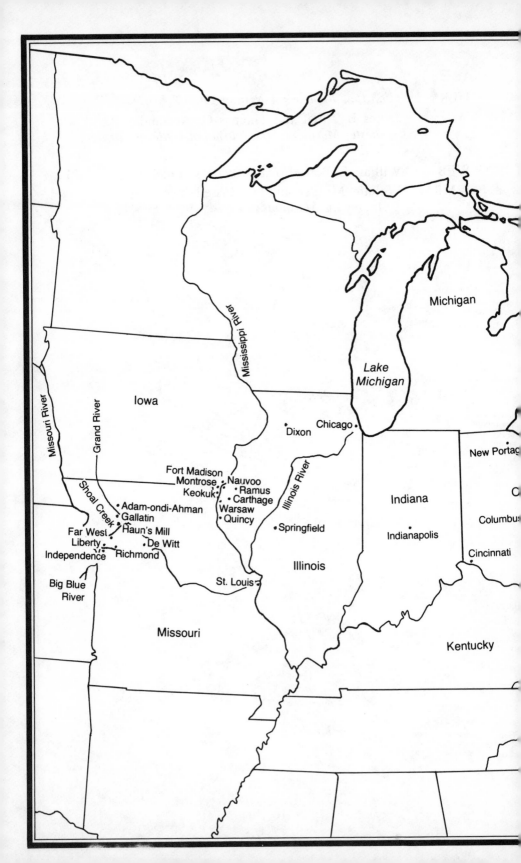

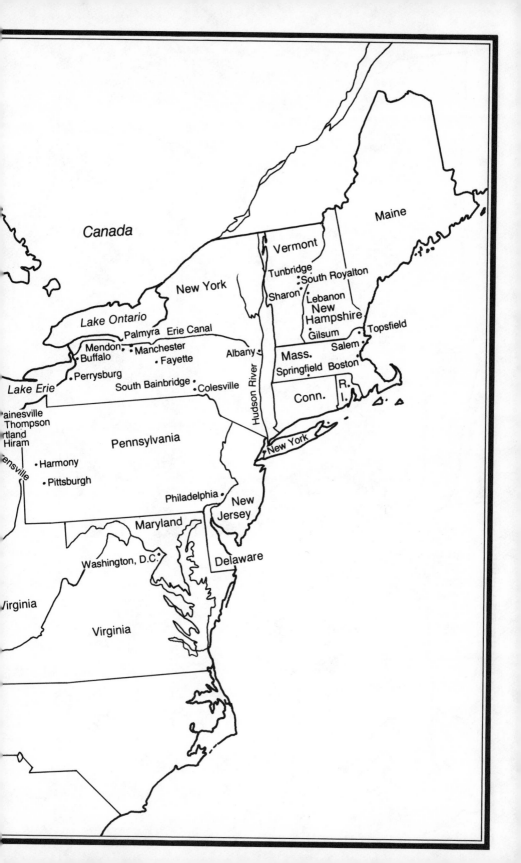

1771-1828

July 12, 1771
> Joseph Smith, Sr., is born at Topsfield, Mass.

July 8, 1775
> Lucy Mack Smith is born at Gilsum, N.H.

Jan. 24, 1796
> Lucy Mack and Joseph Smith, Sr., are married.

About 1797
> The first son of Lucy and Joseph Smith, Sr., is born and dies shortly thereafter.

Feb. 11, 1798/99?
> Alvin Smith is born at Tunbridge, Vt.

Feb. 9, 1800
> Hyrum Smith is born at Tunbridge, Vt.

May 18, 1803
> Sophronia Smith is born at Tunbridge, Vt.

July 10, 1804
> Emma Hale is born at Harmony, Pa.

Dec. 23, 1805
> Joseph Smith, Jr., is born at Sharon, Windsor County, Vt. (A good collection of various descriptions and opinions of Joseph's appearance and life's work are in CHC 2:344-61; FMG 349-65; HA 1-193.)

Between 1806 and 1808
> The Smiths move back to Tunbridge, Vt.

March 13, 1808
> Samuel H. Smith is born at Tunbridge, Vt.

1

Between 1808 and 1810
   The Smiths move to Royalton, Vt. Joseph attends school on Dewey Hill, taught by Deacon Jonathan Rinney.

March 13, 1810
   Ephraim is born to the Smiths at Royalton, Vt. He dies March 24, 1810.

Mar. 13, 1811
   William B. Smith is born at Royalton, Vt.

1811
   The Smith family moves to Lebanon, N.H.

Between 1811 and 1819
   Joseph Smith, Sr., has a series of seven dreams that he interprets as being from God.

July 8, 1812 (?)
   Catherine is born to the Smiths at Lebanon, N.H.

Winter 1812-13
   Hyrum returns home from an academy in Hanover, N.H., with typhoid fever, and most of the other Smith children catch it. Sophronia survives miraculously. As Joseph is recovering, his leg becomes seriously infected. The doctors suggest amputation, but he refuses and, without stimulants, endures as they cut into his leg and operate successfully. Although it is commonly believed that the man who operated on Joseph was an inept backwoods "barber-surgeon," the most recent research has shown that Dr. Nathan Smith at that time was "the only physician in the United States who aggressively and successfully operated for osteomyelitis and thereby prevented amputation." The complex operation given Joseph would not become standard procedure for another century. (See BYS, Sp '77, 319-37; ENS, Mar '78, 58-59.) Joseph uses crutches for several years and limps for life.

1814
   Joseph recovers from his leg operation and travels to visit his Uncle Jesse in Salem, Mass.

   The Smiths move to Norwich, Vt., for three summers of unsuccessful farming.

Mar. 25, 1816
   Don Carlos Smith is born at Norwich, Vt.

2

Summer 1816

Frost falls in the summer, killing the crops, and the Smiths decide to leave Vermont altogether. Joseph, Sr., goes ahead to find new land in New York and then sends for his family. After many problems they make it to Palmyra, Ontario County (now Wayne), N.Y. Palmyra has nearly three thousand people, and Joseph, Sr., works as barrel maker and bricklayer with his sons. Joseph, Jr., works in Martin Harris's fields for fifty cents per day. Lucy Mack Smith paints oilcloth coverings and makes maple syrup, root beer, gingerbread cakes, and boiled eggs to sell.

1818

The Smiths move a couple of miles south of Palmyra to a hundred-acre farm in Manchester.

1819-1820

Religious revivals. Joseph becomes excited about religion. (See BYS, Sp '69, 301-40; DLG, Sp '69, 82-93; DH 49; FWK 1:42-45.)

Spring 1820

The first vision. According to William Smith's testimony, Joseph had heard Rev. George Lane preach a sermon on "what church shall I join" and quoted James 1:5. (FWK 1:42-45.) Joseph ponders the scripture and decides to retire to a nearby grove, where he prays vocally for the first time. He feels the presence of Satan, continues to pray, and has the visitation of the Father and the Son, and is told to join none of the churches.

The first known record of the first vision was not made until 1831 or 1832. (Joseph was first commanded to keep records on April 6, 1830—D&C 21:1.) The well-known version was written in 1839. (For comparisons of the several early versions of the first vision, see BYS, Sp '69, 275-96; IE, Apr '70, 4-13.) The first vision was not taught publicly by the early missionaries and was not published until 1840 by Orson Pratt in England in his missionary tract, "Interesting Account of Several Remarkable Visions and of the Late Discovery of Ancient American Records." (DLG, Aut '66, 29-46; OPJ 465-83.)

July 18, 1821

Lucy, the last child of Joseph, Sr., and Lucy Mack Smith, is born at Palmyra, N.Y.

3

Sept. 21, 1823

Joseph prays for forgiveness for his "foolish errors" and "weaknesses of youth," and is visited three times during the night by an angel named Moroni. Moroni tells him about a hidden book and quotes scriptures from the books of Acts, Joel, Isaiah, and Malachi. Moroni's quotation of Malachi is recorded as D&C 2. (JS-H 1:28-47.) (According to Joseph's neighbors' later testimony, Joseph's "weaknesses of youth" consisted of fighting and drinking—DH 56.)

Sept. 22, 1823

Joseph tries to go to work in the fields, but can't, having been kept awake all night by the angelic visitations. His father tells him to go back to the house, but he faints on the way. Moroni appears again and commands Joseph to tell everything to his father. He does, and his father tells him to go to the place where the angel said the plates had been concealed. Joseph goes there, digs out a large rock with a stick lever, and tries to lift out the plates. He can't. Moroni appears again and explains that Joseph's thoughts have been lusting after wealth and fortune, and he cannot yet have the plates.

Nov. 19, 1823

Joseph's oldest brother, Alvin, dies from an overdose of calomel prescribed by an inept doctor.

Sept. 22, 1824

Joseph is again visited by the angel Moroni.

Sept. 29, 1824

The *Wayne Sentinel* carries Joseph, Sr.'s notice that he dug up Alvin's body on Sept. 25, 1824, to disprove the vicious rumors going around to hurt the Smith family that someone had opened Alvin's grave and mutilated the body.

Sept. 22, 1825

Joseph is again visited by the angel Moroni. (For the possibility of Joseph receiving visitations by other angelic messengers during these years, see FMG 38-39; JD 17:374; JD 21:94; HC 4:537.)

Oct. 1825

Joseph is hired by Josiah Stowell (Stoal) of Chenango Co.,

N.Y., to look and dig for a supposed lost Spanish buried silver mine. Joseph boards at the home of Isaac Hale and meets Isaac's daughter Emma. Their courtship is opposed by Emma's parents.

Nov. 17, 1825
About this time Joseph finishes working for Stowell and returns to work for his father.

Dec. 20, 1825
The Smiths run into financial difficulty, partially through the connivings of others, and are unable to come up with their final house payment. On this date, a Quaker, Lemuel Durfee, takes over ownership of the house, but allows the Smiths to keep residence in it for at least three more years.

Mar. 20, 1826
Joseph stands trial for being a disorderly person. Although some have claimed that Joseph was found guilty of using a seer stone for money seeking, the few known records are confusing, and it has never been substantiated exactly what he was charged with and whether or not he was found guilty. Joseph says that he became known as a money digger by working for Stowell. Apparently digging for treasures is very common in this time and place. The Palmyra newspaper in 1825 states that "we could name . . . at least five hundred respectable men who . . . believe that immense treasures lie concealed upon our green mountains, many of whom have been for a number of years industriously and perseveringly engaged in digging it up." Some claim that Joseph is connected with a man named Walters who charges $3 per day to locate buried treasure. (For this and other claims about Joseph's reputation during this time, see IJB 58-59; FWK 2:73-74; FMG 42-46; DH 65-68.)

Sept. 22, 1826
Joseph is again visited by the angel Moroni.

Nov. 1826
Joseph farms for Joseph Knight, Sr., of Colesville and becomes close friends with Newel Knight.

Jan. 18, 1827
Joseph and Emma wed. Joseph ("very lonely ever since Alvin died") and Emma (stating, "preferring him to any

other man I knew, I consented") leave Emma's home while her father is at church and elope to Squire Tarbill's in South Bainbridge. (BYS, W '74, 202; HC 1:17.) At this time Joseph has again been working for Josiah Stowell. After the wedding they return to the Smith farm in Manchester, where he works for the next season.

Aug. 1827
Joseph returns to Harmony, Pa., to be reconciled with Emma's father and to get her belongings. The 128-mile trip from Manchester to Harmony takes four days by wagon. Soon after, he returns to Manchester.

Sept. 20, 1827
Josiah Stowell and Joseph Knight, Sr., visit the Smith farm.

Sept. 22, 1827
Very early in the morning (just after midnight) Joseph and Emma take Knight's wagon and drive it toward the Hill Cumorah. Joseph is given the plates, Urim and Thummim, and the breastplate. Joseph hides the plates in a fallen hollow birch log and returns home in the morning. A few days later Joseph brings the plates home and devises several hiding places inside the house. When unfriendly visitors surround the house, the Smiths charge out of the house at night shouting military orders, as if the militia was present, to scare off the intruders.

Dec. 1827
After much harassment, Joseph decides to leave Manchester. Martin Harris gives him $50 for the trip, and Joseph and Emma, hiding the plates in a barrel of beans, set out. They are stopped along the way and searched, but make it successfully to Emma's parents. When Joseph refuses to show the plates to Emma's father, they are forced to move out; they move into a small house behind the Hale farm. Joseph eventually buys 13 1/2 acres from the Hales.

Dec. 1827-Feb. 1828
Joseph begins translating a few pages with Emma and her brother Reuben as scribes.

Feb. 1828
Martin Harris brings Hyrum to visit Joseph. Harris ob-

tains a facsimile of the characters and goes to New York City to get a scholarly opinion of them from Dr. Charles Anthon of Columbia University and a Dr. Mitchell. After the meeting, Anthon declares "I cannot read a sealed book." (See Isaiah 29:11.) Martin Harris returns convinced of the book's authenticity. (JS-H 1:63-65.)

Winter 1828

Joseph goes to Joseph Knight, Sr., for financial aid. Knight donates some provisions, a pair of shoes, and $3.

Apr. 12-June 14, 1828

With Martin Harris as scribe, Joseph translates the first 116 pages, sometimes called "the Book of Lehi." During this time, Martin's wife visits Joseph in Harmony for two weeks and badgers him about money and seeing the plates. When she finally returns home, she continues to pressure Martin to at least let her see the manuscript of the record. Joseph refuses twice, but upon the third inquiry to the Lord he is allowed to let Martin take the 116 pages upon the condition that he make a sacred oath to care for them and show them to only a specified few. Martin does this and leaves.

June 15, 1828

Joseph and Emma's first child, Alvin (Alva?), dies within a few hours of his birth. Emma is very ill. Joseph is in torment over the possibility of Martin's losing the manuscript.

July 1828

Three weeks after Martin left, Emma recovered sufficiently to allow Joseph to return to Manchester to learn what happened to Martin and the manuscript. Joseph learns that Martin has lost it and goes through the torments of hell. The Urim and Thummim is taken from Joseph so that he cannot translate. Shortly thereafter, a heavenly messenger returns it to him and through it Joseph receives D&C 3.

Summer 1828

The Urim and Thummim and the plates are taken from Joseph again. Shortly thereafter they are returned and Joseph receives D&C 10. (Some claim that this revelation was given in May 1829—see DLG, W '66, 124.) Joseph returns to Harmony and begins to farm.

Sept. 22, 1828
Joseph's mother says this is the day he was given back the Urim and Thummim.

1829

Jan. 1829

Joseph Knight, Sr., takes Joseph Smith, Sr., and Samuel H. Smith in a sleigh to visit Joseph in Harmony. Knight gives Joseph some money with which to buy paper.

Feb. 1829

During his father's visit, and for him, Joseph receives D&C 4.

Mar. 1829

Martin requests a revelation and Joseph receives D&C 5. By this time, with Emma as scribe, Joseph has translated only 16 pages.

Apr. 5, 1829

Oliver Cowdery hears about Joseph Smith and goes to Harmony to meet him.

Apr. 7, 1829

Joseph begins to translate once again, with Oliver Cowdery as scribe.

Apr. 1829

Joseph receives a revelation (D&C 6) through the Urim and Thummim for Oliver Cowdery. Oliver confesses that he has prayed for a witness about the plates; the revelation is an answer to his prayers. Joseph and Oliver have a difference of opinion about John the apostle—did he die or continue to live? Joseph prays and through the Urim and Thummim receives D&C 7. They continue to translate and Oliver desires the power to translate. Joseph receives D&C 8. Oliver tries unsuccessfully to translate, and Joseph receives D&C 9.

Apr. and May 1829

Joseph and Oliver continue to translate throughout the month of April. After a while local townspeople begin to gather and form into mobs, but they are counteracted by the influence of the Hale family, who have recently become more friendly toward Joseph.

May 15, 1829

The Aaronic Priesthood is restored by John the Baptist. Joseph baptizes Oliver and Oliver then baptizes Joseph. Joseph is to be called the first Elder of the Church and Oliver is to be called the second.

May 25, 1829

Samuel H. Smith, Joseph's younger brother, visits Joseph in Harmony, becomes convinced of the truthfulness of the gospel, and is baptized.

Soon afterwards Hyrum Smith visits, and Joseph, through the Urim and Thummim, receives D&C 11. Shortly thereafter, Joseph Knight, Sr., travels 30 miles from Colesville to bring such supplies as lined writing paper, grain, mackerel, potatoes, and tea, enough to last until they are finished translating. For Knight, Joseph receives D&C 12.

June 1829

Joseph inquires of the Lord concerning his "zealous friends and assistants in the work," the Whitmers. Joseph receives D&C 14 for David Whitmer; D&C 15 for John Whitmer; and D&C 16 for Peter Whitmer, Jr. Joseph and Oliver baptize Hyrum Smith and David and Peter Whitmer in Seneca Lake.

About June 1, 1829

Joseph and Oliver move to the Peter Whitmer home in Fayette (Waterloo), Seneca Co., N.Y. Oliver has been writing to his friend David Whitmer about the progress of the translation, and when the people around Harmony start giving them trouble, Oliver asks David for assistance. David, finding his fields miraculously plowed during the night, sets out in a wagon to bring Joseph and Oliver to the Whitmer home. Joseph continues here until the translation is complete, being supplied free room and board by the generous Whitmer family. Oliver is the primary scribe. As to the manner of translation, Joseph's most elaborate statement was, "Through the medium of the Urim and Thummim I translated the record by the gift and power of God." (HC 4:537.) He also stated in 1831, "it was not intended to tell the world all the particulars of the coming forth of the Book of Mormon." (HC 1:220.) Some contemporaries such as Emma Smith, Martin Harris, and David Whitmer did, however, explain the mode of translation in more detail. (See CHC 1:127-33; FWK 1:70, 190-206; DH 73-74; EE 50-51; PN 29, 80; PC 39-56; JSMS 101-2.)

June 11, 1829

Joseph deposits the title page and obtains the copyright.

June 26, 1829

E. B. Grandin, having turned down an offer to publish the Book of Mormon, publishes the title page in the *Wayne Sentinel.*

Late June 1829

After reading in the Book of Mormon about three witnesses (Ether 5:2-4, 2 Nephi 11:3), Oliver Cowdery, David Whitmer, and Martin Harris ask Joseph to inquire of the Lord to see if they can be those three witnesses. Joseph receives D&C 17, saying they may if they rely on the word of the Lord with "full purpose of heart." "Not many days after" Joseph and the three retire to the woods to pray for the witness. After much prayer they are visited by an angel who shows them the plates. They draw up "The Testimony of the Three Witnesses" and sign it. (HC 1:54-57.) Joseph exclaims, "Now they know for themselves, that I do not go about to deceive the people, and I feel as if I was relieved of a burden which was almost too heavy for me to bear, and it rejoices my soul, that I am not any longer to be entirely alone in the world." (LMS 152.)

"Soon after" eight other witnesses also see and handle the plates. (HC 1:57-58.) "Meantime we continued to translate, at intervals." (HC 1:59.) Joseph and Oliver, anxious to receive the promised Melchizedek Priesthood, pray about it in Father Whitmer's home. In conjunction with this, Joseph receives D&C 18, in which Oliver and David are called to help determine who the Twelve Apostles should be.

Between May 15, 1829, and April 1830 (probably June 1829)

The Melchizedek Priesthood is restored to Joseph and

Oliver by Peter, James, and John. They ordain Joseph and Oliver to the higher priesthood and holy apostleship.

July 1, 1829

According to David Whitmer, the translation at the home of his parents began June 1, 1829, and was completed July 1, 1829. After the translation is completed, Oliver Cowdery copies an entire second manuscript in case of robbery or destruction of the first.

July-Aug. 1829

Joseph tries to get a printer for the book. Having been turned down by E. B. Grandin, publisher of the *Wayne Sentinel,* Joseph goes to Thurlow Weed, who also turns him down, and then to Elihu F. Marshall, who agrees to publish it if proper security is guaranteed. Grandin then consents to do the printing if Martin Harris will guarantee payment.

Aug. 25, 1829

A contract is drawn up with Grandin to print 5,000 copies of the book for $3,000. Martin Harris mortgages his farm to Grandin, agreeing to pay the full amount within 18 months or Grandin can sell the farm.

John H. Gilbert, who set the type, said the book was printed between August 1829 and March 1830. Joseph instructs Cowdery to be very careful with the manuscript: he is to make a second copy, allow only one copy out of his hands at a time, deliver only a few pages at a time—with a guard (Hyrum Smith delivered the first 24 pages, having hidden them under his vest), and leave a guard on duty day and night.

Summer 1829

As soon as 64 pages are printed up, Solomon Chamberlain takes the printed but unbound pages and heads on a mission of 800 miles through Canada (probably the first mission of the Church) telling people to prepare for the coming forth of the full Book of Mormon. When the translation is completed, Joseph returns the plates to the angel Moroni.

Sept. 2, 1829

A new paper, the *Reflector,* begins publication in Palmyra. Abner Cole, using the name Obadiah Dogberry, begins this paper to fight against Mormonism and to discourage the sale of the forthcoming book. Since Cole is printing at the Grandin press, he easily gets copies of printed pages of the Book of Mormon and, beginning in January 1830, publishes whole sections of "Joe Smith's Gold Bible." The matter is eventually submitted to arbitration and Cole is forced to stop printing.

1830

Jan. 2, 11, 13, 22, 1830

The *Reflector* publishes plagiarized sections of "The First Book of Nephi" and "Alma."

Winter 1830

According to David Whitmer, when Martin Harris has problems raising the money to pay for the printing, Hyrum suggests that they go to Canada and sell the copyright. Hyrum asks Joseph, and Joseph receives a revelation that agrees. When Hiram Page and Oliver return from Toronto, having been unsuccessful, they ask Joseph why the revelation failed, and he says, "Some revelations are of God; some revelations are of men; and some revelations are of the devil." (CHC 1:162-66.)

Mass meetings are held in Palmyra to boycott the printing of the book, and Grandin becomes so nervous about his money that he suspends printing. Joseph returns to Palmyra to urge Martin to pay the printer in full, but Martin's wife is opposed, so he refuses.

Mar. 1830

Joseph receives D&C 19, in which Martin Harris is told to repent and pay his debt to the printer.

Mar. 26, 1830

The *Wayne Sentinel* announces that the Book of Mormon has been published and advertises its sale. Within a few days, Martin Harris is on the streets of Palmyra, trying to sell copies for $1.25. Harris is by now legally separated from his wife. As soon as the books are printed, Solomon Chamberlain takes eight or ten copies and goes on a preaching mission, selling one. On this mission he meets

Brigham and Phinehas Young at a reformed Methodist conference.

Mar. 29, 1830
Hyrum and Samuel Smith are suspended from the local Presbyterian church for nonattendance.

Apr. 1830
Joseph receives D&C 20.

Apr. 6, 1830
The "Church of Jesus Christ" is officially organized in the home of Peter Whitmer, Sr., in Fayette, N.Y. Although about thirty people are present, only six—Joseph, Oliver, Hyrum Smith, Peter Whitmer, Jr., Samuel H. Smith, and David Whitmer—become the first legal members of the Church. After prayer, they sustain Joseph and Oliver, who ordain each other to the office of elder in the Church. The sacrament of bread and wine is passed. They lay their hands on each member of the Church for the gift of the Holy Ghost and confirmation as a member of the Church. Some prophesy and all praise the Lord and rejoice exceedingly. Joseph receives D&C 21.

They ordain the other brethren to various offices and leave the house, go to the river, and baptize several, including Joseph's parents, Martin Harris, and Orrin Porter Rockwell. (A&L 47 explains the changes in the name of the Church until it reached the present name— see May 3, 1834, and April 26, 1838. ENS, Jan '71, 39-56, carries excellent paintings of the events on this day.)

Apr. 9, 1830
W.W. Phelps, an anti-Masonic newspaper publisher, buys a Book of Mormon. He later meets Joseph, determines to join the Church, is thrown into prison by some Presbyterian traders to keep him from it, and is finally baptized a year later.

Apr. 11, 1830
First Sunday meeting is held at the home of Peter Whitmer, Sr. Oliver Cowdery gives the first public discourse since the organization of the Church. Six persons are baptized.

Apr. 18, 1830
Seven more are baptized by Oliver Cowdery.

Apr. 1830

Joseph receives D&C 22 and 23. He visits the Knights in Colesville, N.Y. After several meetings, Newel Knight cannot bring himself to pray vocally. He returns from the woods, where he attempted—unsuccessfully—to pray, and his limbs and face become very distorted; he is tossed around the room under the power of Satan. Joseph lays his hands on him and rebukes the devil in the name of Christ, and Newel is healed miraculously in the presence of eight or nine neighbors. This is the first miracle in the Church.

Sometime between June 1830 and Oct. 1830

Joseph begins his translation of Genesis 1:1—5:8, which is now Pearl of Great Price, Moses 2:1—5:43a.

May 1830

Newel Knight visits Joseph Smith in Fayette, N.Y., and is baptized one week after the miracle.

June 1830

The *Reflector* publishes a series of anti-Book of Mormon articles, satirizing it under the title "The Book of Pukei." (See FWK 1:266-98.)

June 9, 1830

The first conference of the Church is held in the Whitmer home, Fayette, N.Y. About 30 attend and the power of the Holy Ghost is manifested; many prophesy, see visions, etc. Shortly thereafter, 11 are baptized, including three of Joseph Smith's siblings.

June 27-28, 1830

The Prophet visits Colesville and the Knight family. On Sunday they dam up the river to baptize over a dozen people, but a mob gathers and tears the dam down, threatening persecution and harm. Early Monday morning the Saints dam up the river again and baptize thirteen people, including Emma Smith. A mob of 50 surround them and watch.

June 28, 1830

During an evening meeting to confirm new members, Joseph is arrested for disorderly preaching. He is taken to trial in South Bainbridge, five miles from Colesville, where James Davidson and John Reid defend him. Josiah

Stowell, his former employer, testifies in his behalf. (J. Stowell was a loyal supporter of Joseph although he never moved west with the Saints—he was 61 and had extensive land holdings.) Immediately after Joseph is acquitted in the first trial, he is arrested a second time, taken back to Colesville, and tried again. After the gathering of a mob and a good deal of alarm, he is again acquitted. Joseph writes that during the trials the Lord comforted the Saints by revealing a "precious morsel": Moses 1:1-42, "The Visions of Moses." (HC 1:98-101.)

June 30, 1830

Samuel H. Smith sets out on one of the first Church missions, trying to sell the Book of Mormon. After much discouragement, he leaves one at the home of John P. Green, the brother-in-law of Brigham Young. He also leaves one with Phinehas H. Young, a brother of Brigham.

July 1830

Joseph and Oliver farm in Harmony, Pa. During this time Joseph receives D&C 24, 25, and 26.

Aug. 1830

Joseph begins to arrange and copy the revelations he has received to date. Oliver moves to the Whitmer home in Fayette, N.Y., and writes Joseph a letter stating that D&C 20:37 is in error and commanding Joseph in the name of God to change it. Joseph goes to the Whitmer home and talks with the Whitmers and Oliver, convincing them that the verse is acceptable.

About this time Isaac Hale, Emma's father, is convinced by a Methodist preacher that Joseph is an imposter. Newel Knight and wife visit Joseph Smith for Knight's confirmation. Joseph sets out to buy wine for the sacrament; he meets a heavenly messenger and is told not to buy wine or strong drink from his enemies. (D&C 27; the first four paragraphs were written in August and the remainder was written in September.)

Joseph and the Whitmers visit the Colesville Branch. They pass miraculously unrecognized through a hostile mob. Since there is also persecution in Harmony, Joseph and his family move to the Whitmer home in Fayette.

Aug. 31, 1830

Hyrum Smith arrives in Fayette, having walked twenty-five miles with a man named Parley P. Pratt, who borrowed a Book of Mormon from a Baptist deacon named Hamblin and read it excitedly. He has now come to N.Y. wanting to meet the Prophet.

Sept. 1830

Hiram Page has been receiving revelations through a seer stone and has convinced Oliver Cowdery and the Whitmers that these were true revelations from the Lord. In response to this Joseph receives a revelation to Oliver Cowdery. (See D&C 28.) Later, in the presence of six elders, Joseph receives D&C 29.

Sept. 1, 1830

Parley P. Pratt is baptized by Oliver Cowdery.

Sept. 19, 1830

Parley P. Pratt baptizes his brother Orson on Orson's nineteenth birthday.

Sept. 26-29, 1830

The second conference of the Church is held at Fayette, N.Y., 62 members attend. On the first day there is much disagreement and discussion about Hiram Page's seer stone but the Church votes unanimously to sustain Joseph Smith. Joy unspeakable and the manifestations of the Holy Ghost attend the three-day conference. During this conference Joseph receives revelations for John, David, and Peter Whitmer, Jr., and Thomas B. Marsh. (See D&C 30, 31.)

Fall 1830

After the conference Hyrum goes to Colesville with his family on his mission. The day he leaves, Joseph Smith, Sr., is imprisoned because of a $14 debt owed to a Quaker. The man offers to forgive the Prophet's father if he will renounce the Book of Mormon, but he refuses. A mob threatens the home of Lucy Mack Smith, but she is saved when 19-year-old William returns and scares the mob away. Joseph, Sr., ends up spending 30 days in jail, but he preaches the gospel while there and converts two men.

Oct. 1830

Joseph receives D&C 32, instructing Parley P. Pratt and Ziba Peterson to accompany Oliver Cowdery and Peter Whitmer on their mission to the Lamanites in the wilderness. These four missionaries leave and preach to Indians near Buffalo, then travel 200 miles until they reach the area of Kirtland, Ohio. Joseph also receives D&C 33.

Oct. 15, 1830

The four missionaries arrive in Mentor, Ohio, and introduce the gospel to Sidney Rigdon. Within a week they preach in Mentor, Euclid, and Kirtland and baptize 17. Sidney Rigdon refuses to debate his former follower, Parley P. Pratt, but agrees to study the Book of Mormon alone, and after two weeks Rigdon also is converted.

Oct. 21, 1830

Joseph translates Gen. 5:28-37, which becomes Moses 5:43-51. The translation of Genesis continues sporadically throughout the following three years.

Oct. 31, 1830

The four missionaries in Kirtland move from Sidney Rigdon's home to the communal family farm of Isaac Morley and there confirm a dozen more members in the Church in Kirtland.

Nov. 4, 1830

Orson Pratt comes to meet Joseph. Joseph receives D&C 34 for him.

Nov. 7, 1830

Missionaries confirm about 30 more new members in Mayfield, Ohio. By this time they have also baptized Sidney Rigdon's friend John Murdock and Dr. Frederick G. Williams, who gives them cash and a horse and accompanies them on their mission to the Lamanites.

About Nov. 20, 1830

The missionaries leave three branches of the Church in Ohio, having baptized about 130 people. Kirtland is presided over by Lyman Wight (another former follower of Rigdon), Warrensville by John Murdock, Mentor by Sidney Rigdon. (The one disciple of Rigdon whom they were not able to convert was Orson Hyde, who preached against the Book of Mormon for awhile and was not baptized until Oct. 30, 1831.)

Dec. 10, 1830

Sidney Rigdon and Edward Partridge, a successful

Painesville hatter, arrive in Fayette from Kirtland to meet Joseph. Joseph later writes that Partridge is "a pattern of piety and one of the Lord's great men." (HC 1:128.)

Dec. 11, 1830

Joseph baptizes E. Partridge. (HC 1:129.)

Mid-Dec. 1830

In response to a visit from Sidney Rigdon and Edward Partridge (see Dec. 10, below), the Lord reveals to Joseph D&C 35 and 36. To encourage the small flock of 70 members in Colesville and surrounding areas, the Lord reveals to Joseph some of the lost books of the Bible. Joseph records the Prophecy of Enoch (what is now Moses 7:1-69). Joseph also receives D&C 37.

1831

Jan. 1831

After traveling almost 1500 miles, the missionaries reach the borders of the Lamanites in Independence, Mo., "after much fatigue and some suffering," and having preached to many tribes of Indians along the way. (See PPP 48-52.)

Jan. 2, 1831

The third conference of the Church is held in Fayette, N.Y., at which time D&C 38 is given.

Jan. 5, 1831

Joseph receives D&C 39 for James Covill, and D&C 40, about Covill.

Late Jan.-Feb. 1, 1831

Joseph, Emma, Sidney Rigdon, and Edward Partridge leave for Ohio in a sleigh. They arrive February 1, and stay in the house of Newel K. Whitney in Kirtland. Joseph recognizes Whitney immediately, although they have never met, explaining that he has seen him in a vision.

Feb. 4, 1831

Isaac Morley has been experimenting with his "common stock" farm for two years. It was called "the family" and they held all things in common. Because of the disharmony that was beginning to emerge, Joseph encourages them to abandon "the family" in favor of "the more perfect law of the Lord." Joseph receives D&C 41, in which Edward Partridge is called to be the first bishop of the Church. (See HC 1:145-48.)

Feb. 9, 1831

In the presence of twelve elders at Kirtland, Joseph receives D&C 42, which introduces the law of consecration.

Mid-Feb. 1831

A woman named Hubble and a man named Hawley have been receiving revelations causing confusion among the Saints. In relation to this Joseph receives D&C 43. He also receives D&C 44.

Feb. 14, 1831

The missionaries in Missouri gather and decide to send one of their number back to Kirtland to visit the branches they organized along the way. P.P. Pratt is chosen and travels about 1,000 miles back to Kirtland, Ohio.

Mar. 3, 1831

Joseph writes Hyrum in Colesville telling him to bring the Saints to Kirtland as soon as possible. Hyrum departs at once, leaving Newel Knight behind to organize the Colesville Saints to come a month later.

Mar. 7, 1831

Due to many false reports, lies, and foolish newspaper stories, Joseph Smith receives D&C 45.

Mar. 8, 1831

Joseph receives D&C 46 and 47.

Mid-Mar. 1831

The Kirtland Saints inquire of Joseph about where the New York Saints will settle. Joseph receives D&C 48. Parley P. Pratt reaches Kirtland from Missouri to find hundreds of Saints now in the Church. At this time Leman Copley, of the sect called Shaking Quakers (Shakers), has joined the Church and Joseph receives a revelation about Leman's former sect. (See D&C 49.)

Apr. 7, 1831

Martin Harris finally sells his 151 acres for $3,000 to cover the Book of Mormon debt.

Apr. 7-June 19, 1831

Joseph is busy translating the Bible.

Apr. 30, 1831

Emma bears a twin son and daughter named Thaddeus and Louisa. They both die within three hours. John Murdock's wife bears twins the same day and she dies. Because Murdock has five other children, the twins are given to Emma to care for. Nine days later she adopts them. They are named Joseph and Julia.

May 1831

Parley P. Pratt returns from his mission to the Shakers in Cleveland, where they rejected the gospel message. As he travels through the branches of the Church, he finds strange spiritual manifestations, such as swooning, barking, contortions, cramps, fits, running around like Indians pretending to scalp each other, scooting on the floor, etc. He and several other elders go to Joseph to try to understand what these spirits mean. Joseph inquires and receives D&C 50. Elder Pratt, having been present when Joseph receives this revelation, describes it in detail. (See PPP 62.)

May 7, 1831

Oliver Cowdery writes a letter from Missouri explaining their work and success and trials among the Indians in that area. (For his speech to the Delaware nation, see HC 1:183-85.)

May 14, 1831

The Colesville Branch, including Joseph's parents and Orrin Porter Rockwell, arrives in Ohio from New York. (For details of the trip see LMS 195-208; BYS, Sp '70, 379-83.) To help Joseph relocate these Saints, the Lord gives him D&C 51. The Colesville Branch settles in Thompson, Ohio, on the thousand-acre farm of Ezra Thayre and Leman Copley. Joseph's parents stay on the Morley farm.

Winter or Spring 1831

Ezra Booth, a Methodist minister; John Johnson, and Johnson's wife and family visit Joseph Smith out of curiosity. Joseph heals Mrs. Johnson's lame arm miraculously. They are all converted.

Spring 1831

Joseph miraculously heals a lady named Chloe Smith.

June 1831

Several earthquakes occur in China and the newspapers carry a satirical story entitled "Mormonism in China" because a Mormon girl prophesied the event six weeks earlier. Because of the accuracy of the Mormon prophecy, Simonds Ryder joins the Church. (HC 1:158.) About this time Luke S. Johnson, Robert Raftburn, Sidney Rigdon, and others go on successful missions throughout Ohio, and the Church membership swells to two thousand.

Joseph receives D&C 53. At this time, the Saints from Colesville have been living the law of consecration and stewardship on land owned by Leman Copley in Thompson, Ohio. Copley apostatizes and begins to persecute the Saints. Newel Knight comes to Joseph seeking advice, and Joseph receives D&C 54. William W. Phelps and his family arrive in Kirtland, having been converted in New York, and seek Joseph's advice. Joseph receives D&C 55. Later he also receives D&C 56.

June 3-6, 1831
The fourth general conference of the Church is held in Kirtland, Ohio. Two thousand persons attend. The previous day Joseph prophesied that "the man of sin" would be revealed. After many evil manifestations of the spirit of Satan descending upon one member after another, Joseph rebukes Satan and many wonderful spiritual manifestations are experienced (including Joseph prophesying that John the Revelator is among the ten tribes and Lyman Wight seeing a vision of the Son sitting on the right hand of the Father). Elders are ordained as high priests for the first time in this dispensation. (HC 1:175-77.) The next day, June 7, Joseph receives D&C 52.

June 19, 1831
Joseph, Sidney Rigdon, Martin Harris, Edward Partridge, W.W. Phelps, Joseph Coe, A.S. Gilbert, and Gilbert's wife leave Kirtland for Missouri. They travel by way of Cincinnati, Louisville, and St. Louis, traveling by stage, canal boat, and the last 250 miles on foot. In Cincinnati Joseph visits with the Rev. Walter Scott, a Campbellite minister who denounces the Saints' beliefs in the gifts of the Spirit.

June 28-July 25, 1831
The Colesville Saints leave Thompson, Ohio, and make their journey to Missouri.

Mid-July 1831
Joseph's party arrives in Independence, Mo. There is a

glorious reunion with missionaries there. Jackson County population at this time is less than 3,000, and land costs $1.25 per acre. Joseph records that the people are nearly a century behind the times; Parley Pratt notes that they are still living in skins and very primitive conditions. (HC 1:188-89.) Because of the primitive land, Joseph wonders how Zion can ever be built in her glory in such a place, and receives D&C 57. The first Sunday after their arrival, W.W. Phelps preaches at the western boundary of the United States to a congregation made up of all races and peoples. Two are baptized.

July 17, 1831

W.W. Phelps, writing to Brigham Young in 1861, claimed that on this day Joseph taught the brethren that plural marriage was a correct principle. (DH 340.) Because Joseph had been translating the book of Genesis about this time, it is thought likely that he might have inquired of the Lord about the propriety of plural marriage as practiced by the ancient patriarchs. For other references indicating that 1831 was the year in which the doctrine of plural marriage was first made known to Joseph, see HC 5:xxix; CHC 2:95-101; FMG 285-86; A&L 69; JD 20:29.

July 25, 1831

The Colesville Branch of about 60 persons arrives in Missouri. Other Church leaders also arrive about the same time. Upon their arrival Joseph receives (on Aug. 1, 1831) D&C 58.

Aug. 2, 1831

Joseph and others help the Colesville Saints begin building their houses in Kaw Township, 12 miles west of Independence, by laying logs for their cabins. The first log is placed by 12 men to represent the laying of the foundation of Zion in Missouri. Sidney Rigdon dedicates the land for the gathering of Zion.

Aug. 3, 1831

The Missouri temple spot is dedicated by Joseph.

Aug. 4, 1831

The first conference in the land of Zion is held in the home of Joshua Lewis in Kaw Township. Fourteen elders and about 30 other members are present. The sacrament is passed and Joseph exhorts them all to righteousness.

Aug. 7, 1831

The funeral of Polly Knight, wife of Joseph Knight, Sr., is held. Polly prayed during her journey to Missouri that she might only be allowed to set foot on the promised land. Shortly after she arrives, she dies, being the first member of the Church to pass away. On the day of her funeral, the Lord tells the Saints through Joseph that those who live in the Lord and die in the Lord are given great promises. (See D&C 59.)

Aug. 8, 1831

Joseph receives D&C 60.

Aug. 9, 1831

Joseph leaves Independence in a canoe with ten elders. After several days of many dangers on the rivers, and after W.W. Phelps sees a daylight vision of the destroyer upon the waters, Joseph receives, on Aug. 12, D&C 61.

Aug. 13, 1831

Joseph meets other elders who have been traveling and preaching. He receives D&C 62, which encourages them.

Aug. 9-27, 1831

Joseph, Sidney, and Oliver travel back to Kirtland. At this time in Kirtland, the Saints want to receive the word of the Lord upon every subject, and therefore Joseph prays about the gathering and the purchasing of lands; he receives D&C 63.

Aug. 31-Sept. 1, 1831

James Gordon Bennett publishes two humorous but anti-Mormon articles in the *Morning Courier* and *New York Enquirer.* Bennett had visited among the Saints with a New York politician named Martin Van Buren and had recorded his thoughts of the "Mormonites" in his journal on June 29, August 7, and August 8, 1831. Bennett, who will become one of the most successful publishers in the nineteenth century, eventually publishes hundreds of more favorable articles about the Church and is called by Joseph Smith, ten years after this, "the high minded and honorable Editor of the *New York Weekly Herald.*" (HC 4:477-78.)

Sept. 1831

Joseph prepares to move to Hiram, Ohio (about thirty-five

miles south of Kirtland), to continue his work with Sidney on the translation of the Bible. In Hiram he stays at the home of John Johnson, a recent convert. A broadside is published containing Joseph's translation of Matthew 24. (It differs slightly from the present version found in the Pearl of Great Price.)

Sept. 11, 1831
D&C 64 is received.

Sept. 12, 1831
Joseph and his family move into the Johnson home in Hiram and there he prepares to recommence his translation of the Bible, working on Matthew 26:71a—Mark 8:44 until early November. A conference is held in which W. W. Phelps is instructed to buy a press and type in Cincinnati for the purpose of publishing a monthly newspaper in Missouri, to be called the *Evening and Morning Star.* The conference also votes to stop Ezra Booth from preaching as an elder. Booth was converted by a miracle when Joseph healed the arm of Mrs. Johnson, but had since apostatized. He is probably the first apostate to publish articles against the Church. Among other things, he accuses Joseph of lightmindedness, levity, jesting, joking, and having a hot temper.

Oct. 1831
Joseph receives D&C 65.

Oct. 11, 1831
A conference is held in Hiram, Ohio, at the Johnson home. The elders are instructed as to how meetings were held anciently.

Oct. 21, 1831
A conference is held in Kirtland, Ohio. Joseph and Sidney are sent there to settle the trouble caused by two brethren abusing one of Newel K. Whitney's children.

Oct. 25-26, 1831
A conference is held in Orange, Ohio. When the subject of consecrating one's worldly goods is brought up, Joseph volunteers that although he has no goods in the world to consecrate, he will consecrate himself and his family. Joseph also says, "God had often sealed up the heavens because of covetousness in the Church." (TPJS 9.) At the

request of William E. McLellin, Joseph prays and receives D&C 66, a revelation directed to McLellin.

Oct. 30, 1831

Orson Hyde, a clerk in the Gilbert and Whitney store and a former Campbellite preacher under Sidney Rigdon, is baptized in Kirtland. (HBB 29 gives this date: HC 1:217 places this occurrence on the first Sunday of October.)

Nov. 1, 1831

A conference is held in Hiram, Ohio. The Saints decide to print 10,000 copies of the Book of Commandments (the collection of Joseph Smith's revelations up to this date). Oliver is chosen to take the collection to Missouri for printing. Joseph receives the Lord's preface to the revelations, D&C 1.

Mid-Nov. 1831

Shortly after D&C 1 is given, there is some question and criticism about the language in the revelations, and Joseph receives D&C 67. In it, the Lord bears witness that the revelations are from him, and challenges the wisest among the elders to write a revelation on his own to see if he can duplicate Joseph's ability. After this revelation is received, McLellin tries to write a commandment but fails. Joseph records, "It was an awful responsibility to write in the name of the Lord." After this episode, the faith of the elders is increased, and they draw up a testimony to Joseph's revelations, which can be seen in D&C, p. iv. (HC 1:226.) Four elders inquire of Joseph the mind of the Lord concerning them, and he receives D&C 68.

Nov. 1-12, 1831

Joseph spends his time reviewing the Book of Commandments and attending four conferences within two weeks—the last held in Hiram, Ohio. The Church sustains the printing of the book, stating the revelations are worth the temporal riches of the whole earth. In answer to inquiry, Joseph receives D&C 70.

Nov. 3, 1831

The elders desire to know many things concerning the gathering and the preaching of the gospel; and in response to this, Joseph receives what is called an appendix to his former commandments, D&C 133. The Book of Commandments and Revelations is dedicated by Joseph's prayer, after which he receives D&C 69.

Nov. 15, 1831

The commandments are ready to be taken to Missouri for printing, and Oliver Cowdery and John Whitmer leave for Independence. Thereafter Joseph spends his time on translating the scriptures with Sidney Rigdon as scribe, which he calls "this branch of my calling." (HC 1:238.) Joseph does this until he receives D&C 71, which calls Joseph and Sidney on missions.

Dec. 3, 1831

Joseph and Sidney travel to Kirtland to begin their mission.

Dec. 4, 1831

Joseph and Sidney meet with the elders and members in Kirtland, and Joseph receives D&C 72.

Dec. 4, 1831-Jan. 8 or 10, 1832

Joseph and Sidney go on their missions to southern Ohio and throughout the state, preaching the gospel to counteract the anti-Mormon articles being written by Ezra Booth.

Dec. 19, 1831

In Independence, Bishop Partridge purchases 63 acres and 43 square yards for the Church for $130.

1832

Jan. 1832

Joseph recommences the translation, working until the time of the next conference. During this time he asks the Lord for an explanation of 1 Corinthians 7:14 and receives D&C 74.

Jan. 10, 1832

Until this time Joseph and Sidney Rigdon have been in the southern part of Ohio, preaching the gospel, after which they return to Hiram. Joseph receives D&C 73, telling the elders to continue preaching until their next conference.

Jan. 25, 1832

Conference is held at Amherst, Ohio. For the first time Joseph is sustained and ordained as President of the High Priesthood. He then receives D&C 75.

Feb. 16, 1832

Joseph returns to Hiram, Ohio, and continues translating the New Testament with Sidney Rigdon as scribe. While translating John 5:29, they wonder if there isn't some sort of gradation in rewards in the next life because of people's varied degrees of righteousness. In response to this question they receive a series of visions, known as D&C 76. About this vision Joseph writes, "The sublimity of the ideas; the purity of the language; the scope for action; . . . the rewards for faithfulness, and the punishments for sins, are so much beyond the narrow-mindedness of men, that every honest man is constrained to exclaim: '*It came from God.*'"

According to Philo Dibble, this vision was given in the

presence of about 12 others. Joseph and Sidney would stare into space. One would say "What do I see?" And then he would say what he was seeing and the other would say "I see the same"; and then they would repeat the process. At the end of the vision, Dibble reports that Joseph sat calmly and firmly while Sidney was pale and limp, and that Joseph remarked with a smile, "Sidney is not used to it as I am." Sidney stayed up that night recording the vision. (HC 1:252-53; HA 67-68.)

Feb. 16, 1832-Feb. 2, 1833
Joseph translates John 5:30-Revelation 22.

About Mar. 1, 1832
Joseph continues to translate the scriptures. In response to Joseph's questions about the Revelation of John, the Lord gives him D&C 77.

Mar. 3, 1832
Hyrum sells six copies of the Book of Mormon to a peddler and receives as pay ten yards of calico, some cotton cloth, four tin pans, some other tins, and a six-pound cheese. The normal price was eight books for $10, or two books for $2.50.

Mar. 8, 1832
Joseph ordains Jesse Gause and Sidney Rigdon to be his counselors in the Presidency of the High Priesthood.

Before Mar. 20, 1832
About this time several people apostatize from the Church and become enemies of Joseph. Simonds Ryder (see June 1831) leaves the Church because a note signed by Joseph and Sidney spelled his last name with an "i" instead of a "y." Ryder deduces that if the Spirit could be mistaken in spelling his name, it could also be mistaken in other matters it had given to Joseph. Leaving the Church with Ryder are Eli Johnson, Edward Johnson, and John Johnson, Jr. (three sons of John Johnson, Sr., in whose house Joseph was then staying). These men accuse the Prophet of immorality and of trying to steal their father's wealth by teaching him the law of consecration. In addition, Ezra Booth accuses Joseph of too much joking and jesting and of losing his temper. Perhaps for this reason, the Lord begins using pseudonyms in the revelations. As

31

Joseph continues to translate the Bible he receives D&C 78. Following that, he receives D&C 79, 80, and 81.

The original handwritten copy of D&C 81 mentions Jesse Gause as the one called to be the counselor to Joseph Smith, but his name has been crossed out and the name of Frederick G. Williams inserted. Although Elder Williams is called as a counselor to Joseph Smith at this time, he will not be set apart until March 1833.

About this time Joseph receives a letter from Missouri which states that the printing press is set up and ready to print the *Evening and Morning Star*. A prospectus of that paper is included.

Mar. 24, 1832

Joseph is sitting up late with his 11-month-old adopted son, who has the measles, when about a dozen men break into the house, drag the Prophet from the house, strip his clothes from him, and begin to pour hot tar all over his body. At this time he sees others of the mob pulling Sidney Rigdon from his house. Because Sidney is unconscious, Joseph supposes that he is dead and begins to plead for his own life. The mobbers break a vial of nitric acid against his mouth, trying to poison him. In the process they break a tooth, causing him to have a slight whistle for life. One man says, "That's the way the Holy Ghost falls on folks!" and jumps on Joseph, ripping off his remaining clothes and scratching his fingers into Joseph's skin. Joseph pulls the tar away from his mouth so he can breathe. Two men rush out of the house to help Joseph and, each assuming that the other is from the mob, start attacking each other. In this fight, the collar bone of John Johnson, Sr., is broken. When the mob finally flees, Joseph tries to return to the house; when Emma sees him she thinks the tar is blood and faints. Joseph spends the night with his friends, who pull and rip off the pieces of tar and skin. Simonds Ryder, the Johnson sons, and Ezra Booth are thought to have led the mob.

Mar. 25, 1832

The people assemble for Sunday worship and Joseph preaches a sermon, never mentioning the episode of the night before, even though he knows that several of the mob are in the audience. That day he baptizes three.

Sidney Rigdon, whose head was dragged across the

frozen and rough ground until he became unconscious from the tarring and feathering, goes delirious for several days. The morning after the tarring and feathering, he asks his wife for a razor with which to kill Joseph, and then asks Joseph for a razor with which to kill his wife. Several days later Sidney preaches that the keys have been taken from this people and will be given to another people. He also will not allow praying. Joseph eventually has to take away Sidney's preaching license until he repents and returns to a normal state of mind.

Mar. 29, 1832

Joseph's adopted son, Joseph Murdock Smith, dies from a cold caught when he was pulled from Joseph's arms during the mobbing. (Some claim this child was the first martyr in the Church; see BYS, W '74, 205.)

Apr. 1, 1832

Joseph leaves Hiram, Ohio, for Missouri with Newel K. Whitney, Peter Whitmer, and Jesse Gause. They go around Kirtland for fear of another mob. A mob does follow them as far as Cincinnati, 300 miles away. The Missouri Saints felt jealousy of the Kirtland Saints because Joseph had spent so much time in Kirtland and had picked so many of the leaders from there.

Apr. 4, 1832

Joseph buys paper for the newspaper being printed by W.W. Phelps. He sends Emma a letter telling her to stay at the Whitney store in Kirtland. However, when Emma arrives, an aunt who is visiting the Whitneys makes it impossible for her to stay there. During Joseph's absence she is shuffled from the home of one member to another; she is very lonely, having no place to stay and having just lost a child.

Apr. 14, 1832

Brigham Young is baptized, confirmed and ordained an elder in Mendon, N.Y. He also converts his brother Joseph, who later becomes president of the First Quorum of Seventy. Two days after Brigham's baptism, Heber C. Kimball is also baptized.

Apr. 24, 1832

Joseph arrives in Independence, Mo., by stage and greets the brethren there.

Apr. 26, 1832

A conference is held at which Joseph is acknowledged as the President of the High Priesthood just as he had been at the Amherst conference on the previous January. He receives D&C 82.

Apr. 27, 1832

Joseph transacts business to make the Saints more independent of their enemies, who seem to be moving in all around them.

Apr. 28-29, 1832

Joseph visits and enjoys a reunion with the Colesville Saints, who have settled in Kaw Township.

Apr. 30, 1832

Joseph returns to Independence and receives D&C 83.

May 1, 1832

A council of the Church meets in Independence and decides to print only 3,000 copies of the Book of Commandments (10,000 had originally been planned at the Hiram Conference of Nov. 1, 1831). W.W. Phelps is assigned to print the hymns selected by Emma Smith. It is decided that the Church stores in Kirtland and Independence should be joined as one firm, with a different company name for each.

Between May 6 and June 1832

Joseph leaves Independence with Sidney Rigdon and Newel K. Whitney and travels to Kirtland, mostly by stage. At one point in the journey the horses bolt; Bishop Whitney attempts to jump from the coach and breaks a leg. Sidney proceeds to Kirtland while Joseph and Bishop Whitney stay in Greenville, Indiana, for four weeks while the latter's leg heals. Joseph sets his leg and administers to him. At one point Joseph eats something poisonous and vomits blood so badly that he dislocates his jaw. Bishop Whitney administers to him at once and he is healed but loses much hair from his head. The day they are ready to leave, Joseph, as a seer, prophesies the events of the upcoming day, and they all come to pass.

June 1832

Joseph arrives back in Kirtland and spends most of the summer translating the Bible. The first issue of the *Eve-*

ning and Morning Star is published in Independence, with W.W. Phelps as editor. The press is 12 miles from the western boundary of the United States and 120 miles west of any other press in the country. Publication in Missouri continues until July 1833.

June 6, 1832

While staying in Greenville, Joseph writes a very personal letter to Emma, stating that he has visited a grove just out of the town almost daily to "give vent to all the feelings of my heart in meaditation and prayr I have Called to mind all the past moments of my life and am left to morn [and] Shed tears of sorrow for my folly in Sufering the adversary of my Soul to have so much power over me as he has had in times past but God is merciful and has forgiven my Sins and I rjoice that he Sendeth forth the Comforter unto as many as believe and humbleeth themselves before him. . . . God is my friend in him I shall find comfort I have given my life into his hands I am prepared to go at his Call I desire to be with Christ I Count not my life dear to me only to do his will. . . ." (BYS, Su '71, 517-20; for other personal notes by Joseph Smith, see ENS, Ap '77, 11.)

July 1832

The second issue of the *Evening and Morning Star* is published, stating that Zion (Missouri) is too poor and that the Saints should not come from Ohio without consulting with their local bishop.

July 20, 1832

Frederick G. Williams commences working as Joseph's scribe, and continues until January 1836.

July 1832

The *Upper Missouri Advertiser* begins publication by W. W. Phelps as a weekly paper for the Missouri Saints.

Aug. 1, 1832

Jesse Gause sets out on an eastern mission with Zebedee Coltrin.

Aug. 19, 1832

Zebedee Coltrin returns to Kirtland because of illness. Jesse Gause (set apart as Joseph's counselor on March 8, 1832) continues east and soon disappears from all Church history records.

Sept. 22-23, 1832

At this time many pairs of elders are returning from their successful eastern missions, and Kirtland is filled with great joy. Joseph and six elders receive D&C 84.

Oct. 1832

Joseph settles pregnant Emma and adopted daughter Julia in a house (formerly a store) owned by Newel K. Whitney and A.S. Gilbert. Joseph and Bishop Whitney take a short trip to Albany, Boston, and New York. They negotiate a loan for $15,000 or $20,000 in goods for the Church's new venture of a general store in Kirtland. When Joseph returns to Kirtland he sets up the store, but it fails miserably because he is overly generous. If he turns down people's credit, they leave the Church; when he decides that the worth of a soul is more important than the worth of dry goods, he extends credit to almost anyone and the store soon fails.

Oct. 13, 1832

While in New York Joseph writes a very tender and personal letter to Emma showing his concern over her delicate health during the last stage of her pregnancy, and expressing his fascination with New York City. (See BYS, W '74, 205.)

Nov. 1832

The *Evening and Morning Star* announces that there are 830 members in Missouri.

Nov. 6, 1832

Joseph Smith III is born in Kirtland to Joseph and Emma after a very hard labor. Joseph is their first child to live. Just after the son is born the Prophet returns from his eastern trip.

Nov. 8, 1832

Brigham Young, Joseph Young, and Heber C. Kimball of Mendon, N.Y., arrive in Kirtland to meet Joseph Smith for the first time. They find him chopping and hauling logs in the woods. That evening they have a meeting, and during prayer Brigham begins speaking in tongues. Some ask Joseph Smith about it and he says it is the pure Adamic language. Joseph records this as the first time he has heard the gift of tongues in the Church. (HC 1:295-297.)

Summer 1831-Nov. 27, 1832

Sometime between these dates, the first part of Joseph's personal history is recorded by Frederick G. Williams. This record includes the first presently known written account of the first vision.

Nov. 27, 1832

Being concerned about the mechanics of the law of consecration as it is being practiced in Missouri, Joseph sends a letter to W.W. Phelps in Independence. Part of his communication is later published as D&C 85.

Dec. 1832

At this time there are many national troubles, especially between the government of the United States and the state of South Carolina. President Andrew Jackson's protective tariff has been opposed by South Carolina; and on Nov. 24, 1832, the legislature of South Carolina declares that as of Feb. 1, 1833, Jackson's tariff will no longer apply to that state, and that they will secede if President Jackson tries to enforce the law. On Dec. 10 President Jackson issues a proclamation against South Carolina and threatens to march forty thousand government troops against them. During this crisis, on Christmas day 1832, Joseph receives D&C 87, the Civil War prophecy.

Dec. 6, 1832

Joseph receives D&C 86.

Dec. 27, 1832

Joseph receives D&C 88, "The Olive Leaf which we have plucked from the Tree of Paradise, the Lord's message of peace to us." (HC 1:316.) The Saints are commanded to build a house to the Lord.

1833

Jan. 4, 1833

Joseph writes a long letter to New York newspaper editor N.E. Seaton. The letter explains the plan of God in the latter days, the coming bloodshed, and the reasons for the plagues that are covering the land (such as the Asiatic cholera). Joseph says, "I think that it is high time for a Christian world to awake out of sleep. . . . this is what has caused me to overlook my own inability, and expose my weakness to a learned world. . . . I step forth into the field to tell you what the Lord is doing, and what you must do to enjoy the smiles of your Savior in these last days." (HC 1:312-16.)

Jan. 14, 1833

A conference is held in the Kirtland Mills (Kirtland, Ohio). Orson Hyde and Hyrum Smith are appointed to write a letter to Zion (Missouri) telling the people not to complain against Joseph, to repent, that they are loved by the Kirtland Saints, and that the School of the Prophets will commence in two or three days. Joseph writes to W.W. Phelps in Independence, sending him D&C 88, the "Olive Leaf," and telling him to make the *Star* more interesting: "For if you do not render it more interesting than at present, it will fall, and the Church suffer a great loss thereby." (HC 1:316-17.)

Winter 1833

Joseph spends most of the winter translating the scriptures, sitting in conferences, writing letters, and attending the School of the Prophets. Brigham Young, Joseph Young, and Heber C. Kimball spend the same time on a mission to the area around Kingston, Canada. They baptize 45 persons and organize three branches.

Jan. 22-23, 1833
A conference is held with several high priests and elders. Joseph speaks in another tongue, as do other elders. The next day they assemble again and participate in the ordinance of the washing of feet. (See John 13:4-15.) Each elder washes his own feet and then Joseph washes their feet. Joseph receives a father's blessing from Joseph Smith, Sr. F.G. Williams then asks permission to wash Joseph's feet, and does so. They partake of the sacrament.

Jan. 24, 1833
According to Zebedee Coltrin, the School of the Prophets commenced on this day.

Feb. 2, 1833
On this day Joseph records, "I completed the translation and review of the New Testament, on the 2nd of February, 1833 and sealed it up, no more to be opened till it arrived in Zion." (HC 1:324.) It appears that Joseph translated Genesis 24:42a-Malachi 4:6 between this date and July 2, 1833.

Feb. 12, 1833
Joseph writes a second letter to Mr. Seaton (see Jan. 4, 1833) requesting that he publish Joseph's whole letter, not just part of it, as it has been given by a commandment of God.

Feb. 26, 1833
A solemn assembly is held in Zion (Missouri), to discuss D&C 88 and the various letters of Jan. 14, 1833.

Feb. 27, 1833
Joseph receives D&C 89. According to Brigham Young the School of the Prophets was meeting in Joseph's kitchen, a small room in the house attached to the store owned by Bishop Whitney. As the brethren would gather after breakfast, they would immediately light their pipes, filling the room with smoke, or they would begin to chew tobacco, spitting it on the floor. After the complaints of his wife, Joseph prayed about the problem and received the above revelation. (See JD 12:157-58.) (For the health fads of the day, see A&L 95.)

Mar. 8, 1833

Joseph receives D&C 90.

Mar. 9, 1833

Joseph has come to the portion of the scriptures called the Apocrypha, and wonders whether or not to translate it. He receives D&C 91.

Mar. 15, 1833

Brother Lake's preaching license is withdrawn because he claimed to receive revelations. He was under the influence of an evil spirit. The same day Joseph receives D&C 92.

Mar. 18, 1833

The School of the Prophets is held with great joy. Sidney Rigdon and Frederick G. Williams are ordained by Joseph to be members of the First Presidency. This is the first official organization of the First Presidency since the Church was restored. The sacrament is passed and Joseph promises that the pure in heart will see a heavenly vision; many do.

Apr. 1833

The School of the Prophets closes until fall.

Apr. 6, 1833

In Jackson County, Missouri, about 80 Saints gather at the ferry on the Big Blue River on the Jackson County border line to celebrate and worship. They rejoice in the fact that it is the third anniversary of the organization of the Church and 1800 years since the day Christ died. This is the first time the birth of the Church is celebrated. They also discuss, and publish in the *Star*, the signs of the last days, including the fact that 60 million people have died of the Asiatic cholera in the past 15 years.

Apr. 13, 1833

Joseph answers a letter to Brother Jared Carter stating that "it is contrary to the economy of God for any member of the Church . . . to receive instructions for those in authority, higher than themselves." (HC 1:338.)

Apr. 18, 1833

A mob of 300 "old settlers" gathers at Independence to decide on plans to destroy or expel the Mormons from Jackson County. After they spend all day trying to decide on various plans, their liquor gets the worst of them and they break up in a "Missouri row." These "old settlers," largely from the southern states, came to Jackson County before the Saints, and could not move on because anything west of Missouri had been designated by President Jackson as Indian territory. They watched with some resentment as ever-increasing numbers of the religiously oriented northerners flocked into Jackson County claiming that God had given the county exclusively to them. Acts of violence began as early as the spring of 1832, when the homes of some Saints were stoned and windows broken. In the fall of 1832, some haystacks were burned, houses shot into, and people insulted; and as recently as February 20, a mob of 50 or 60 men armed with whips and guns attacked at least one household. The group on this date constitutes the first organized resistance to the Mormons in Missouri.

Apr. 21, 1833
Joseph writes to the brethren in Zion, telling them not to print any of the new translation of the Bible in the *Star*, that it will be printed in a volume by itself, and the New Testament and Book of Mormon will be bound together in one volume.

Apr. 30, 1833
A conference of high priests is held in the schoolroom in Kirtland, and various business is attended to.

May 6, 1833
On this date Joseph receives D&C 93. He also receives D&C 94.

May 25, 1833
Joseph's uncle John Smith and cousin George A. Smith from Potsdam, N.Y., arrive in Kirtland. They are the only relatives of the family of Joseph Smith, Sr., who have thus far received the gospel, outside of Joseph's immediate family.

June 1, 1833
There is great excitement in Kirtland as the Saints anticipate the commencement of the building of the house of the Lord. Although the Church is very poor, a letter is sent throughout the Church asking for subscriptions for the house. Joseph receives D&C 95.

June 4, 1833

A high priests conference considers the matter of what to do with the French farm. Joseph prays and receives D&C 96.

June 5, 1833

George A. Smith hauls the first load of stone for the building of the temple. Others commence digging the foundation. (For stories of the great sacrifice and dedication made by all connected with the building of the Kirtland Temple, see WEB 125-27; OFW 67-70.)

June 6, 1833

A conference of the High Priesthood is held, and Orson Hyde is chosen as a clerk to the First Presidency.

June 25, 1833

Joseph writes to Bishop Partridge in Missouri about the law of consecration, stating that there must be a balance between the will of the bishop and the will of the people, that it must be done by the mutual consent of both parties. He also mentions plans for a second edition of the Book of Mormon.

The plat for the city of Zion is made known and the plan of temples is sent to the brethren in Zion. (See the description in HC 1:357-62. For an analysis of Joseph's city plan and of the later cities actually built by the Saints and a comparison of them to many other rural American city plans of his day, see BYS, W '77, 223-33.) Joseph says that when one city is full, they will build another, "and so fill up the world in these last days . . . for this is the city of Zion." (HC 1:358.)

Summer 1833

About 1200 Saints have gathered in Jackson County, Mo. The School of the Prophets was established there. P.P. Pratt writes that all is peaceful and plentiful, there are no law suits or broken promises, robberies, idleness, Sabbath breaking—"In short, there has seldom if ever, been a happier people upon the earth than the Church of the Saints now were." (PPP 93-94.)

July 1833

The *Evening and Morning Star* publishes an announcement titled "Free People of Color." So that any Mormon

Negroes can migrate into Missouri without being captured as slaves, the announcement quotes the law that allows free Negroes to come and go unhindered. The southern settlers in Missouri, whose animosities toward the Mormons have been building all along, are infuriated by this announcement. They join together to form a secret constitution to rid themselves of the Mormons "peaceably if we can, forcibly if we must." They accuse the Mormons of (1) pretending to claim personal revelations, miracles, tongues, and thereby blaspheming God; (2) being deluded fanatics; (3) increasing in numbers daily; (4) being the very dregs of society; (5) raising sedition among the slaves; (6) inviting free Negroes and mulattoes of other states to become Mormons and move to Missouri; (7) declaring that God has given the state of Missouri to them. (HC 1:374-76.)

July 2, 1833

Joseph writes to the Brethren in Zion stating among other things that his translation of the Bible has just been finished.

July 16, 1833

The *Evening and Morning Star* publishes an extra edition stating that the previous article entitled "Free People of Color" has been misunderstood. The intention of the article was not only to stop free Negroes from immigrating to Missouri, but also to stop them from joining the Church altogether.

July 20, 1833

The retraction does nothing to alleviate the animosity of the other settlers. On this day several hundred assemble and declare that the Mormons must leave at once. They proceed to W.W. Phelps's printing press and destroy it and tear down his house. The Book of Commandments, which was on the press at the time, is destroyed, and a few people gather up extra pages from which come the extremely rare 160-page copies of the book presently extant. The mob then covers Bishop Edward Partridge and Charles Allen with acid and tar and feathers. Bishop Partridge is so meek that the crowd is humbled and finally stops its attack. The Rev. Pixley, one of the leaders of the mob, gives the Saints 15 minutes to leave town.

July 23, 1833

The mob again attacks the Saints in Independence. Six saints—John Corrill, John Whitmer, W.W. Phelps, A.S. Gilbert, Bishop Partridge, and Isaac Morley—offer themselves as a ransom for the Saints if the mob promises not to pursue the other Saints. They are forced to sign a treaty stating that half the Saints will leave Jackson County by January 1, 1834, and the rest will leave the following April. It is evident that the Lt. Gov. Lilburn Boggs is playing a large part in the mob action. Boggs, in fact, has contended with the Mormons for purchase of several of the lands that Mormons now own. In Kirtland at this time, 24 elders—six at each corner—set the cornerstone of the Kirtland Temple.

Aug. 1833

Joseph receives D&C 99.

Aug. 2, 1833

Joseph receives D&C 97.

Aug. 6, 1833

Joseph receives D&C 98, part of which explains the Lord's law of retribution.

Between Aug. 1833 and Sept. 4, 1833

Sometime between these dates Oliver Cowdery leaves Missouri and travels to Kirtland with the terrible news of the persecutions in Jackson County.

Sept. 4, 1833

Joseph writes to Vienna Jaques in Independence, thanking her for her pecuniary offerings and also stating in reference to the Missouri persecutions, "I am not at all astonished at what has happened to you, neither to what has happened to Zion, and I could tell all the whys and wherefores of all these calamities. But alas, it is in vain to warn and give precepts, for all men are naturally disposed to walk in their own paths." (HC 1:407-9.) (Earlier in the year Joseph had written several letters to Missouri telling the brethren to repent or terrible troubles would come.)

Sept. 11, 1833

A council meets in Kirtland to consider the expediency of a press there and proposes that the paper be called the *Latter Day Saint Messenger and Advocate.* The *Star* will also be transferred to Kirtland, with Oliver Cowdery as editor. A council is held in Jackson County, Missouri. Bishop Partridge is acknowledged as head of the Church in Zion, and ten high priests are chosen to preside over the ten branches there. W.W. Phelps sings a song about the tribulations of the Nephites in tongues and Lyman Wight interprets the tongues.

Sept. 28, 1833

Orson Hyde and W.W. Phelps are dispatched to Governor Dunklin of Missouri with a petition, signed by almost all of the members there, that outlines the history of the abuses against the Mormons, including the destruction of the press, the tarring and feathering, the offering of six lives as ransom and the members' being forced to sign the illegal agreement to leave the state.

Oct. 1, 1833

Joseph sends Oliver Cowdery to New York with $800 to buy a new press.

Oct. 5-Nov. 4, 1833

Joseph, Sidney Rigdon, and Freeman Nickerson leave Kirtland on a mission to Upper Canada and return to Kirtland. Their mission follows this itinerary:
Elk Creek (Oct. 8).
Westfield (Oct. 10).
Westfield with Nash, an infidel (Oct. 11).
At Perrysburg, N.Y., with Father Nickerson (Oct. 12).
Lodi, Canada (Oct. 14).
Upper Canada (Oct. 18).
Mount Pleasant, near Brantford County (Oct. 20).
Colburn Village (Oct. 22).
Colburn, Waterford, and Mount Pleasant (Oct. 24).
Joseph preaches at Mount Pleasant and baptizes twelve (Oct. 27).
Sacrament, confirmation, two are baptized (Oct. 28).
Two are baptized and confirmed; the gift of tongues is experienced (Oct. 29).
They leave for Kirtland (Oct. 29).
They reach Buffalo (Nov. 1).
They reach Kirtland at 10 A.M. (Nov. 4).

Oct. 11, 1833

Joseph, on this mission, records in his journal that he has

"much anxiety about my family." (HC 1:419.)

Oct. 12, 1833
Joseph receives D&C 100 "while Joseph and Sidney are on the mission in Perrysburg, N.Y."

Oct. 19, 1833
Governor Dunklin of Missouri answers the petition of the Saints, advising them to go to the local justices of the peace for protection and to sue in the local courts for property damage.

Oct. 20, 1833
The Church officials in Missouri announce their intentions to defend themselves, having purchased powder and lead in Clay County. The Missourians look upon this as breaking the treaty agreement of July 23, 1833.

Oct. 26, 1833
A mob of about 50 meet together and vote "to a hand to move the Mormons." (CHC 1:343.)

Oct. 30, 1833
The Saints receive an offer from lawyers Wood, Reese, Doniphan, and Atchison to defend the Saints for the sum of one thousand dollars (two hundred and fifty dollars each).

Oct. 31-Nov. 7, 1833
The mobs begin a reign of terror in Missouri.

Oct. 31, 1833
A mob of 50 attacks houses west of the Big Blue River, whipping and stoning women, men, and children.

Nov. 1, 1833
On this Friday night, a mob moves to attack the Colesville Branch, which is located on the prairie about 13 miles west of Independence. Two advance spies contact Parley P. Pratt and hit him on the head with their guns, drawing blood. The other Saints are aroused and capture these two, keeping them for the night. This causes the rest of the mob to postpone their attack. Violence breaks out against the Saints' homes in Independence. The home of A.S. Gilbert is destroyed. The Gilbert and Whitney store is destroyed; goods are thrown everywhere. Other houses are attacked and windows are broken, with Saints whipped and driven into the wilderness.

Nov. 2, 1833

The Saints in Independence move a half mile away from the city into the wilderness and camp there in groups of 30. Another mob attacks the Saints located on the Big Blue River, six miles from Independence. David Bennett, who has been sick in bed, is beaten terribly, and one of the mob receives a bullet in his thigh.

Nov. 3, 1833

Several Saints go to the justices of the peace, who refuse to issue peace warrants because they fear the mob. The friends of the Saints warn them to leave Independence at once because the mob has warned that tomorrow "would be a bloody day." (HC 1:429.)

Nov. 4, 1833

The mobs, 40 or 50 with guns, begin their destruction. They meet 30 Mormons, with 17 guns, led by David Whitmer. At sunset there is a battle, and two of the Missourians are killed (including one who had claimed, "With ten fellows, I will wade to my knees in blood, but that I will drive the Mormons from Jackson County"). Andrew Barber is also shot and dies the next day (the first Mormon to die in battle). Philo Dibble is wounded and lies dying for several days until Newel Knight administers to him; then Dibble immediately vomits up several quarts of blood and the bullet with which he was wounded. That evening the Gilbert and Whitney store is totally demolished, and several of the Saints are advised to go to jail, as that is the only safe place in town. Later that night, however, they return home. (HC 1:429-32.)

Nov. 5, 1833

Early in the morning A.S. Gilbert, Isaac Morley, and John Corrill are taken to prison and shot at on the way. Rumors spread that Lt. Gov. Boggs is behind the mob. Rumors also spread that the three prisoners will be shot, and 100 Saints gather to protect them. Before a full-scale war breaks out, however, the Saints decide to surrender their arms if the Missourians also promise to disarm. The Mormons later discover that the leaders of these harassers seem to be Lt. Gov. Boggs, the Rev. Isaac McCoy, Judge S.D. Lucas, and almost every other local government official. In the evening of November 5 and 6 about 150 women and children flee to the prairie with only six men to protect them.

Nov. 6, 1833
W.W. Phelps, A.S. Gilbert, and William E. McLellin send a letter to Governor Dunklin explaining their side of the Missouri problems.

Nov. 7, 1833
The Saints are driven from Jackson County to Clay County, Ray County, Van Buren County (and from Van Buren County to Lafayette County). On both sides of the Missouri River, 1200 homeless Saints gather, destitute, camping out in tents.

Nov. 13, 1833
At 4:00 A.M. a meteoric shower fills the sky with "the falling of the stars." The destitute Saints camped along the Missouri look upon this as a favorable sign from heaven. According to one source, in the fall of 1833 Joseph Smith, Jr., had prophesied, "forty days shall not pass, and the stars shall fall from heaven." (HA 69; HC 1:439.)

Nov. 19, 1833
Joseph records some personal notes and his personal opinion of his counselors: Sidney Rigdon is a great and good man but has several faults so that one cannot place confidence in him; Frederick G. Williams "is one of those men in whom I place the greatest confidence and trust, for I have found him ever full of love and brotherly kindness." (HC 1:443-44.)

Nov. 22, 1833
Don Carlos Smith, Joseph's youngest brother, comes to live with Joseph to learn the art of printing.

Nov. 25, 1833
Orson Hyde and John Gould arrive from Missouri to tell Joseph and the brethren in Kirtland the terrible news of the happenings there.

Dec. 1, 1833
Oliver Cowdery and Newel Whitney arrive in Kirtland with a press from the East.

Dec. 5, 1833
Joseph receives a letter from W.W. Phelps further outlin-

ing the Missouri persecutions. About this time Joseph writes Bishop Partridge in Missouri instructing him to seek redress at the law but not to sell any Jackson County lands.

Dec. 6, 1833

The Missouri elders petition Governor Dunklin for assistance in restoring them to their homes, for military protection, and for a court of inquiry once it is safe for Mormons to testify. This includes the statement that the protection of the Saints in Jackson County by force of the militia must be made to last until the Saints can receive "strength from our friends to protect ourselves." (HC 1:452.)

Dec. 10, 1833

Joseph writes to the persecuted Saints in Missouri, stating that "when we learn your sufferings, it awakens every sympathy of our hearts; it weighs us down; we cannot refrain from tears, yet we are not able to realize, only in part, your sufferings." (HC 1:453-56.)

Dec. 12, 1833

A letter arrives stating that the Saints who had moved to Van Buren County will also be driven from there.

Dec. 15, 1833

W.W. Phelps writes to Joseph that Gov. Dunklin will restore the Saints to Jackson County, but that he has no constitutional power to protect the Saints once they have been restored to the county, and the mob is swearing to kill them if they return. (There is evidence that this becomes the underlying motivation for the march of Zion's Camp in May 1834—to protect the Saints once they have been restored, not to restore them by force, as is commonly supposed. See BYS, Su '74, 406-20.)

Dec. 16, 1833

Joseph receives D&C 101.

Dec. 18, 1833

The press is dedicated and the first issue of the *Evening and Morning Star* is published, with Oliver Cowdery as editor. Joseph Smith, Sr., is ordained the first patriarch of the Church. The Prophet records his personal blessings upon his parents and his brothers (including the statement concerning the pride of his brother William, which will prove to be prophetic in the troubles that occur during December 1835 and January 1836).

Dec. 24, 1833
Four aged families are driven out of Independence, Missouri. These are Revolutionary War veterans, and one was a bodyguard to George Washington.

Dec. 26, 1833
A Church court is held in Kirtland. Three persons are excommunicated and two others repent.

Dec. 27, 1833
The remains of the press in Independence are sold, and $300 of that money goes to lawyers for fees.

Dec. 29, 1833
In Richland, New York, Elders Zera Pulsipher and Elijah Cheney call at the home of Wilford Woodruff. He is at work, but his wife tells him of the preaching meeting that the elders will hold that evening. When he hears of the meeting he goes at once to the sermon and stands and bears testimony and is converted.

1834

Jan. 1, 1834

The scattered Saints in Missouri hold a conference in Clay County with Bishop Partridge presiding. They decide to send Lyman Wight and Parley P. Pratt as messengers to Kirtland.

Jan. 8, 1834

Work is progressing rapidly on the temple in Kirtland. However, threats of mob violence become so bad that guards sleep at the temple with their rifles. At one A.M. a cannon owned by the enemies of the Church fires 13 rounds. The Church in Kirtland is poverty stricken because of the great expense of the temple building.

Jan. 11, 1834

Joseph and five others in Kirtland pray (1) that the Lord will protect their lives; (2) that the Lord will protect the lives of those in the United Order; (3) that Joseph will be given the victory over the threats against his life by apostate Doctor Philastus Hurlburt; (4) that the Kirtland bishop will get enough money to pay off the Church's debts; (5) that the printing press will be protected; and (6) that the Lord will deliver up Zion.

Jan. 22, 1834

The elders in Kirtland send a long letter of comfort and exhortation to the Saints in Missouri.

Jan. 28, 1834

Joseph prays again for protection from Doctor Hurlburt. (Hurtburt's threats will eventually result in a trial—see April 4, 1834.)

Jan. 31, 1834

Joseph prays that the *Star* might get 3,000 new subscribers within the next three years.

Feb. 4, 1834

Gov. Dunklin of Missouri writes to Elders Phelps, Morley, Whitmer, Partridge, Corrill, and Gilbert, stating that although he sympathizes with the Saints, he regrets to say that the president of the United States alone has the power to call out the militia, and Dunklin himself has too little power to help.

Feb. 12, 1834

A high priests and elders council is held in Kirtland. Joseph explains that a man's heart must be pure before judging any matter. He explains the strict propriety of councils held in ancient days as compared with the present situation where one man will be uneasy, another sleeping, another praying.

Martin Harris is tried before the court for accusing Joseph of not understanding the Book of Mormon, of wrestling too much, and of drinking when he was translating the Book of Mormon. Martin Harris repents, stating that he meant that these things happened before the book was translated. He is forgiven. Leonard Rich is also called before the council for breaking the Word of Wisdom and for selling revelations at extortionate prices. He confesses and is forgiven.

Feb. 17, 1834

The first stake of the Church is organized in Kirtland. The minutes of that first high council meeting are eventually published as D&C 102.

Feb. 18, 1834

Joseph reviews the minutes of the first high council meeting. He ordains two assistant presidents and 12 high councilmen. Joseph Smith, Sr., and John Johnson, Sr., give their sons special blessings.

Feb. 19, 1834

The first case is brought before the high council. Ezra Thayre accuses Curtis Hodges, Sr., of preaching so loudly and inarticulately that several of the people ran to the Church to see if someone was hurt. Hodges admits his error, repents, and says "he had learned more during this trial than he had since he came into the Church." He is forgiven. (HC 2:33-34.)

Feb. 20, 1834

At a meeting of the high council it is decided that no official member of the Church is worthy to hold an office if he breaks the Word of Wisdom once it has been properly explained to him. Three Saints in Missouri return to Jackson County briefly and are severely beaten with clubs by a mob.

Feb. 22, 1834

Parley P. Pratt and Lyman Wight arrive in Kirtland, Ohio, having traveled the eight hundred mile journey from Missouri on foot and in utter poverty.

Feb. 24, 1834

Elders Pratt and Wight report to the brethren in Kirtland that there has been no progress toward the recovery of Mormon possessions in Jackson County in the past three months; Gov. Dunklin promised to give the Saints an armed force to guard them while they returned to Jackson, but refused to keep that force in Jackson as a continued protection of them; unless some other force of the Saints were there, they would be driven out again. Twelve Mormon witnesses under protection of 50 members of the Liberty Blues (the militia ordered out by Gov. Dunklin at the request of the Mormons) assemble at Independence for court proceedings for their lost lands. They find that there is no hope of criminal prosecution in Independence against the Missourians. Joseph receives D&C 103, which commands him to organize a group of men to go down to Missouri.

Feb. 26-Mar. 28, 1834

Joseph goes east to obtain volunteers for the march to Zion.

Feb. 26   Joseph leaves Kirtland with Parley P. Pratt.

Feb. 27   They stay at Brother Roundy's. Joseph receives several letters from missionaries in Canada that tell him of their great success there.

Feb. 28   They stay with a kind stranger.

Mar. 1   They arrive in Westfield.

Mar. 2 Sunday. Parley P. Pratt preaches to the small branch in the morning. Joseph preaches in the afternoon.

Mar. 4 They travel to Villanova.

Mar. 5 They reach Brother Nickerson's. Joseph is filled with the spirit of prophecy; several volunteer to go to Zion.

Mar. 6 Another meeting is held at Brother Nickerson's. Some unbelievers cause the meeting to end in complete confusion.

Mar. 7 They reach Ellicotville. There is no place to stay, so they travel on another mile in the mud and rain.

Mar. 8 They reach Palmersville.

Mar. 9 Joseph preaches at the schoolhouse.

Mar. 10 They stop over with Warren A. Cowdery (Oliver's brother) in Freedom, N.Y.; after preaching, one Methodist is baptized.

Mar. 11 Heman T. Hyde is baptized.

Mar. 12 They travel 36 miles to Father Bosley's.

Mar. 14 They stay at Father Beaman's (who had been a friend of Joseph's even before the Book of Mormon was published).

Mar. 17 A conference of elders is held in Avon, N.Y. Joseph outlines the purpose of the mission.

Mar. 19 They begin the journey back to Kirtland.

Mar. 20 Joseph finds a man in China, N.Y., who agrees to keep them for the night for money. Joseph comments that "there are more places for money than for the disciples of Jesus, the Lamb of God."

Mar. 21 They reach six miles east of Springville.
They reach Vinson Knight's in Perrysburgh.

Mar. 23 They arrive at Father Nickerson's in Perrysburgh; meeting is held.

Mar. 25 They reach Westfield.

Mar. 27 They meet Sidney Rigdon in Springfield.

Mar. 28 Joseph reaches Kirtland to find that his family is well; Parley P. Pratt continues his journeying with another companion. (HC 2:40-45; PPP 108-

13 describes Elder Pratt's feelings about traveling with Joseph.)

Mar. 31, 1834

A young man, Ira J. Willis, goes into Jackson County, Missouri, looking for a stray cow. He is captured by Moses Wilson, who, with six other men, whips Willis in a cruel and savage way. Joseph writes, "May God reward Moses Wilson according to his works." (HC 2:46.)

Apr. 1-9, 1834

Joseph goes to Chardon, Ohio, for the court case of Philastus Hurlburt, who has threatened Joseph's life. Hurlburt loses the case and is forced to pay a $200 to $300 bond and keep the peace for six months.

Apr. 10, 1834

The Missouri Saints send a petition to the president of the United States with 114 signatures asking redress for the Jackson County expulsion. Between January 9 and May 15, 1834, the Saints send literally dozens of petitions and letters to various U.S. government officials (in accordance with D&C 101:79-90). (Copies of many of these are in HC 1:472-93.) The United Order in Kirtland is dissolved by order of the high council. Each person is given his own stewardship.

Apr. 11, 1834

Joseph attends a meeting wherein Brother Tyler is restored to the full fellowship of the Church.

Apr. 12, 1834

Joseph spends the day fishing near Lake Erie and visiting the brethren.

Apr. 13, 1834

Joseph is sick and unable to attend his Sunday meetings.

Apr. 15, 1834

Joseph hauls hay and plows and sows oats for Frederick G. Williams.

Apr. 17, 1834

Sidney Rigdon speaks in the Kirtland Temple about the redemption of Zion, and Joseph asks members to contribute all they can. They receive $29.68 for the redemption of Zion.

Apr. 18, 1834

Joseph travels to New Portage for conference. As he is about to stop to help a sick man on the road, he is warned by the Spirit and keeps going. The man is soon joined by two others who chase Joseph. He escapes safely, however.

Apr. 19, 1834

They travel to Norton, Ohio. Elders Sidney Rigdon, Oliver Cowdery, and Zebedee Coltrin give Joseph a blessing. Those present then lay their hands upon the head of Sidney and "confirm upon him the blessings of wisdom and knowledge to preside over the Church in [Joseph's] absence." Elders Cowdery and Coltrin are also given blessings. (HC 2:51.)

Apr. 21, 1834

A conference is held in Norton, Ohio. Joseph says, "Take away the Book of Mormon and the revelations, and where is our religion? We have none: for without Zion and a place of deliverance, we must fall." (HC 2:52.)

Apr. 22, 1834

Joseph returns to Kirtland.

Apr. 23, 1834

A high council meeting is held in Kirtland. Joseph receives D&C 104.

Apr. 24, 1834

The Missouri Saints inform Gov. Dunklin that a force of Saints from the East will be marching to Missouri to protect them when Gov. Dunklin fulfills his promise to restore them under guard to their lands in Jackson County.

Apr. 24-30, 1834

The old settlers in Missouri learn that the Saints are expecting an armed force from the East, and they begin permanent destruction of the Saints' remaining homes in Jackson County. About 170 houses are burned to the ground this week.

May 1, 1834

W.W. Phelps writes to Joseph Smith stating that the rumor of a Mormon army coming to Missouri has caused the mobs to burn the houses throughout Jackson County. Over 20 men from Kirtland with four luggage wagons travel to New Portage, 50 miles distant, to prepare for the

March of Zion's Camp to Missouri. They wait there for the others to arrive from Kirtland.

May 3, 1834

A conference is held in Kirtland. The various terms by which people call the Church, such as "Mormonite," are discussed and it is decided that the name of the Church should be altered to "The Church of the Latter-day Saints."

May 5-July 3, 1834

The march of Zion's Camp from Kirtland to Missouri: This group of Saints marches about nine hundred miles in three weeks to protect the Saints in Missouri from the other Missourians if and when Gov. Dunklin restores them to their Jackson County lands. Beginning with about 100 men, the numbers eventually swell to 204 men, 11 women, and 8 children. Joseph divides them into companies of 12 men each, and each company has 2 cooks, 2 firemen, 2 tentmen, 2 watermen, 2 wagoneers and horsemen, 1 runner, and 1 commissarian. A man marches in front of the group carrying a white flag with the red letters *PEACE* on it. They take whatever old weapons they can get. Joseph has the best weapons of all, including a good sword, rifle, a very aggressive bulldog, and a fine pair of silver-mounted pistols with brass barrels, which were captured in the War of 1812. Joseph travels incognito, calling himself Squire Cook. Every morning at four o'clock and every evening a trumpet blast signals for the men to kneel for their prayers.

May 5   Joseph and his company leave for Missouri with horses, wagons, firearms, etc. They make 27 miles the first day. George A. Smith's new boots blister his feet so Joseph gives him his own boots.

May 6   They reach New Portage, 50 miles from Kirtland, and are joined by other brethren. At this point, they all consecrate their money into the common fund to be divided up at the end of the trip.

May 7   The company now has 130 men and about 20 baggage wagons. The company is divided and organized into 12 companies, each to choose its own captain.

May 8   They travel 12 miles to Chippeway.

May 9 The *Painesville Telegraph* reports that Joseph has told his troops he is ready for martyrdom. The company reaches Wooster.

May 10 They reach Richfield township. A circular signed by Oliver Cowdery and Sidney Rigdon is sent to the Saints asking them to volunteer and join Zion's Camp. This circular states that Gov. Dunklin promised to use the state militia to reinstate the Saints.

May 11 Sunday. Elder Sylvester Smith preaches and the sacrament is passed. Eight more join the group.

May 12 They travel 35 miles.

May 13 The roads are very bad. They are forced to haul the wagons out of mud holes with ropes. Parley P. Pratt breaks his harness.

May 14 They reach Belle Fountain. Sylvester Smith begins to grumble because of a shortage of bread.

May 15 They come close to Springfield. Moses Martin falls asleep on guard duty.

May 16 Joseph says he is very depressed in this place because he senses there was a great deal of bloodshed here at one time; he says, "Whenever a man of God is in a place where many have been killed, he will feel lonesome and unpleasant, and his spirit will sink." Many of the men worry about milk sickness. They pass through Dayton, Ohio; some people ask them who they are, and they answer very evasively: they are from the East, they are going west, sometimes one leads them and sometimes another! There is a court-martial that evening for Moses Martin. He is acquitted, but Joseph gives him a stern warning. (HC 2:66-68.)

May 17 They travel 40 miles and camp across the Indiana state line. Guards are set up to watch for spies. Sylvester Smith is warned about his rebellious spirit. They are told to humble themselves so the Lord will not send a scourge.

May 18 It is Sunday morning. Many of the horses are found to be sick; only Sylvester Smith's horse dies. The sacrament is passed and there is

58

preaching. About this time, the Saints in Clay County, Mo., begin making their own arms for their own defense.

May 19 They travel 31 miles to Henry County.

May 20 They travel 25 miles through terribly muddy roads, sometimes with mud coming over the tops of their boots. Once again they give evasive answers to strangers' questioning.

May 21 They reach Indianapolis and are warned that they will not be allowed to pass through the city. They split up so that one or two of them walk through a back road at a time; thus no one in the city realizes that a whole company of men has passed through the city, and the townspeople are left wondering "when that big company would come along." (HC 2:70.)

May 22 They reach Belleville.

May 23 They reach four miles from Greencastle.

May 24 They cross the Wabash River on ferry boats and reach the Illinois state line by night.

May 25 No Sunday meeting is held, but they spend the day washing, baking, and preparing to continue the journey. A spy in disguise enters the camp and tells them that they will never cross the Mississippi River alive.

May 26 They cross a 16-mile prairie. They have to strain the "wigglers" out of their water before they can drink it. They finally come to a well of water, for which they all rejoice. They camp a mile west of the Embarras River. Joseph Smith tells the men not to hurt the rattlesnakes they find, stating that "men must become harmless, before the brute creation; when men lose their vicious dispositions and cease to destroy the animal race, the lion and the lamb can dwell together, and the sucking child can play with the serpent in safety." Brethren carry the snakes out on sticks. Joseph tells them not to kill any animal on the trip unless it is absolutely necessary for food. Joseph then shoots a squirrel. The brethren decide to cook it and eat it so that it will not be wasted, and Joseph is glad they listened to his precept more than his example, "which was right." Parley P. Pratt and Amasa Lyman return to the group bringing twelve new men. They see the reflection of the rising moon and think it is an enemy campfire. Everyone gets ready for battle until they realize their mistake and have a good laugh about it. (HC 2:71-72.)

May 27 The angels of God go before the group. One man falls asleep on a rattlesnake but is not harmed. When others want to kill the rattlesnake, the man, Solomon Humphreys, says, "You shan't hurt him, for he and I had a good nap together." (HC 2:74.)

May 28 They reach Decatur township, suffering for lack of food and water. One horse dies.

May 29 They are detained until noon, having to buy a new horse. Some murmur. To divert their attention, Joseph organizes the camp into three parts for a sham battle. Many of the captains show surprisingly good military sense; but Heber C. Kimball cuts his hand when grabbing another man's sword. Joseph chastizes Zebedee Coltrin for giving him (Joseph) good bread while some of the other brethren are forced to eat sour bread, stating that he wants no partiality in the food. The Missouri brethren write to Gov. Dunklin.

May 30 Two brethren go ahead in disguise to spy out circumstances in Missouri. Many of the horses become bloated from eating dried corn and prairie grass. Ezra Thayre makes a medicine of tobacco, copperas, cayenne pepper, and water or whiskey, which seems to cure the horses. The two spies return saying that people are somewhat excited.

May 31 A man asks them if they could use $100. An hour later, he returns with $100, wishing he could give them more. At noon a man comes into camp drunk; it turns out he is probably a spy faking drunkenness.

June 1 Sunday. They are camped near Jacksonville. Many of the townspeople, suspecting that this group is composed of Mormons, come to hear them preach. However, each elder preaches according to his own particular religious upbringing, and therefore the townspeople cannot decide whether these preachers are Baptists, Campbellites, Reformed Methodists, Restorationists, etc.

June 2 In spite of enemy threats, they are ferried across the Illinois River.

June 3 They travel past some ancient Indian mounds and Joseph tells about the ancient warriors and the Prophet Zelph (story of the white Lamanite) and Onandagus. Joseph also prophesies that a scourge will come upon the camp because of murmuring, and some will "die like sheep" unless they repent. Many murmur about the food, but Joseph's company gladly eats the partially spoiled hams that others refuse to eat. A double guard is posted for what turns out to be a false alarm. (HC 2:79-82.)

June 4 The group encamps on the banks of the Mississippi River and begins to cross it, which takes two days. During this time, Sylvester Smith complains bitterly about Joseph and his bulldog, finally stating, "If that dog bites me, I'll kill him." Joseph answers, "If you kill that dog, I'll whip you." Some brethren report that Sylvester and Joseph were about to start fighting until the brethren broke them up, and Brigham Young later reports that Joseph finally turned to the men and asked them if they were not ashamed of such an evil spirit, and said, "I am." (HC 2:82-83; DH 173.)

June 5 The elders in Clay County, Mo., write to Gov. Dunklin asking when he will supply the military guard to return the Saints to Jackson County.

June 6 Gov. Dunklin writes to Col. J. Thornton about the Mormon problem, stating that he wishes they could work out a peaceful compromise with their enemies, but he has limited powers to get involved in the conflict.

June 7 Zion's Camp reaches the Allred settlement of the Church members at the Salt River and stays until June 12.

June 8 Sunday. There is preaching in the morning. Hyrum Smith and Lyman Wight join the camp with volunteers from Michigan. The camp now totals 205.

June 12 Lyman Wight is elected general of the camp. Joseph chooses 25 lifeguards for himself, with Hyrum as captain and George A. Smith as armorbearer. Joseph sends Parley P. Pratt and Orson Hyde with a message to Gov. Dunklin to see if he will fulfill his promise to reinstate the Mormons in Jackson County to their lands.

June 13 H.C. Kimball's horse gets loose and the guards are chastized.

June 14 Two men are chased by "four suspicious fellows on horseback." Others ride throughout Jackson County yelling, "The Mormons are coming, the Mormons are coming!" and also setting fire to some houses. (HC 2:91-93.)

June 15 Parley P. Pratt and Orson Hyde return to camp with the message from Gov. Dunklin that he will not fulfill his promise to reinstate the Mormons to their lands. Bishop Partridge also visits the camp.

June 16 One man swears to kill the Mormons or else the buzzards can eat his flesh. His boat sinks, he drowns, and his body floats downstream until he gets lodged on an island; the buzzards end up eating his flesh. There is also a thunderstorm this day, which for the first time satisfies the men's thirst. Martin Harris begins to boast that he can handle snakes without fear, and he gets bitten and poisoned. Joseph reproves him, stating that if a man is bitten by accident he might ask in faith for the Lord to heal him; however, men should never provoke miracles from the Lord. In Liberty, Mo., the Mormons and non-Mormons gather at the courthouse. Both sides offer to buy each other out, but feelings are too intense and nothing is settled.

June 17 They cross the Wakenda River and Joseph proposes that they go eight or ten miles across the prairie; however, Lyman Wight, Sylvester Smith, and others oppose this because they want the comforts of water and wood by the shore of the river. There is much disputation in the camp.

June 18 Two brothers find that they have slept accidentally over rattlesnakes, but they remove the rattlesnakes without any harm. They go seventeen miles across the prairie before breakfast, and then proceed to Richmond. Joseph feels very unsafe about that location. Rumors are spreading that about 50 Jackson County men are coming to attack the Saints.

June 19 At dawn they march nine miles. A black woman along the road warns them that a company of men are lying in wait for them. A wagon breaks, and they camp between the Little Fishing River and Big Fishing River. A mob of over 300 begins to move toward Zion's Camp. However, during the night a huge hailstorm hits the area and the river rises 30 feet within 30 minutes, so that no one can possibly cross it, and the Saints are protected from the mobs across the river.

June 20 Zion's Camp moves five miles onto the prairie.

June 21 Col. Sconce and two others visit the camp asking why the men have come to Missouri. Joseph stands and tells them of the sufferings of the Saints in Jackson County, stating that "we had come one thousand miles to assist our brethren, to bring them clothing, etc. and to reinstate them on to their own lands; and that we had no intention to molest or injure any people, but only to administer to the wants of our afflicted friends; and that the evil reports circulated about us were false, and got up by our enemies to procure our destruction." After this speech the men congratulate Joseph and offer their help. (HC 2:105-6.) Ezra Thayre and Joseph Hancock come down with the cholera. Joseph states that because of murmuring, disobedience, and lack of humility before God, some in the camp "should die like

63

sheep with the rot." The Clay County Saints write another letter concerning their grievances. (HC 2:106-7.)

June 22 The sheriff of Clay County, Cornelius Gillium, enters the camp. Joseph reveals his identity for the first time. Gillium publishes the Saints' proposition for a peaceful compromise: that each side choose six men to decide what compensation is honestly due the Mormons. Joseph receives D&C 105.

June 23 When Zion's Camp gets within five or six miles of Liberty, at the pleadings of Gen. Atchison, the Saints' lawyer, they decide not to enter Liberty because of the feelings of the people there. They turn and cross the prairie going toward A.S. Gilbert's residence. A high priests council meets and calls Edward Partridge, W.W. Phelps, Isaac Morley, John Corrill, John Whitmer, David Whitmer, and numerous others to go to Kirtland to receive their endowments with power from on high. A.S. Gilbert says that he cannot do it. Some are very angry because Joseph turned away from Liberty and because they would not get a chance to fight. Some say they would prefer death to returning without a fight.

June 24 A severe outbreak of cholera hits the camp. The guards fall to the earth because of the sudden attack of this disease. Joseph tries to administer to heal several, "but I quickly learned by painful experience, that when the great Jehovah decrees destruction upon any people, and makes known His determination, man must not attempt to stay His hand." Joseph himself is hit with the disease whenever he tries to heal another. (HC 2:114.)

June 25 Zion's Camp is separated into small bands, and several members disperse among the other Missouri Saints. Joseph writes to the lawyers Doniphan and Atchison stating that he has dispersed the camp. The neighbors will give them no water because they are afraid of the cholera. Several die the first day. Because there is no wood available on the prairie, dead Saints are buried in blankets. The attack lasts for four days. Sixty-eight get sick from the cholera and 14 die.

June 26 The Saints again write to Gov. Dunklin, stating that "the shedding of blood is, and ever has been, foreign and revolting to our feelings." (HC 2:117-18.)

June 29 A.S. Gilbert dies from the cholera. Although a faithful Saint, Gilbert lacked self-confidence concerning his public-speaking abilities, and had recently said that he would "rather die than go forth to preach the Gospel to the Gentiles." (HC 2:118-19.)

July 1 Young Jesse Smith, who had been placed in the care of his cousin Joseph, dies after Joseph labors long and hard with him. Jesse had been playing at the river with other young members of Zion's Camp when he said that he felt guilty having so much fun while others were sick and dying, and he died shortly thereafter. Joseph tells the camp that if they will humble themselves, the plague will be stopped from that moment forward. They do, and it ceases.

July 3 The second stake of the Church is organized in Clay County, Mo. David Whitmer is president with W.W. Phelps and John Whitmer as assistant presidents. Twelve high councilmen are also chosen. Joseph authorizes General Lyman Wight to officially discharge the members of Zion's Camp and give them permission to return home. The common funds are redistributed, amounting to $1.14 per person.

Various opinions have been expressed through the years about the planning and outcome of Zion's Camp. Some have said the plan to attack Jackson County and forcibly restore the lands to the Saints was a major failure. Others have justified it on the grounds that, although it did not restore the Saints to Jackson County, it gave future leaders of the Church "an experience that we never could have gained in any other way." (JD 13:158.) However, some recently discovered publications of that time seem to indicate that it was never the plan for Zion's Camp to restore the land to the Missouri Saints. Rather, having received the promise by Gov. Dunklin that he would use the state militia to restore the lands, the purpose of Zion's Camp was only to protect the Saints once they had already been restored. Because Gov. Dunklin never fulfilled his promise to restore the lands, Zion's Camp was helpless to do anything else but dissolve as it did. (For a complete discussion, see BYS, Su '74, 406-20.)

July 8, 1834

Joseph meets in the eastern part of Clay County at the home of Thomas B. Marsh. According to several records, at this time Joseph ordained David Whitmer to succeed him as President of the Church. However, the testimony differs as to certain conditions set upon this ordination. (See BYS, W '76, 194; DH 183; HC 3:32.)

July 9, 1834

Joseph starts for Kirtland with his brother Hyrum, Frederick G. Williams, and others.

July 12, 1834

The high council of Zion sends out various leaders to visit the different branches of the Church.

July 31, 1834

About this time, many Church members were practicing various spiritual gifts, and Church courts were held on several different days to decide whether or not these gifts actually came from God.

Aug. 11, 1834

The Kirtland high council meets to investigate a charge by Sylvester Smith that, on the march of Zion's Camp, Joseph was a "Tyrant—Pope—King—Usurper—Abuser of men—Angel—False Prophet—Prophesying lies in the name of the Lord—Taking consecrated monies." This begins a long series of Church court proceedings with Joseph and Sylvester accusing each other of wrong actions. After several months the matter is finally resolved when Sylvester Smith publishes a public confession and apology of his shortcomings in the *Messenger and Advocate,* written on Oct. 28, 1834. (For a full discussion, see HC 2:142-60.)

August 16, 1834

Joseph writes the Missouri high council "to be in readiness to move into Jackson County in two years from the eleventh of September next, which is the appointed time for the redemption of Zion." (HC 2:145.)

Sept. 1, 1834

Joseph acts as a foreman in the temple's stone quarry and labors with his own hands.

Sept. 18, 1834

There is a conference at New Portage, Ohio. Joseph anoints with oil; heals and prays for a sister; and speaks about false spirits.

Sept. 24, 1834

The high council again tries to publish the Book of Commandments (which was being published when the press was destroyed on July 20, 1833).

Oct. 1834

Joseph's old enemy, Philastus Hurlburt, gets together with Eber D. Howe to publish *Mormonism Unvailed* [sic]. This includes many affidavits against the character of Joseph Smith, supposedly by people who knew him in his youth in New York. This also includes a new explanation for the writing of the Book of Mormon, claiming that Sidney Rigdon and Joseph Smith had stolen and republished a manuscript of a novel written by a Solomon Spaulding. This is the second anti-Mormon book published. The first was *Delusions* in 1832, a reprint of Alexander Campbell's 1831 articles in the *Millennial Harbinger*.

Oct. 1-15, 1834

Joseph works on the Lord's house. He decides to stop printing the *Evening and Morning Star,* as it was intended as a Missouri paper, and in its place, the *Latter-day Saint Messenger and Advocate* will be published. In the first issue, Oliver Cowdery makes a list of seven Latter-day Saint articles of faith. This magazine will be published until September 1837.

Oct. 16-20, 1834

Joseph travels with five others to Michigan. They have a

good journey, and are amused when a man tells Oliver Cowdery that he has heard that Joseph Smith was dead. Joseph is greatly pleased with the preaching in Michigan. Afterwards they return to Kirtland.

Nov. 1834
Joseph writes that "no month ever found me more busily engaged than November. . . . I made this my rule: *When the Lord commands, do it.*" He writes several letters of instruction to the high council. (HC 2:170-71.)

Nov. 25, 1834
Joseph is preparing for the reopening of the School of the Prophets and receives D&C 106.

Nov. 29, 1834
Joseph and Oliver unite in prayer and covenant that "if the Lord will prosper us in our business and open the way before us that we may obtain means to pay our debts . . . we will give a tenth to be bestowed upon the poor in His Church." Joseph also prays that the Lord might give him the prosperity he gave to Jacob and his other servants. (HC 2:174-75.)

Nov. 30, 1834
Joseph prophesies that the Lord will soon send assistance to deliver the Saints from debt.

Dec. 1, 1834
The School of the Elders is resumed and well attended. Joseph begins to deliver his seven lectures on theology (Lectures on Faith).

Dec. 5, 1834
Joseph ordains Oliver Cowdery to be an assistant president of the Church.

Dec. 9, 1834
Joseph and Emma receive their patriarchal blessings from Joseph, Sr. (For details of the blessings, see BYS, W '74, 206-8.)

Mid-Dec. 1834
A letter from Gov. Dunklin rekindles the hopes of the Missouri Saints. He says he will not reinstate them to their lands by force, but that they must go through the local

courts. Kirtland High School is established, with the First Presidency as the trustees. The enrollment grows to 130, at which time the 30 youngest students are dismissed. Penmanship, arithmetic, English grammar, and geography are taught. Joseph writes that "the year closed without bringing anything to pass for the relief of the Saints in Missouri." (HC 2:178.)

1835

Jan. 1835

The School of the Elders meets all month and Joseph prepares the Lectures on Faith (theology) for publication in the book of Doctrine and Covenants, which the committee is now compiling. The School of the Elders also arranges for the calling of "Twelve Apostles" according to the revelation of June 20, 1829. (See D&C 18.)

Feb. 1835

The *Northern Times,* a weekly political paper in support of the Democratic party, is commenced by the Kirtland Saints. This paper will eventually favor the election of Martin Van Buren.

Feb. 8, 1835

Joseph meets with Brigham and Joseph Young on Sunday and tells them, "Brethren, I have seen those men who died of the cholera in our camp; and the Lord knows, if I get a mansion as bright as theirs, I ask no more." Joseph then asks them to gather the members of Zion's Camp for a special conference to be held the next Saturday. (HC 2:181.)

Feb. 14, 1835

A large meeting is held in Kirtland. Joseph speaks about the coming of the Lord, stating, "The coming of the Lord, which was nigh—even 56 years should wind up the scene." (In 56 years Joseph would have been 85 years old; see D&C 130:14-17.) The members of Zion's Camp are seated separately from the others. Chapter 15 of John is read. Joseph talks about calling of the Twelve. The three witnesses of the Book of Mormon pray, and choose 12 from the members of Zion's Camp: Lyman E. Johnson, Brigham Young, Heber C. Kimball, Orson Hyde, David W. Patten, Luke S. Johnson, William E. McLellin, John F. Boynton, Orson Pratt, William Smith, Thomas B. Marsh, and Parley P. Pratt. Lyman E. Johnson, Brigham Young, and Heber C. Kimball are then set apart by the three witnesses, one witness each setting apart one apostle.

Feb. 15, 1835

Another meeting is held, where six more are ordained: Orson Hyde, David W. Patten, Luke S. Johnson, William E. McLellin, John F. Boynton, and William Smith. (Thomas B. Marsh and Orson and Parley P. Pratt are out of town at this time.)

Feb. 21, 1835

Parley P. Pratt is ordained to the Twelve. Oliver Cowdery gives instructions to the Twelve.

Feb. 27, 1835

Joseph meets with nine of the Twelve and stresses the importance of keeping records, expressing his own personal sorrow for not having kept a record of many of the important dates of earlier Church history, which he cannot remember. And if he had such records, "I would not part with them for any sum of money." (HC 2:198-200.)

Feb. 28, 1835

The Church is assembled and the seventies are called from those who went on the Zion's Camp march. Joseph Young is called to be the senior president; the other presidents are Hazen Aldrich, Levi W. Hancock, Sylvester Smith, Leonard Rich, Zebedee Coltrin, and Lyman Sherman. Several (about forty) are ordained by Joseph Smith, Sidney Rigdon, and Oliver Cowdery.

Mar. 1, 1835

Joseph Smith preaches about taking the sacrament unworthily and ordains more seventies.

Mar. 8, 1835

More men are ordained to be seventies.

Mar. 12, 1835

Joseph meets with the Twelve; it is proposed that they take their first mission to the eastern states. An itinerary is drawn up.

Mar. 28, 1835

The Twelve meet together and confess their many short-comings in regard to light-mindedness and vanity. They pray and ask Joseph to request a revelation to comfort them in their travels. Joseph receives D&C 107. The School of the Prophets closes in the last week of March.

Apr. 1835

Various conferences are held; work on the temple progresses.

Apr. 26, 1835

The Twelve and the Seventies meet in the unfinished temple. Joseph instructs them concerning their first mission. Orson Pratt and Thomas B. Marsh have finally arrived in Kirtland and are set apart as members of the Quorum of the Twelve.

May 2, 1835

Joseph seats the Twelve according to age for seniority, and instructs them, saying that they have no authority to go into Zion (Missouri) or into any of the stakes where there is a high council. Their duty is to go abroad. When the Twelve pass a decision, it is in the name of the Church; therefore it is valid.

May 4, 1835

The Twelve leave on their first missions for Pennsylvania and New York.

Mid-May 1835

Brethren arrive in Kirtland from Missouri. New assignments are made. John Whitmer replaces Oliver Cowdery as editor of the *Messenger and Advocate*. Frederick G. Williams is appointed editor of the *Northern Times*. W.W. Phelps moves in with Joseph to assist him in compiling the Doctrine and Covenants.

May 26, 1835

W.W. Phelps, having just arrived in Kirtland, writes to his wife about the remarkable unity of the Saints at that place, stating, "They keep the word of wisdom, drink cold water, and don't even mention tea and coffee; they pray night and morning." (DH 188.)

June 1835

The *Messenger and Advocate* publishes an article to the

Missouri Saints outlining their duties: the high council is to administer the spiritual affairs of the Church, while the bishop should administer the temporal affairs. Joseph receives a brief visit from a Mr. Hewitt of the Irvingite Church in Scotland, which also believes in apostles, prophets, pastors, and gifts of tongues.

June 6, 1835

A conference is held in New Portage, Ohio, presided over by Oliver Cowdery. Some are tried for breaking the Word of Wisdom, and some new members are baptized.

June 18, 1835

Joseph preaches on the evangelical (patriarchal) order.

June 25, 1835

There is a meeting in Kirtland for the purpose of collecting and subscribing money for the building of the temple. The amount of $6,232.50 is added to the list.

July 3, 1835

Michael Chandler comes to Kirtland to exhibit four Egyptian mummies and two rolls of papyrus. He brings them to Joseph for translation. Joseph interprets and Chandler gives Joseph a certificate saying Joseph's interpretation is the "most learned." (HC 2:235.)

July 5, 1835

Some of the Saints purchase the mummies, and Joseph commences translations on the papyrus with W.W. Phelps and Oliver Cowdery as scribes. "To our joy [we] found that one of the rolls contained the writings of Abraham, another the writings of Joseph of Egypt." (HC 2:235-37.)

July 9, 1835

Joseph goes to Cleveland for a Church court.

July 19, 1835

"The remainder of this month, I was continually engaged in translating an alphabet to the Book of Abraham, and arranging a grammar of the Egyptian language as practiced by the ancients." (HC 2:238.) On this same date, W.W. Phelps writes to his wife, "These records of old times, when we translate them and print them in a book, will make a good witness for the Book of Mormon." (BYS, Su '71, 394.) (In reference to the above Phelps letter, Hugh Nibley argues that because Phelps said "we translate them," all of Joseph Smith's notes, Egyptian grammars, etc., were not necessarily prepared by Joseph alone, if at all. Phelps apparently tried his hand at some of these things too, and scholars should be careful not to attack Joseph for the alphabet and grammar if they were, in fact, only vain attempts by W.W. Phelps. See BYS, Su '71, 350-99.)

Aug. 17, 1835

A general assembly of the Church is held in Kirtland to present the Book of Doctrine and Covenants of the Church of the Latter-day Saints for approval. Two articles of beliefs of the Church are also approved at this time. One concerning marriage states that "inasmuch as this Church of Christ has been reproached with the crime of fornication and polygamy, we declare that we believe that one man should have one wife, and one woman but one husband, except in case of death, when either is at liberty to marry again." (HC 2:246-47.) Joseph Smith is not at this meeting, but is in Michigan preaching.

At this same conference, an article of beliefs concerning governments and laws in general is approved for publication and it becomes D&C 134.

Aug. 19, 1835

Church court tries Almon W. Babbitt on charges of breaking the Word of Wisdom and stating that the Book of Mormon is not essential to salvation. He claims that he was only following the example of Joseph and others. He is reproved, and he finally repents and is forgiven.

Aug. 23, 1835

Joseph returns to Kirtland after visiting Michigan.

Aug. 28, 1835

Joseph preaches on the duties of wives. The Twelve hold a conference in Farmington, Maine.

Sept. 1, 1835

Joseph writes a letter to the elders of the Church, which is subsequently printed in the *Messenger and Advocate*. The message explains the beliefs of the Church and outlines the problems in Missouri. Joseph admits that some members may have caused some of the problems in Missouri because "many, having a zeal not according to knowledge, and not understanding the pure principles of the doctrine of the Church, have no doubt, in the heat of enthusiasm, taught and said many things which were derogatory to the genuine character and principles of the Church; and for these things we are heartily sorry, and would apologize, if apology would do any good." Joseph's message carried over into three issues of the *Messenger and Advocate.* (See HC 2:253-72.)

Sept. 2-8, 1835

Joseph goes to New Portage, Ohio, with Oliver and Sidney for a conference and to deal with many spiritual and temporal affairs of the Church.

Sept. 14, 1835

The high council convenes in Kirtland and decides to pay Joseph, Sr., $10 per week for the expenses he incurs as patriarch. Frederick G. Williams is to be paid the same as scribe. Oliver Cowdery is appointed as recorder of the Church. It is decided that Emma Smith will make a selection of sacred hymns to be printed by W.W. Phelps.

Sept. 16-19, 1835

Joseph attends to various Church courts and high council meetings.

Mid-Sept. 1835

The first edition of the Doctrine and Covenants (*Doctrine and Covenants of the Church of the Latter-day Saints: carefully selected from the Revelations of God*) comes off the press, bound and printed (including the "Lectures on Faith"). This is an expanded version of the Book of Commandments, which had been destroyed on July 20, 1833.

Sept. 23, 1835

Joseph receives many visitors during the day. He prays for the salvation of Ezra Thayre. A Brother Noah Packard donates one thousand dollars for the building of the temple. Joseph prays that Packard be blessed a hundredfold. Joseph prays for his own prosperity and freedom from debt: "My heart is full of desire today, to be blessed of the God of Abraham with prosperity, Until I shall be able to pay all my debts, for it is the delight of my soul to be honest. O Lord, that thou knowest right well. Help me, and I will give to the poor." (HC 2:281.)

Sept. 24, 1835

The high council meets at Joseph's home to discuss a plan to go to Zion (Missouri) for its redemption in the spring, "to live or die on our own lands." They begin to take a subscription of those who will go, hoping to get 800 or 1,000 emigrants. (HC 2:282.)

Sept. 26, 1835

The Twelve return from their missions to the East. The First Presidency meets with them to discuss some letters written about them, explaining several problems that occurred. They decide that the Twelve were justified and the complaints unfounded. Some confess; all are forgiven.

Oct. 1, 1835

Joseph labors on the Egyptian alphabet with Oliver Cowdery and W.W. Phelps, and comes to understand some of the principles of astronomy as understood by Abraham. (An alphabet and grammar has been published and Egyptian scholars have attacked its accuracy. But others argue it is the work of Phelps and Cowdery, not Joseph. See BYS, Su '71, 355, 359-62.)

Oct. 4, 1835

On Sunday morning Joseph goes with John Corrill to a meeting in Perry, Ohio; but because of a confusion in time, the meeting is not held. However, on the way they see two deer in the forest, and Joseph rejoices at the creations of God.

Oct. 5, 1835

Joseph is at home, fatigued from the long ride in the rain the previous day. He meets with the Twelve in the evening and instructs the men about going to Missouri with their families next season.

Oct. 7, 1835

Joseph goes to his father's home to administer some mild herbs to him. Joseph records a blessing on Bishop Whitney, for his generosity to the poor.

Oct. 8, 1835

Joseph stays with his father, about whom he is very worried.

Oct. 10, 1835

Joseph stays with his father again and finds him failing

rapidly. Oliver Cowdery is elected as a delegate to the state gubernatorial nominating convention by the Geauga County Democratic Convention.

Oct. 11, 1835
After secret prayer Joseph hears the voice of the Lord: "My servant, thy father shall live." He is greatly relieved. (HC 2:289.)

Oct. 13, 1835
Joseph visits his father, who has very much recovered, which causes everyone to marvel at the miracle.

Oct. 15, 1835
Joseph labors in his father's orchard, gathering apples.

Oct. 16, 1835
Joseph baptizes Ebenezer Robinson.

Oct. 17, 1835
Joseph is troubled by domestic problems and dismisses his boarders.

Oct. 23, 1835
Joseph assembles with several others and they unite in a special prayer requesting release from their debts.

Oct. 26, 1835
Joseph goes to court in Chardon to contest the case of his brother Samuel, who is accused of avoiding military duty. Joseph feels that they would have won the case if they had brought the necessary evidence, but Samuel is fined $20 and has to sell his cow. Joseph writes, "The money which they have thus unjustly taken shall be a testimony against them, and canker, and eat their flesh as fire." (HC 2:292.)

Oct. 27, 1835
Joseph goes into the field to pray for Samuel's wife, who is on the verge of death as she tries to deliver a child. Dr. Frederick G. Williams arrives and helps her deliver the child successfully.

Oct. 29, 1835
A high council court is held at which Joseph and his brother William begin a series of serious disagreements. William has accused Brother and Sister Elliot of whipping their 15-year-old daughter. Joseph defends the Elliots, claiming that the child was at fault. Joseph returns home

to converse with the parents of Bishop Whitney in hopes of baptizing them. When he returns to the high council, Joseph's mother, Lucy Mack Smith, testifies in the Elliot case. Joseph objects to her testimony, because the matter has already been settled. William Smith accuses Joseph of doubting their mother's testimony, and Joseph tells him he is out of order. Feelings are roused and they are on the verge of a fist fight when their parents intervene, and, after much debate, order is finally reestablished. The court finds both parents and daughter at fault, and they all confess.

Oct. 30, 1835
William Smith is censured by the high council.

Oct. 31, 1835
Hyrum Smith, in a spirit of meekness, tries to work with Joseph and William to settle the differences between them. Joseph offers to confess his faults if William will also confess his. William then becomes infuriated and begins to spread stories about Joseph. He convinces another brother, Samuel, that Joseph is wrong and William is right.

Nov. 1, 1835
Joseph receives a revelation chastizing Reynolds Cahoon for dishonesty. He preaches at Church and confirms a number of children who had been baptized.

Nov. 2, 1835
Plastering and the hard finishing on the outside of the temple have begun. Joseph is busy setting up the School of the Elders. He goes with Sidney Rigdon, Oliver Cowdery, and Frederick G. Williams to Willoughby College to hear a Dr. Piexotto lecture on physics. They learn that he will come to Kirtland to teach Hebrew. Joseph receives a revelation for Elder Williams, saying that he should go to New York to preach the gospel.

Nov. 3, 1835
Joseph receives a revelation for the Twelve, stating that they must humble themselves and be patient with his brother William. He then dedicates the School of the Elders, promising a "glorious endowment that God has in store for the faithful." (HC 2:300-301.)

Nov. 4, 1835
Joseph spends the day at school.

Nov. 5, 1835
Several of the Twelve have come to Joseph to hear and discuss the Nov. 3, 1835, revelation to the Twelve.

Nov. 6, 1835
Joseph meets a man from the East who is surprised that he looks just like any other man, having suspected a prophet to be "something more than a man." Joseph reflects that "Elias was a man subject to like passions as we are, yet he had such power with God, that He, in answer to his prayers, shut the heavens that they gave no rain for the space of three years and six months." (HC 2:302.)

Nov. 7, 1835
Joseph receives a revelation concerning Isaac Morley and Edward Partridge, stating that the Lord is well pleased with them and that they should tarry for a little while in Kirtland and attend the school.

Nov. 8, 1835
Joseph chastizes Emma for leaving the Sunday meeting before partaking of the sacrament. She weeps.

Nov. 9-11, 1835
Joseph receives visits from Joshua, the Jewish minister (Robert Matthias), who explains several interesting doctrines of his own. After several visits and lectures, Joseph tells him that his doctrine is of the devil. Joshua identifies his true identity as an ex-convict. Upon commandment of God, Joseph casts him from his home.

Nov. 14, 1835
Joseph receives a revelation to Warren Parrish, who is called to become Joseph's scribe.

Nov. 16, 1835
Joseph receives a letter from Harvey Whitlock, in which Harvey repents of his past sins. Joseph answers him, stating, "Let it suffice that I say that the very flood gates of my heart were broken up—I could not refrain from weeping. I thank God that it has entered into your heart to try to return to the Lord." He also sends him a revelation from the Lord stating that his sins have been forgiven and that he should return to the Church. (HC 2:312-16.)

Nov. 17, 1835

Joseph exhibits the alphabet of the ancient records to Mr. Holmes, and goes with him and Frederick G. Williams to see the mummies.

Nov. 18, 1835

Emma is sick. Joseph attends an elder's debate on the subject "Was it, or was it not, the design of Christ to establish His Gospel by miracles?" After a three-hour debate the negative side wins. Joseph feels that the debate is unhealthy because of too much passion; ill feelings are made manifest in defending one's own views whether right or wrong. (HC 2:317-18.)

Nov. 19, 1835

Joseph visits the workmen in the temple and spends the rest of the day translating the Egyptian record.

Nov. 20, 1835

Oliver Cowdery returns from New York and gives Joseph several Hebrew and Greek grammar books.

Nov. 21, 1835

Joseph spends the day studying the books, especially the Hebrew alphabet. In the evening, he meets with the Hebrew class to make arrangements for a Hebrew teacher. Joseph expresses his dissatisfaction with Dr. Piexotto.

Nov. 24, 1835

Joseph performs his first marriage ceremony, solemnizing the ceremony between Newel Knight and Lydia Goldthwaite. He remarks that marriage is an institution of heaven and began in the Garden of Eden, and that it needs the authority of the priesthood.

Nov. 27, 1835

Christian Whitmer (one of the Eight Witnesses) dies. He has been serving as a high councilor in Missouri.

Nov. 13-30, 1835

Joseph is involved with the Church courts, visitors, translations, letter writing, various Church business, and recovering from a cold caused from the extreme snow outside.

Dec. 2, 1835

Joseph is criticized and made fun of while on a family sleigh ride to Painesville.

Dec. 10, 1835

Joseph and David Whitmer administer to Angeline Works, who says she feels much better.

Dec. 11, 1835

Two fires erupt in the board kiln and shoemaker shop.

Dec. 12, 1835

Joseph spends a day in reading and translating and showing his Egyptian records to some hostile visitors. In the evening he attends a debate at William Smith's.

Dec. 13, 1835

Joseph attends church and later attends a marriage where he remarks on the subject of matrimony and on the duties of husbands and wives. He then seals the marriage.

Dec. 15, 1835

Orson Hyde visits Joseph to hand him a letter explaining certain grievances. He feels the temple committee store (the committee that was in charge of building the temple also ran a store in Kirtland) has been more lenient with credit toward William Smith than toward Hyde. He thought that the Twelve were to be equal in all things, either richness or poverty. Joseph is very upset about Hyde's complaint.

Dec. 16, 1835

Joseph exhibits the Egyptian records to several people, explaining Abraham's view of the planetary system. In the evening he goes to a debate at William Smith's. After the debate, there is some discussion about whether or not this sort of debate should continue. Joseph feels that the debates should be ended, but William Smith grows angry and wants to continue them. The argument finally breaks out into a fight, and William Smith "used violence upon my person." (HC 2:334-35.)

Dec. 17, 1835

Joseph talks with Orson Hyde. They work out their differences successfully so that Hyde's mind is satisfied. Joseph's parents visit him to discuss the difficulty between him and William.

Dec. 18, 1835

William Smith submits a letter to Hyrum, begging for forgiveness because of the fight with Joseph and asking to be released from his apostleship because of his temper. Joseph answers, encouraging him to keep his apostleship, to control his temper, and "if at any time you should consider me to be an imposter, for heaven's sake leave me in the hands of God, and not think to take vengeance on me yourself. . . . David sought not to kill Saul, although he was guilty of crimes that never entered my heart." (HC 2:338-43.)

Dec. 23, 1835
Joseph studies the Greek language.

Dec. 25, 1835
Joseph enjoys Christmas at home with his family, "the only time I have had this privilege so satisfactorily for a long period." (HC 2:345.)

Dec. 26, 1835
Joseph studies Hebrew. Lyman Sherman comes and asks for the word of the Lord concerning him. Joseph receives D&C 108.

Dec. 28, 1835
The Quorum of the Seventy meet to report on their missions "since they were ordained to that Apostleship." (HC 2:346.)

Dec. 29, 1835
William Smith is charged with speaking disrespectfully about Joseph and "attempting to inflict personal violence on President Joseph Smith, Jun." Joseph Smith, Sr., gives 15 patriarchal blessings. (HC 2:346-47.)

Dec. 31, 1835
Joseph records that some people have accused him of pretending to have the mummies of the bodies of Abraham and Joseph, which he denies. He describes the writings of the book of Abraham, "beautifully written on papyrus, with black, and a small part red, ink or paint, in perfect preservation." (HC 2:348. The papyri were rediscovered in 1966, and since that time scholars have translated several of them to determine whether or not they have any possible connection with Abraham. However, a papyrus fitting Joseph's above description has not yet been found.)

1836

Jan. 1, 1836

The Smith family meets with Martin Harris to help reconcile the differences between Joseph and William. Joseph Smith, Sr., opens with a powerful prayer. William confesses his faults and asks for Joseph's forgiveness. Joseph asks for forgiveness from William. The women are then called in and they all promise to support and uphold each other. "While gratitude swelled our bosoms, tears flowed from our eyes." Joseph closes the meeting with prayer. The men then unitedly lay their hands on the head of George A. Smith, and he is immediately healed of a very painful rheumatic infection that covered his body. (HC 2:353-54.)

Jan. 2, 1836

Church court is held against William Smith, but William confesses his faults and is forgiven.

Jan. 4, 1836

Joseph meets with others to organize a Hebrew School, but the contracted Dr. Piexotto is delayed and they decide not to use him. Elders McLellin and Hyde are appointed to find a new teacher. The completed upper west room of the temple is consecrated and dedicated by prayer as a translating room for Joseph and the others. In the evening, several meet at the temple to organize a singing school, and a committee of six is chosen to supervise the singing department.

Jan. 5, 1836

Joseph attends the Hebrew school, which is divided into

classes. Orson Pratt argues with Joseph about the pronunciation of a Hebrew letter.

Jan. 6, 1836

Orson Pratt confesses his fault in arguing over something as trivial as pronunciation of a Hebrew letter. William E. McLellin hires a Hebrew professor, Dr. Joshua Seixas, for seven weeks for $320. Joseph records his views on the American Indians and his views on Andrew Jackson's policies concerning the Indians.

Jan. 7, 1836

Joseph attends a huge feast given by Newel K. Whitney. According to the instructions of the Savior, all the poor, lame, and blind are invited.

Jan. 8, 1836

The plastering and hard finishing on the exterior temple walls are completed.

Jan. 12, 1836

Joseph explains solemn assemblies to the First Presidency of the Church.

Jan. 13, 1836

Joseph meets in council with the Missouri and Kirtland stake presidencies. Various changes in assignments in priesthood are made at this time; vacancies are filled. New officers are then set apart. Sidney Rigdon is administered to and healed from an ailment. Sidney then speaks on the subject of endowment and the meeting is concluded. Joseph records, "This has been one of the best days that I ever spent." (HC 2:364-68.)

Jan. 14, 1836

The Hebrew class meets in anticipation of the arrival of the Hebrew professor, Dr. Seixas of Hudson, Ohio. Rules of order for the House of the Lord in Kirtland are then drawn up. These include such things as that no sermons are to be interrupted by the "ill manners or ill breeding, from old or young, rich or poor, male or female, bond or free, black or white, believer or unbeliever"; no one is to be insulted within the temple; no one is to run up and down the stairs or explore the House; no one is to carve in the wood with knives, pencils, etc.; no children are to play inside the building; and all people should be treated with respect in the building. (HC 2:368-69.)

Joseph meets with the First Presidency and the Twelve and gives them special instructions concerning problems among them—too harsh language being used in chastening, the necessity of forgiveness, and so on. Joseph says, "The Twelve are not subject to any other than the first Presidency . . . and where I am not, there is no First Presidency over the Twelve." (HC 2:372-75.)

Jan. 17, 1836

A large meeting is held this Sunday. The quorums are arranged in order. After several speak, others begin to confess their faults, and "the gift of tongues came on us also, like the rushing of a mighty wind." (HC 2:375-76.) In the afternoon, Joseph performs the marriages of three couples.

Jan. 19, 1836

The School of the Prophets commences their reading of the Bible in Hebrew. Joseph records that he is very excited about this. He prays that the Lord will "speedily endow us with the knowledge of all languages and tongues." (HC 2:376-77.)

Jan. 20, 1836

Joseph performs the marriage of John Boynton and Susan Lowell.

Jan. 21, 1836

Joseph and the First Presidency meet in the attic story of the printing office, where they begin the ordinance of washing bodies in pure water. They also anoint their heads. Later, in the west schoolroom in the temple, they anoint their heads with holy oil. In the next room the other high Church councils meet, awaiting this ordinance. They bless Father Smith; he is anointed with oil and blessed as patriarch. Father Smith then blesses each member of the Presidency. At this time Joseph receives a vision of the celestial kingdom, now known as Joseph Smith's Vision of the Celestial Kingdom. Other brethren of the bishopric and high councils of the Church also share in these ordinances and visions, and the brethren sing and pray and rejoice until one or two o'clock in the morning.

Jan. 22, 1836

Joseph meets in the evening with the Twelve and the Presidency of the Seventy. Elder Thomas B. Marsh is set apart as President of the Council of the Twelve and anointed with oil; angels administer to them. Other gifts of the Spirit are witnessed. Gov. Dunklin writes a letter to the brethren in Kirtland stating that there is really nothing that he can do to help the Saints in Missouri, for "want of a constitutional power." (HC 2:383-84.)

Jan. 26, 1836

Mr. Seixas arrives from Hudson to begin teaching the Hebrew class.

Jan. 28, 1836

Another meeting is held in the temple in which several Church officers and counselors are anointed with oil. Once again the visions of heaven and angels are open to many.

Jan. 30, 1836

Joseph attends Hebrew school, and Mr. Seixas, the teacher, examines the record of Abraham and announces it original. Joseph attends Hebrew school six days a week during this time. (For the effect that the study of Hebrew had upon Joseph and his later writings, see DLG, Su '68, 41-55.)

Jan. or Feb. 1836

The first hymnal, *A Collection of Sacred Hymns, for the Church of the Latter Day Saints,* selected by Emma Smith, is published by F.G. Williams, & Co., at Kirtland (dated 1835). W.W. Phelps has been working on the collection since Sept. 11, 1835. It contains 90 hymns (words only, no music).

Feb. 1, 1836

Joseph attends Hebrew school. He later explains the gospel to Mr. Seixas, who listens cordially.

Feb. 6, 1836

Several councils of the Church are called together to receive the seal of their blessings in the temple. However, there is much confusion among several of the quorums, and the Spirit is not felt. The Quorum of the Seventy does enjoy "a great flow of the Holy Spirit . . . which was like fire in their bones." William Smith of the Twelve sees a vision of the Twelve and the Seventy in England.

Feb. 7, 1836

Joseph meets with the Presidency of the Church, in the presence of the Seventy, to choose a second Quorum of the Seventy.

Feb. 12, 1836

Joseph studies Hebrew in the day, and in the evening meets with several quorums in the temple school room. He talks about many members who bring persecution on the Church, "in consequence of their zeal without knowledge." (HC 2:394.)

Feb. 15, 1836

Hebrew school continues translating the Bible from Hebrew. Professor Seixas being absent in the afternoon, Joseph unites in prayer with the other brethren asking that, just as Seixas has been their teacher in Hebrew, they may become his teacher in the gospel, that he might believe the Book of Mormon and be baptized.

Feb. 16, 1836

Joseph continues translating, making good progress. "Extremely cold weather, and fine sleighing." (HC 2:396.)

Feb. 19, 1836

Joseph talks with Seixas about religion. He believes the Lord is striving with Seixas because he is a chosen vessel, and that he will eventually join the Church; "but I forbear lest I get to prophesying upon his head." (HC 2:397.)

Feb. 22, 1836

The lower room of the temple is ready for painting, and Brigham Young will superintend it. The sisters meet to begin making for the temple a white canvas curtain called the veil.

Mar. 1836

Throughout this month Joseph studies Hebrew six days a week, translating Genesis. Several people are baptized.

Mar. 3, 1836

Elijah Abel, a Negro, is ordained an elder and receives his patriarchal blessing from Joseph Smith, Sr.

Mar. 5, 1836

The board kiln burns again for the fifth or sixth time this winter.

Mar. 12, 1836

A drunk man freezes to death in the night. Joseph writes, "How long, O Lord, will this monster intemperance find its victims on the earth!" (HC 2:406.)

Mar. 13, 1836

Joseph meets with the Presidency and the Twelve to discuss leaving for Zion by May 15, 1836.

Mar. 23, 1836

Joseph attends school. Two persons are baptized. It is a pleasant day for sleighing.

Mar. 26, 1836

Saturday. Joseph meets with the Presidency to arrange for the solemn assembly to take place the next day.

Mar. 27, 1836

The Kirtland Temple is dedicated. The doors to the temple are open at seven A.M. Joseph seats the people. Almost 1,000 enter; many others are turned away. Contributions in excess of $950 are given. At nine A.M. Sidney Rigdon opens the service and speaks for two and a half hours on the need for belief in "present revelation," at one point drawing tears from many. He says that in spite of the many houses of worship built on the earth, this is the only one built by divine revelation. Songs of hosanna are sung. The audience rises to sustain the First Presidency. The Twelve are sustained "as Prophets, Seers, Revelators, and special witnesses to all nations of the earth." (HC 2:417.) The Presidents of the Seventy are sustained as "Apostles and special witnesses to the nations, to assist the Twelve in opening the Gospel kingdom among all people." Other officers are also sustained. "The vote was unanimous in every instance." (HC 2:418.) Another hymn is sung. Joseph offers the dedicatory prayer, which was given by revelation. It is recorded as D&C 109.

The dedication is then unanimously accepted and the Lord's Supper is administered. Others rise to speak. President Frederick G. Williams testifies that an angel entered the window. David Whitmer also testifies that he saw an angel. President Brigham Young gives a short speech in tongues, which David W. Patten interprets; Elder Patten then speaks in tongues himself. The meeting is adjourned at about four o'clock.

In the evening 416 brothers meet for the ordinance of the washing of feet. George A. Smith begins to prophesy, and a noise "like the sound of a rushing mighty wind" fills the temple; all arise and feel the invisible power, and experience visions, angels, the gift of tongues. People in the neighborhood hearing unusual noises and seeing the bright light above the temple run toward it to see what is happening. (HC 2:410-28.)

Mar. 29, 1836

Joseph attends the last lecture in Hebrew taught by Professor Seixas before Seixas leaves Kirtland. Joseph meets with other brethren in the Lord's House. They partake of the bread and wine of the Lord's Supper, tend to the ordinance of the washing of feet, and continue in the house all night, prophesying about the glory of God.

Mar. 30, 1836

About 300 brothers meet in the temple to attend to the ordinance of the washing of feet. A contribution is taken. The Lord's Supper is passed and their fast is broken. Joseph instructs the elders that "it was not necessary for them to be sent out, two by two, as in former times, but to go in all meekness, in sobriety, and preach Jesus Christ and Him crucified; not to contend with others on account of their faith, or systems of religion, but pursue a steady course. This I delivered by way of commandment; and all who observe it not, will pull down persecution upon their heads, while those who do, shall always be filled with the Holy Ghost; this I pronounced as a prophecy, and sealed with hosanna and amen." Joseph then tells the quorums that he has completed the organization of the Church, "that I had given them all the instruction they needed." (HC 2:430-32.)

Joseph returns to the temple about nine P.M. and continues with the brethren prophesying and speaking in tongues until five o'clock the next morning. The Savior appears to some; angels administer to others; and "it was a Pentecost and an endowment indeed." (HC 2:432-33.)

Mar. 31, 1836

The temple is again dedicated for those who could not enter the previous Sunday. The meeting progresses in a manner similar to that of March 27.

Apr. 1, 1836

Leman Copley, who had left the Church several years earlier and who had testified against Joseph in his suit with Philastus Hurlburt, returns to Joseph to repent and confess his wrongs. He puts his confession in writing and asks for baptism again. Joseph readily forgives him.

Apr. 2, 1836

The Presidency meets to discuss the raising of money for the redemption of Zion. Church publications are discussed.

Apr. 3, 1836

Joseph attends meetings in the temple. Thomas B. Marsh and David W. Patten speak in the morning. In the afternoon Joseph assists in distributing the Lord's Supper to the members. The veils are then dropped and Joseph and Oliver Cowdery retire to the pulpit behind them, bow themselves in prayer, and receive the vision recorded as D&C 110.

Apr.-May 1836

Joseph devotes his time to the "spiritual interests of the brethren; and particularly in devising ways and means to build up Kirtland." (HC 2:441.)

May 16, 1836

Joseph is involved in Church courts concerning a variety of charges, such as drinking, family neglect, adultery, un-Christian-like conduct, and lying.

May 17, 1836

Joseph's grandmother, Mary Smith, wife of Asael Smith, arrives in Kirtland after a 500-mile trip. She is 93 years old and is satisfied that Joseph is the prophet. Her husband, Asael, once predicted that a prophet would be raised up in their family.

May 27, 1836

Grandmother Mary Smith dies. Sidney Rigdon preaches the brief funeral sermon.

June 2, 1836

Oliver Cowdery receives a letter from W.W. Phelps noting that Far West, Missouri, is a good place for the Saints to settle.

June 16, 1836

Church courts are held in which two elders are tried for lack of charity and want of benevolence to the poor. Orson Hyde writes the "first genuine Mormon missionary tract," which is published in August 1836 in Toronto, Canada, under the title: "A prophetic warning to all the churches, of every sect and denomination, and to every individual into whose hands it may fall." (BYS, Su '72, 510-11.)

June 20, 1836

Frederick Granger Williams Smith is born to Joseph and Emma in Kirtland. He is named after Joseph's second counselor.

June 22, 1836

Joseph's father and uncle go on a mission to the East to give patriarchal blessings throughout the Church.

June 28, 1836

Elder Warren Parrish writes that several elders have been mobbed, arrested, and kicked out of Tennessee for preaching the gospel.

June 29, 1836

A public meeting is held in Liberty, Clay County, Missouri, in which the local citizens decide that to avoid a civil war the Saints must leave Clay County. They accuse the Saints of coming into the county friendless and penniless, of arriving in large numbers, of being nonslave holders, and of communicating with the Indian tribes.

July 1, 1836

The Mormons meet in Clay County to deny several of the charges that are made against them; however, under protest, they agree to leave.

July 18, 1836

Gov. Dunklin sends a letter to the Missouri Saints saying that although he sympathizes with them, the public considers them obnoxious and has determined to expel them;

and it is therefore useless for him to go against the overwhelming public sentiment. He tells them that if they cannot convince their fellow inhabitants that they are totally innocent, they had better leave the county, because "all I can say to you is that in this Republic the *vox populi* is the *vox Dei*" (the voice of the people is the voice of God). (HC 2:461-62.)

July 25, 1836

Joseph and the First Presidency in Kirtland send a letter to the Missouri Saints advising them not to give any further offenses. Joseph, Hyrum, Sidney, and Oliver leave Kirtland for New York. From New York they go to Salem, Mass.

At this time the Church is in dire financial stress, the Kirtland Temple having cost between $40,000 and $60,000. A brother named Burgess comes to Joseph and says that he knows of a large amount of money hidden away in a cellar of a certain house in Salem, Mass., which had belonged to a widow. The woman has died, and he is the only person who knows of the whereabouts of the treasure. Joseph and the others take him at his word and decide to go to Salem to gain the treasure for the financial welfare of the Church. When they reach Salem, Burgess claims that the town has changed so much that he cannot find the house, and soon afterwards he leaves them there. Joseph hires a house in Salem and they stay there for approximately a month, visiting various sections of the surrounding country from time to time. While in Salem, Joseph records his thoughts concerning Puritanism and its terrible religious intoleration and persecution of other sects; burning of witches; torturing, whipping, and burning Catholics; and so on. He quotes the Savior's statement, "By their fruits you shall know them." (HC 2:464-65.)

Aug. 1836

Orson Hyde publishes his missionary tract, "A Prophetic Warning . . . ," in Toronto, Canada.

Aug. 6, 1836

In Salem, Joseph receives D&C 111. Brigham Young and Lyman E. Johnson join the group in Salem. Brigham has been traveling with Joseph Young throughout the East and has baptized a good number of people. In Boston they baptized 17 people.

Aug. 11, 1836

The Rev. Truman Coe writes a description of Mormonism in the *Ohio Observer,* including the statement that "they believe that the true God is a material being, composed of body and parts; and that when the Creator formed Adam in his own image, he made him about the size and shape of God himself." This is one of the earliest recorded statements concerning the Mormon belief on this doctrine. (BYS, Sp '77, 354.)

Sept. 1836

Joseph returns to Kirtland sometime this month.

Fall 1836

Various members of the Twelve are on successful missions in the East and in Canada.

Oct. 1836

The Missouri Saints continue to gather at Shoal Creek, later known as Far West.

Oct. 2, 1836

Joseph's father and uncle return to Kirtland after a 2,400-mile trip visiting dozens of eastern branches.

Oct. 18, 1836

Sidney Rigdon deposits $12 for 2,000 shares of stock in the Kirtland Safety Society. He later receives another 1,000 shares and pays $818 by November 16, 1836.

Nov. 2, 1836

Several of the brethren meet in Kirtland and draw up the articles of the "Kirtland Safety Society," with Sidney Rigdon as president and Joseph Smith as cashier. They dispatch Orson Hyde to Columbus, Ohio, to gain a banking charter from the legislature. They dispatch Oliver Cowdery to go to Philadelphia to get printing plates for the printing of their banknotes.

Nov. 25, 1836

Wilford Woodruff returns to Kirtland from a mission in Missouri, Kentucky, Arkansas, and Tennessee, after baptizing over 100 people, many of whom immigrated to Kirtland.

Dec. 1, 1836

The Missouri Saints gather at Far West and petition for an act of incorporation for a new county exclusively for Mormons. Alexander Doniphan, the Saints' lawyer and a Missouri Democrat, introduces the bill into the state legislature.

Dec. 20, 1836

Elijah Abel is ordained a seventy by Zebedee Coltrin. Abel was apparently reordained on April 4, 1841.

Dec. 22, 1836

A special conference is called in Kirtland as a result of the financial embarrassment of the Saints in Kirtland. The branches abroad are instructed not to send only the poor people to Kirtland, for they have no monies with which to pay for things. The gathering to Kirtland is stopped, and donations and monies are requested from the other branches. At this time large tracts of land in Kirtland have been purchased and planned into lots. The long-range plan is for a large city. A printing establishment, sawmill, and tannery have been founded, all of which prove to be unprofitable. And the only people coming into Kirtland seem to be the poor converts, who only add to the problems of the Church.

Dec. 29, 1836

Gov. Boggs of Missouri signs into law a compromise bill forming two smaller counties out of a larger one; this forms Caldwell and Daviess counties. It is understood that Caldwell County will be reserved exclusively for the Mormons, although some of them also settle in Daviess County. In a short space of time, 4900 Saints move into Caldwell County and settle near Far West and other places.

1837

Jan. 1, 1837

Oliver Cowdery returns to Kirtland with the printing plates he has purchased in Philadelphia. At the same time, Orson Hyde returns from Columbus, Ohio, with the disappointing news that the bank charter has been rejected by the state legislature. Joseph records that the charter was denied "because we were 'Mormons.'" However, at this time the antibanking wing of the Democratic Party has just won control of the state legislature, and those in power are turning down all bank applications.

Jan. 2, 1837

The Kirtland Safety Society meets and revises its articles. They decide to go ahead with the bank in spite of the lack of legal charter from the state government, but they call it the "Kirtland Safety Society *Anti*-Bank-*ing* Company." (CHC 1:401.) They determine to have a capital stock of at least $4 million, with shares costing $50 each. There would be 32 managers. In the *Messenger and Advocate* Joseph prints a notice, to "take stock in our Safety Society . . . bring thy sons from far, their silver and their gold (not their bank notes) with them, unto the name of the Lord thy God." (HC 2:473.)

Jan. 6, 1837

The new banknotes begin circulation. There is a short boom, but within three weeks the bank announces it will stop redeeming the notes in specie (gold).

Jan. 12, 1837

The local papers run a series of articles stating that there is a law fixing a $1,000 fine on anyone caught circulating unauthorized bank bills. A month later, one of the same papers editorializes that the 1816 law that stipulated the penalty is obsolete. Nevertheless, the earlier articles discouraged people from trading with the Kirtland money.

Jan. 23, 1837
Sidney Rigdon announces that the bank will no longer give out specie for the Kirtland banknotes. Many people in Kirtland have honored the notes, but no other bank will honor them, and when this is learned, there is a run on the bank.

Jan. 24, 1837
Local papers carry the notice that the Mormons are no longer redeeming their banknotes in gold coin, but will only exchange the notes for land. The notes have therefore only circulated freely for less than three weeks. After this date the Kirtland Anti-Banking Company notes are issued at a greatly decreased rate. The average price paid for a $50 share is about 26¼ cents. They were never sold at full face value of $50 per share.

Jan.-March 1837
Because so little hard cash is necessary to buy notes with such a high face value (for instance $52.50 would buy notes with a face value of $10,000), many begin to foolishly believe that they have made their fortune. City lots jump from $150 to $500-$1000. In the ensuing weeks and months, the spirit of speculation spreads through Kirtland.

The second edition (5,000 copies) of the Book of Mormon is printed in Kirtland. The Kirtland High School is held in the attic of the Kirtland Temple. Approximately 140 students attend in three different departments. H. N. Hawes, Esq., is the professor of Greek and Latin.

Feb. 1837
The Missouri Saints gather in Caldwell County to build houses and to prepare to plant crops.

Feb. 8, 1837
Samuel D. Rounds swears out a writ against Joseph Smith, Sidney Rigdon, and others, charging them with the civil action of banking without legal authority. This case is

brought to court on March 24, 1837, and tried before a jury in October 1837. Sidney and Joseph are fined $1000 each, but appeal the case.

April 3-6, 1837

A conference of the Church is held in Kirtland, with a solemn assembly held on April 6 for the purpose of the washing of feet, anointing, and receiving various instructions. Other meetings are held by different quorums, leading up to a general meeting on April 6. The seventies who have previously been ordained high priests are released from their callings as seventies, and new seventies are called and ordained. Joseph explains that the Melchizedek Priesthood is "no other than the Priesthood of the Son of God." He also says, "After all that has been said, the greatest and most important duty is to preach the Gospel." He talks about "embarrassment, of a pecuniary nature," stating that $6,000 is still needed by the members in Missouri, and $13,000 is needed for the debts caused by the building of the Lord's House in Kirtland. The sacrament of the Lord's Supper is passed, using bread and water. This is the first mention of water being used in the sacrament instead of wine. (HC 2:475-80.)

April 3-5, 1837

W.W. Phelps and John Whitmer are accused by other members of the Church in Missouri of using Church funds to buy large sections of land in their own name and selling those sections to Church members for a profit. (Phelps and Whitmer have been the counselors to Stake President David Whitmer, who was absent. Elders David W. Patten and Thomas B. Marsh, among others, speak against them.)

April 7, 1837

Phelps and Whitmer agree to turn the land back over to the Church to be divided among the Saints. City plans for Far West are drawn up, and a committee is appointed for the building of a temple there.

April 24, 1837

David W. Patten prefers a charge against Lyman Wight in Missouri, accusing him of teaching false doctrine. Wight had said the Church was under a telestial law because the Lord does not use a whip under a celestial law. Wight then took some of the Church members outdoors to whip them "into shape." It is decided that Wight must acknowledge that he had been teaching abominable doctrines before he would be forgiven.

May 10, 1837

Eight hundred banks nationwide suspend payments about this time in the "Panic of 1837," as a depression hits the nation. Suspended payments in New York City alone amount to over $100 million. Within a week, the banks in Ohio suspend payment.

May 1837

With the great depressing of prices, poor Saints who had thought to get rich quick through speculation find themselves suddenly poor again. The spirit of apostasy hits every quorum in the Church. Many blame Joseph personally because he was deeply connected with the Kirtland Safety Society. At least five of the Quorum of the Twelve begin to speak against the Prophet.

May 28, 1837

The Presidency of the Church at Far West resolve unanimously not to fellowship any member of the Church who will not observe the Word of Wisdom literally.

May 29, 1837

Frederick G. Williams, David Whitmer, Parley P. Pratt, Lyman E. Johnson, and Warren Parrish are accused of pursuing a course that is considered injurious to the church of God. A Church court is called to try them. Referring to the charges against Pratt, Sidney Rigdon says he cannot sit in judgment and leaves the stand. Oliver Cowdery then does likewise. Williams leaves also. Confusion breaks out and the court is closed without a decision. Lyman E. Johnson and Orson Pratt bring charges against Joseph Smith for "lying and misrepresentation—also for extortion—and for speaking disrespectfully against his brethren behind their backs." (BYS, Su '71, 327.)

Late in May 1837 while Joseph is on a mission in Michigan, members of the Twelve and others meet in the temple to drop Joseph as prophet of the Church. They want to replace him with David Whitmer. Brigham Young and a few others defend the Prophet and are called a "lick skillet" for doing so. Jacob Bump, a former boxer, almost gets into a fist fight with Brigham, but the meeting breaks up in confusion. (IJB 342-43; JD 11:11.)

June 3, 1837

Grandison Newel takes Joseph to court in Painesville, accusing him of conspiring to take Newel's life. Joseph is put under a $500 bond to keep the peace, but at the next hearing he is discharged due to lack of evidence.

June 4, 1837

God reveals to Joseph that "something new must be done for the salvation of His Church." Joseph sets apart Heber C. Kimball to preside over the England Mission, "the first foreign mission of the Church of Christ in the last days." While Joseph is ordaining Elder Kimball, Orson Hyde comes in, repents of his negative feelings, and asks to be allowed to go to England also. He also is set apart.

June 8, 1837

Joseph transfers his shares in the Kirtland Safety Society to Oliver Granger and Jared Carter, as do many other shareholders between this date and June 20.

June 11, 1837

A high council meeting is held at Far West, Mo. The high councilors resolve that no Church member should sell spiritous liquors or trade with any person who does. Joseph meets to instruct those called to England (Heber C. Kimball, Orson Hyde, Joseph Fielding, and Dr. Willard Richards). They are told to preach only the first principles of the gospel, and *not* to teach about the gathering, the vision (D&C 76), or the book of the Doctrine and Covenants.

June 12-14, 1837

Joseph is sick, too sick to raise his head from his pillow to bid farewell to those leaving on their missions. While he is sick, enemies say he is suffering from the curse of God for teaching the Church things that are contrary to godliness. On June 14 Dr. Levi Richards gives Joseph some herbs and mild food, and suddenly his health is restored.

June 22, 1837

The elders going to England meet other elders in New York (for a total of seven) and engage passage on the ship *Garrick*.

July 1, 1837
The *Garrick* sails for Liverpool.

July 2, 1837
Last entry is made in the records of the Kirtland Safety Society. After this date the society did not operate. (For a discussion on the failure of the society, see BYS, Su '77, 391-472.)

July 3, 1837
Fifteen hundred Saints gather in Far West, Mo., to break ground for a temple. Their numbers increase daily, but anti-Mormon forces are also gathering in Daviess County.

Before July 7, 1837
Previous to this date, Joseph had resigned from his office in the Kirtland Safety Society, having turned over management to Warren Parrish and Frederick G. Williams. Joseph comments "that no institution of the kind, established upon just and righteous principles for a blessing not only to the Church but the whole nation, would be suffered to continue its operations in such an age of darkness, speculation and wickedness." (HC 2:497.) About this time Joseph accuses Parrish of stealing $25,000 from the Kirtland Safety Society, thus bringing about its ruin. When he goes to Williams to get a search warrant, Williams refuses and Joseph threatens to drop Williams from the Presidency. Williams still refuses, and Joseph drops him from the Presidency. There seems to be little evidence that Parrish did steal any amount in specie (hard cash) from the Safety Society; however, there is evidence that he did print notes without authorization. (For further discussion, see BYS, Su '77, 499; LJA 427-28; BYS, Su '72, 432-36.)

July 16, 1837
Orson Hyde preaches on board the *Garrick*. Heber C. Kimball secretly heals a sick child.

July 20, 1837
The *Garrick* anchors on the River Mersey at Liverpool, and the brethren go to Preston, 30 miles away.

July 23, 1837
Heber C. Kimball, Orson Hyde, and others preach at the church of the Rev. James Fielding in Preston, England.

(James Fielding is a brother of Elder Joseph Fielding, who had gone with Elders Kimball and Hyde to England.) This is the first instance of preaching outside the United States and Canada. On this same day, Joseph receives D&C 112.

July 26, 1837

In England, the Rev. Fielding begins to fear he will lose his flock if the elders continue to preach there. He does not allow them to preach any longer.

July 27, 1837

Joseph tries to leave for a Canadian mission, but is detained all day in a lawsuit at Painesville. A man who had wanted Joseph to pay for his cooking stove had sworn out a writ against him. Joseph gives his watch as security.

July 28, 1837

Joseph stays at home until night and then leaves Kirtland and travels 30 miles to Ashtabula, Ohio.

July 29, 1837

Joseph remains in Ashtabula. During the day he bathes at the beach, and in the afternoon he takes a boat to Buffalo.

July 30, 1837

Joseph separates from Brigham Young and Albert P. Rockwood and heads for Toronto with Sidney Rigdon and Thomas B. Marsh. On the morning of this day, in Preston, England, Elders Russell, Hyde, and Kimball have a terrible experience with the devil, being knocked about by an invisible force. They finally rebuke the evil spirit. At ten A.M. at the River Ribble they baptize nine members. George D. Watt runs a race with another for the honor of being the first to be baptized in England in this dispensation and wins; nine thousand spectators watch. Some years later when Heber Kimball told Joseph about the experiences with Satan, Joseph recorded, "When I heard of it, it gave me great joy, for I then knew that the work of God had taken root in that land. . . . The nearer a person approaches the Lord, a greater power will be manifested by the adversary to prevent the accomplishment of His purposes." (OFW 129-32.)

Aug. 1837

The *Messenger and Advocate* prints a warning: "Beware of speculators, renegades, and gamblers, who are duping the unwary and unsuspecting, by palming upon them those bills, which are of no worth here. I discountenance and disapprove of any and all such practices." (HC 2:507.) A newspaper to be called *Elder's Journal* is announced. Joseph Smith will be the editor.

Aug. 4, 1837

Jenetta Richards, daughter of the Rev. John Richards, is the first to be confirmed in England. The ordinance is performed by Heber C. Kimball. Jenetta will later marry Dr. Willard Richards while he is on a mission, which causes a great deal of bickering among the new English converts. The Saints also dislike her because she wears nice clothes (representing the upper class). She takes to wearing her worst clothes.

Aug. 5, 1837

The Saints in Far West agree to build a relatively modest house of the Lord, with Bishop Partridge as treasurer for the venture. Elder Goodson in England, in direct violation of Joseph's orders, reads D&C 76 publicly, "which turned the current feeling generally, and nearly closed the door in all that region." (HC 2:505.)

Aug. 6, 1837

The elders in England begin to be persecuted, being called "thieves" and "sheep stealers" by other ministers. (HC 2:506.)

Aug. 28, 1837

The Ohio banks (except Kirtland) that had suspended payment because of the national depression resume payments at this time.

Late August 1837

Joseph returns to Kirtland, having preached, baptized, and blessed the Saints in Canada.

Sept. 3, 1837

A general conference is held in Kirtland. The body of the Church unanimously sustains Joseph as the president. Joseph presents Sidney Rigdon and Frederick G. Williams for a sustaining vote and Elder Williams is not sustained. Joseph introduces Oliver Cowdery, Joseph Smith, Sr., Hyrum Smith, and (Uncle) John Smith as assistant counselors, stating these, with the others, are to be considered as the heads of the Church. They are sustained unanimously. The Twelve Apostles are presented for a sustaining vote. Luke S. Johnson, Lyman E. Johnson, and John F. Boynton are rejected and disfellowshipped. Boynton, being the only one present, tries to confess his sins and explain his reasons, stating that he had been told that the bank had been instituted by the power of God and would never fail; so his faith was shaken when it did fail. Joseph states that he said the bank would survive only if it was conducted on righteous principles. Another vote is taken in Elder Boynton's case, but he still is not sustained. In other proposed sustainings, objections are made against Martin Harris, John Johnson, Joseph Coe, Joseph Kingsbury, and John P. Greene.

While Joseph was on his mission to Canada in August, dissension in the Church was everywhere. Calling themselves the "Old Standard," Warren Parrish, Martin Harris, Luke S. Johnson, John F. Boynton, and others claimed that they should lead the Church and should control the temple. The "Old Standard" arrived with weapons during one Sunday meeting and threatened to take the temple by force from Joseph Smith, Sr., who was presiding at that meeting. The congregation scattered in fear, the police came in and took out the offenders, and order was finally restored. A young woman who was staying at David Whitmer's home prophesied through a black stone that Joseph had fallen because of transgression, and Church leadership would fall on David Whitmer or Martin Harris. The apostates held many meetings with her and formed their new group. These are the reasons for the lack of sustainings at the September conference. (For further discussion, see IJB 350-52; LMS 241-43; CHC 1:403-4.) Although Joseph has Oliver Cowdery sustained at this time, he announces that Oliver is in transgression. Joseph hopes that he will humble himself.

Sept. 4, 1837

Joseph writes to Zion (Missouri), apologizing for the recent problems and stating, "Brethren, we have waded through affliction and sorrow thus far for the will of God, that language is inadequate to describe. Pray ye therefore with more earnestness for our redemption. You have undoubtedly been informed by letter and otherwise of our difficulties in Kirtland, which are now about being settled." (HC 2:508.) He receives a revelation stating that the Lord is not pleased with John Whitmer and W.W. Phelps.

Sept. 9, 1837
A high council is organized in Kirtland.

Sept. 10, 1837
A meeting is held at the Lord's House in Kirtland. Luke S. Johnson, Lyman E. Johnson, and John F. Boynton of the Twelve, and John P. Greene confess their sins; they are received back into fellowship and return to their former offices.

Sept. 17, 1837
A conference is held in Kirtland. One hundred nine missionaries are called on various missions.

Sept. 18, 1837
The Kirtland bishopric sends a letter to the other branches of the Church, explaining the financial embarrassment involved in the debt caused by building the house of the Lord, and asking the Saints to send a tithe in gold and silver for the relief of Kirtland and the building of Zion.

Sept. 27, 1837
Joseph, Sidney Rigdon, William Smith, and Vincent Knight leave Kirtland for Missouri.

Oct. 1837
The *Elders' Journal* begins publication, replacing the *Messenger and Advocate.* Only two issues will be published in Kirtland. In the case begun the previous February by Samuel D. Rounds, suing Joseph for his banking activities, a jury trial is held and Joseph and Sidney are fined $1,000 each.

Oct. 30, 1837
A plan is presented to the high council for the re-organization of the Church by a group that claims Moroni had appeared to Collins Brewster.

Nov. 1, 1837
About this time Joseph arrives in Far West, Mo.

Nov. 6-7, 1837
At a meeting in Far West it is decided that the building of the house of the Lord will be postponed until the Lord

reveals that it is his will to have it commence. At a general conference on Nov. 7, Frederick G. Williams is again objected to as second counselor and he is replaced by Hyrum Smith, who is accepted unanimously. When David Whitmer is about to be sustained, there is some debate; but after Joseph's remarks about him, he is unanimously accepted as stake president. John Whitmer, after confessing his errors, is sustained as first assistant president. W.W. Phelps confesses and is sustained as the second assistant president. The apostles and the bishopric are also sustained, and the congregations ban trading with liquor, tobbaco, coffee, tea shops, etc.

Nov. 10, 1837
About this time Joseph leaves Far West to return to Kirtland.

Nov. 20, 1837
The high council at Kirtland brings charges against several people who are following revelations given to Collins Brewster, supposedly translated by him from the book of Moroni. Moses Norris ordained Brewster a prophet. Fellowship is withdrawn.

Dec. 1837
John F. Boynton is excommunicated.

Dec. 6, 1837
The Far West high council approves a motion to pay themselves and other Church officials $1.50 per day for Church work.

Dec. 10, 1837
Joseph reaches Kirtland. While he was gone, Warren Parrish, John F. Boynton, Luke S. Johnson, Joseph Coe, and others had tried to overthrow the Church. Under the name "Church of Christ," and calling themselves the "Reformers" or the "Old Standard," they called those who supported Joseph heretics, took over the temple frequently, and tried to run Joseph's followers out of town. Those who defended Joseph are sharply criticized and, according to one testimony, "there were not 20 persons on earth that would declare that Joseph Smith was a prophet of God." (TFO 45.) At one point, someone claimed that Moses was a rascal, the prophets were tyrants, Jesus a despot, Paul a liar, and all religion "a

fudge." (DH 214-15; IJB 353-54.) Shortly after returning to Kirtland, Joseph calls a meeting of elders in the temple. Joseph and Sidney give forceful speeches against the apostates. This group, led by Oliver Cowdery, John Whitmer, and David Whitmer, as well as Boynton, Parrish, and the Johnsons, speak against Joseph. The meeting breaks up in confusion. Nearly 50 leaders of the apostates are excommunicated. Threats of violence continue.

Dec. 22, 1837

Brigham Young, as one of the most vocal defenders of Joseph, begins to fear for his life as the violence grows. He flees from Kirtland on horseback.

Dec. 25, 1837

In England the missionaries hire the "Cock Pit" for preaching. They meet there this Christmas day with 300 Saints for the first conference held in England. They teach the Word of Wisdom to the Saints, the first time that it is publicly taught in England. Joseph closes his record of this year with the comment, "Apostasy, persecution, confusion, and mobocracy strove hard to bear rule at Kirtland, and thus closed the year 1837." (HC 2:529.)

1838

Jan. 1838

"A new year dawned upon the Church in Kirtland in all the bitterness of the spirit of apostate mobocracy." (HC 3:1.) Grandison Newel has another warrant out for Joseph's arrest. This time it is on the charge of fraud. Joseph has been in constant legal difficulty in the past year. Foreclosures, warrants for his arrest, trials, seizure of property, and any other possible legal maneuvers have been used against him. Joseph's mother claims that this is either to gain his property or to get him put into jail. The "Reformers" plan to sue Joseph for debt, and if he is unable to pay, they will take over ownership of the Egyptian mummies being kept in the temple. They threaten to burn them.

Jan. 12, 1838

Joseph receives three revelations, the contents of which are now unknown. Joseph flees from Kirtland on his horse, "Old Charley," with Sidney Rigdon and rides 60 miles the first day. According to one story, a repentant apostate warns Joseph of a plot to assassinate him. The mob appears before Joseph can escape. He is quickly placed in a box nailed onto an ox cart. He is then driven out of town to safety, gets his horse, and rides off. (See IJB 355.)

Jan. 13, 1838

At Norton, Ohio, Joseph and Sidney wait 36 hours for their families to arrive.

Jan. 15-16, 1838

The printing press in Kirtland, formerly owned by the

Church but attached for debt payment in December, burns down. Those loyal to Joseph blame the apostates. The apostates, of course, blame those loyal to Joseph.

Jan. 16, 1838

The families travel in wagons toward Far West, Mo. Joseph reaches Dublin, Indiana, where he stays for nine days with Brigham Young. Destitute, he asks Brigham Young if he has any advice for him. Joseph cuts wood to sustain himself, being totally without finances; a member sells his farm for $300 and donates it to him. His enemies chase him for two hundred miles, often crossing his tracks or looking for him when he is hidden in the same house with just a partition between them.

Feb. 5, 1838

A general assembly of the Church is held at Far West, Mo., to decide whether or not David Whitmer, John Whitmer, and W.W. Phelps should continue as the (stake) presidency of the Church in Missouri. The assembly is repeated at other Mormon settlements for the next four days. After lengthy arguments, there is an almost unanimous vote to reject these three as presidents. Whitmer and Phelps are accused of having used $1400 of Church funds to buy Missouri lands and then selling them to the Saints for a profit. They are also accused of having sold lands in Jackson County, which constituted a denial of the faith (because of the prophecies concerning the eventual return to Jackson County). David Whitmer has also been charged with breaking the Word of Wisdom.

Feb. 10, 1838

The high council meeting is held at Far West. It is recommended that several members volunteer for military duty even though, as licensed ministers, they are exempt. Thomas B. Marsh and David W. Patten are appointed to lead the Church until Joseph arrives. Joseph and Sidney Rigdon are, at this time, each leading a party by a different route toward Missouri.

March 1838

Joseph records the political motto of the Church, which praises the U.S. Constitution and democracy but warns, "woe to tyrants, mobs, aristocracy, anarchy, and toryism, and all those who invent or seek out unrighteous and vexatious law suits, under the pretext and color of law, or office, either religious or political. Exalt the standard of Democracy!" (HC 3:9.)

D&C 113 is recorded, which contains the Prophet's answers to certain questions concerning Isaiah.

March 14, 1838
Joseph and Emma, who is pregnant, arrive in Far West to the open arms of their eager friends. They move into the home of George W. Harris. Every few days more Saints arrive.

March 29, 1838
Joseph writes a letter to the Kirtland Saints saying that because of the many lawsuits in the past seven years he could not leave Kirtland in a good situation, "but if there are any wrongs, they shall all be noticed, so far as the Lord gives me ability and power to do so." (HC 3:9-12.)

Spring 1838
The town of Far West begins to develop, with 1,500 Saints, 150 houses, 6 stores, and 1 schoolhouse, which is also used for a church. Later, other Saints will arrive from Kirtland and the population will swell and spill over out of Caldwell into Ray, Daviess, and Carroll counties. Sidney Rigdon builds the biggest house, with double logs; it includes an endowment room. Of the 5,000 people living in Caldwell, 4,900 are Mormons.

April 4, 1838
Sidney Rigdon and his group reach Far West after suffering many afflictions along the way.

April 6-7, 1838
General conference is held at Far West, where they celebrate the anniversary of the organization of the Church. New appointments are made. Thomas B. Marsh is made stake president of Far West with Brigham Young and David Patten as his counselors. John Whitmer is asked to return the copies of the Church historical record that he had made, but he seems reluctant to do so.

April 11, 1838
Oliver Cowdery is accused in a Church court:

1. For bringing lawsuits against the brethren.

2. For trying to destroy the character of Joseph Smith by accusing him of adultery.

3. For not attending meetings.

4. For denying the faith by refusing to be governed by the revelations in temporal affairs.

5. For selling lands in Jackson County.

6. For sending an insulting letter to the high council.

7. For leaving his holy calling and working for filthy lucre.

8. For being connected in suspect businesses.

9. For leaving the work of God for the work of the world.

April 12, 1838

All charges except for four, five, and six are sustained, and Oliver Cowdery is excommunicated from the Church.

April 13, 1838

Five charges are brought against David Whitmer. He withdraws fellowship from the Church before they can cut him off. Elders Luke S. Johnson and Lyman E. Johnson are also cut off.

April 17, 1838

Joseph receives D&C 114. This same date he also receives a revelation for Brigham Young.

April 20, 1838

Heber C. Kimball and Orson Hyde leave Liverpool for America, leaving Joseph Fielding as mission president, and Willard Richards and William Clayton as his counselors. Since they arrived in Great Britain nine months earlier, about 1500 people have been converted and 26 branches established. Until the return of the Twelve two years later, almost as many would leave the Church in England as would join, due to a series of internal problems. (See WC 7-11.)

April 26, 1838

Joseph receives D&C 115.

April 27, 1838

Joseph begins writing the history of the Church from its beginning to this date.

May 1838

Joseph spends the month in writing his history, preaching sermons, attending Church courts, and traveling.

May 6, 1838

Sunday. Joseph preaches, cautioning the Saints to beware of men who come among them growling and whining for money. He also explains astronomy as understood by Abraham.

May 7, 1838

Elder Reynolds Cahoon and Parley P. Pratt arrive in Far West from New York City.

May 8, 1838

Joseph publishes in the *Elders' Journal* answers to frequently asked questions concerning basic Mormon beliefs, the origin of the Book of Mormon, Joseph Smith as a prophet, the communal order, polygamy, the Mormons' view of abolition, Joseph's reputation as a money digger (Joseph admits to it but says he only got $14 a month for it).

May 11, 1838

William E. McLellin is tried in a Church court for lustful desires and for lack of confidence in the Church leaders. (McLellin is eventually cut off from the Church; yet 50 years later he testifies, "I have no faith in Mormonism as an ism, even from its start . . . but when a man goes at the Book of Mormon he touches the apple of my eye. He fights against truth—against purity—against light—against the purest, or one of the truest, purest books on earth." BYS, Su '70, 486.)

May 18-June 1, 1838

Joseph leaves Far West and travels to the northern part of the state, comforting the poor, etc. He then returns to Far West.

May 19, 1838

Joseph marches across the Grand River to the mouth of Honey Creek and from there takes a boat 18 miles to Lyman Wight's home. Wight lives at the foot of Tower Hill, a name Joseph gives the hill because of some ruins, which he designates as an old Nephite altar or tower. One-half mile from Lyman Wight's ferry, the brethren reach a place called Spring Hill; the Lord names it Adam-ondi-Ahman, "because, said He, it is the place where Adam shall come to visit his people, or the Ancient of Days shall sit, as spoken of by Daniel the Prophet." (HC 3:34-35. For a discussion of the Nephite tower see BYS, Su '73, 553-76 and BYS, Aut '72, 27-35.) The above-quoted explanation of the name Adam-ondi-Ahman, is now found as D&C 116.

June 2, 1838
Alexander Hale Smith is born to Emma in Far West. He is named for Joseph's friend and lawyer, Alexander Doniphan, and is also given Emma's maiden name, Hale.

June 4, 1838
Joseph leaves Far West for Adam-ondi-Ahman with Sidney Rigdon and Hyrum.

June 5, 1838
They reach Col. Lyman Wight's house in the rain and survey the area for several days.

June 17, 1838
John D. Lee and wife, Aggatha, are baptized in Far West.

June 19 or 17 (?), 1838
Sidney Rigdon delivers the famous "Salt Sermon" based on Matthew 5:13. At this time there are so many dissenters in Missouri that many of the loyal Saints feel that the old settlers of Missouri will be stirred up against the Saints by the apostates. This sermon is Sidney's warning to the apostates that they, like the salt, "have lost his savour, . . . it is thenceforth good for nothing but to be cast out and to be trodden under foot of men." He implies that the apostates will be literally trodden under foot if they do not move out at once.

Shortly thereafter, a printed notice addressed to Oliver Cowdery, David Whitmer, John Whitmer, W.W. Phelps, and Luke E. Johnson is circulated, warning them to leave Missouri at once, under threat of physical violence. This is signed by 84 leading Saints, the first of whom was named Sampson Avard. Joseph Smith and Sidney Rigdon did not sign this petition. The apostates flee from Missouri at once, hoping their families will follow them shortly.

About this time, a secret oath-bound society of some of the Saints is formed with the intent of using unlawful violence against the enemies of the Church. They first form to drive out the dissenters and apostates; then they turn against nonmember Missourians living in the area. They swear themselves to secrecy, silence, and loyalty in hidden meetings with oaths and signs of recognition. They eventually adopt the name Danites. Their leader, Sampson Avard, turns from defending the Church to attacking it in November 1838. (For further details concerning the Danites, see BYS, Su '74, 421-50; BYS, Aut '72, 36-61; SB 215-86.)

June 28, 1838

The Adam-ondi-Ahman Stake is organized. John Smith, Joseph's uncle, is made stake president, with Reynolds Cahoon and Lyman Wight as counselors. "Adam-ondi-Ahman," a hymn composed by W.W. Phelps, is the meeting's closing song.

July 4, 1838

The Saints hold a Fourth of July celebration in Far West. The cornerstones for the temple are laid (in accordance with D&C 115:8). Sidney Rigdon gives a highly emotional speech declaring the Saints' "Declaration of Independence"from mobs and persecutions; he states, "We have not only when smitten on one cheek, turned the other, but we have done it, again and again, until we are weary of being smitten, and tired of being trampled upon. . . . We will never be the aggressors; we will infringe on the rights of no people; but shall stand for our own until death. . . . We this day then proclaim ourselves free, with a purpose and a determination, that never can be broken, No never! *No Never!!* NO NEVER!!!" (This oration is published in a pamphlet; see BYS, Su '74, 517-27.)

July 6, 1838

Joseph receives a letter from Heber C. Kimball and Orson Hyde in Kirtland expressing good feelings. He also receives a letter from his brother, Don Carlos Smith, requesting funds for his group of people who are trying to travel from Kirtland. Don Carlos states that he sold all of Joseph's goods for $45.74, and now has $25 left over to get 28 people and 13 horses 500 miles.

July 6-Oct. 4, 1838

The Kirtland Camp of Saints travels from Kirtland to Adam-ondi-Ahman, Mo. On March 6, 1838, a meeting of the seventies in the Kirtland Temple had decided to move the Saints from Kirtland to Missouri. On July 6, 1838, a wagon train, over a mile long with over 500 Saints, leaves Kirtland for Missouri. Because of great suffering and discouragement, by the time the group reaches Springfield, Ill., about halfway, only 260 are left. They reach Adam-ondi-Ahman on October 4, 1838. (For a day-by-day account of the three-month journey, see HC 3:87-148.)

July 8, 1838

Tithing is instituted for the Church. Joseph prays inquiring how much property the Lord requires for a tithing, and receives D&C 119. Also given are D&C 120, 117, and 118. Another revelation is received: W.W. Phelps and Frederick G. Williams are told that because of transgressions, their former standing had been taken away; however, they may now be again ordained elders in the Church and preach the gospel. (Although Phelps does not take advantage of this revelation, Williams does.)

July 9, 1838

A conference is held in which the new members of the Twelve are officially notified and called into the quorum.

July 10, 1838

Joseph visits Adam-ondi-Ahman with several others. When the Saints are slow to consecrate their lands to the Church, he proposes an alternate plan wherein the Church would lease the property from 10 to 99 years without interest.

July 26, 1838

The First Presidency, high council, and bishop's court meet at Far West to dispose of Church lands. It is decided that all Church lands will be put into the hands of the bishops. It is also decided that the traveling expenses of the First Presidency will be defrayed, and that the Church will use its influence to stop the selling of liquor in Far West.

July 28, 1838

Joseph leaves Far West for Adam-ondi-Ahman to help

settle the brethren from Canada who have just moved there.

Aug. 6, 1838

A fight breaks out when the Mormons are prevented from voting in the election at Gallatin (near Adam-ondi-Ahman). Because of the rumored activities of the Danites, and because of the pamphlet publication and circulation of Rigdon's Fourth of July speech, anti-Mormon feeling had been building once again in Missouri. Two weeks before the election, Judge Joseph Morin warned Mormons that William Peniston, an anti-Mormon candidate, had threatened to use force to keep Mormons from voting against him. When several Saints come to Gallatin to vote, they are attacked and a fight breaks out. Although Gallatin, the Daviess County seat, has only ten houses and three saloons, rumors spread that two Mormons have been killed and that thirty Saints have beat off a mob of two hundred. Other rumors of both Mormon and mob vengeance circulate rapidly.

Aug. 7, 1838

Joseph, in Far West, receives the report from Gallatin that two or three Saints have been killed while trying to vote. He leaves for Gallatin with Sidney Rigdon, Hyrum Smith, and 15 or 20 others (who take arms for protection).

Aug. 8, 1838

Joseph and the others meet with Adam Black, justice of the peace, and ask him to sign a letter stating that he had nothing to do with the mobs at Gallatin. Black later testifies that he was forced to sign the documents under threat of violence, and others state that Sidney Rigdon pulled a sword on Black.

Aug. 10, 1838

William P. Peniston swears out a warrant to Judge Austin A. King against Joseph and Lyman Wight stating that they have an army of 500 armed men, and with a force of 120 have threatened the life of Justice Adam Black and forced him to sign the affidavit of August 8.

Aug. 11, 1838

Joseph leaves Far West to visit the Canadian Saints at the Forks of the Grand River. A committee arrives in Far

West accusing the Saints of disturbing the peace on Aug. 8. A general meeting is held at the city hall, where the Mormons and non-Mormons answer each others' accusations.

Aug. 13, 1838

Joseph and his men are chased 12 miles by a mob. Joseph learns that Judge King has issued a warrant for the arrest of both him and Lyman Wight because of the incident on Aug. 8.

Aug. 16, 1838

Judge Morin and a sheriff come to arrest Joseph. He says he is always willing to submit to the laws of the land, but asks not to be tried in Daviess County because of his many enemies there. The sheriff decides not to serve the writ. Lyman Wight, however, defies the sheriff's authority, and when the story is published, state officials take immediate action against the Saints.

Aug. 20, 1838

Joseph organizes the Saints into several agricultural companies.

Aug. 28, 1838

Joseph spends several days at home. Adam Black swears out an affidavit stating that 154 men threatened his life on Aug. 8. Joseph calls him a liar.

Aug. 30, 1838

Governor Boggs, having heard of Lyman Wight's defiance of the law officers, orders General Atchison (Joseph's former lawyer) to call out 400 of the militia in preparation against the Mormons. Joseph and Sidney Rigdon spend considerable time talking with John Corrill, who is on the verge of apostasy.

Fall 1838

Under the advice of Alexander Doniphan, the Saints form into "armies of Israel," which are two armed units organized and ordered into the field by General Doniphan in Caldwell County and General Parks in Daviess County (both are officers of the state militia). Thus, when these troops are ordered into battle in October, the Saints consider themselves as duly authorized state troops fighting against illegal mobs.

Sept. 1, 1838

The First Presidency, with the help of a surveyor, establish the city of Zion, 15 miles from Far West, as a place of safety to which the Saints can flee. Joseph records that the Saints have been very peaceable in spite of the rising storm about them.

Sept. 2, 1838

General Atchison of Liberty comes to Joseph to give him legal advice, convincing him to submit to trial.

Sept. 3, 1838

James Mulholland commences writing for Joseph as his scribe. Joseph begins dictating to him what will become Joseph's six-volume history of the Church, including the best-known version of the first vision. (For details about Joseph's previous and later scribes, see BYS, Sp '71, 439-73.)

Sept. 4, 1838

As rumors of mob violence increase, Joseph hires General Atchison and Alexander Doniphan to represent the Saints. Joseph and Sidney Rigdon commence studying law under them with the hope of passing the bar within 12 months.

Sept. 5, 1838

Joseph swears out an affidavit relating his side of the incident with Adam Black, claiming that he never threatened the man's life.

Sept. 7, 1838

Joseph stands trial for the incident with Adam Black before Judge Austin A. King (a Methodist whose brother had been killed in the anti-Mormon riots of Jackson County in 1833—FMM 90). Joseph is accused of having threatened Adam Black's life on Aug. 8, 1838. In spite of the lack of hard evidence, the judge gives in to fear of mobbers and fines Joseph and Lyman Wight a $500 security bond. William P. Peniston is the prosecuting attorney. Rumors reach Joseph that a mob has gathered to attack Adam-ondi-Ahman. A few brethren from Far West have left for Adam-ondi-Ahman to assist the Saints there.

Sept. 9, 1838

Captain William Allred and ten men learn of a wagon full

of guns and ammunition that were going to the mob that was planning an attack on Adam-ondi-Ahman. Allred finds the wagon broken down, arrests three illegal gun carriers, and distributes the guns to the Saints for their protection. The three prisoners are taken to Far West for trial. At this time, the mob has also been taking prisoners from time to time and sending out rumors of torture, in order to "make us commit the first act of violence." (HC 3:74-75.)

Sept. 10, 1838

Judge King orders that the guns be returned to the government and that the prisoners be freed. He also advises General Atchison to take 200 men and to break up the gathering forces in Daviess and Caldwell Counties.

Sept. 12, 1838

The gunrunners are tried in Far West. Governor Boggs receives a communication from Daviess County charging the "Mormons" with every crime imaginable. Sixty or more mobbers enter the town of De Witt (Carroll County) and warn the Saints to leave at once.

Sept. 14, 1838

William Dryden tells Governor Boggs that he, with ten men as guards, has tried to serve a writ against certain Saints for the incident of Aug. 8 with Adam Black, but the "Mormons" are so well armed that it is impossible to enforce any laws in Caldwell or Daviess counties.

Sept. 15, 1838

Alexander Doniphan writes to Major General Atchison stating that he and his 200 men marched to Far West, received the confiscated weapons and the three prisoners from the Saints, and, to keep the peace, camped between the Saints' forces led by Lyman Wight and the mob forces led by a Dr. Austin of Carroll County.

Sept. 20, 1838

Dr. Austin, after much of his force has been disbanded, takes 100 to 150 men and goes 50 miles southwest to the town of De Witt and besieges that community until October 11, 1838. They give the citizens of De Witt an ultimatum to leave the state by October 1 or face extermination.

Sept. 24, 1838

Governor Boggs orders several generals to discharge their troops, having heard that peace has been restored in Daviess and Caldwell Counties.

Sept. 26, 1838

Lyman Wight and 15 to 20 Saints promise to go to trial at Gallatin. Two committees representing each party agree that the Saints will buy out the land owned by the non-Mormons in Daviess County.

Late Sept. 1838

Local newspapers debate the Mormon question, some stating that the Mormons have broken their promise to stay within Caldwell County by spreading to other counties. Other papers say that a law requiring that members of any religion stay within a certain county is unconstitutional.

Oct. 1, 1838

Generals Atchison, Doniphan, and Parks organize the mobs into militia units and then disband them. Many of them travel 50 miles southeast to De Witt in Carroll County and join Austin's mob surrounding that town.

Oct. 2, 1838

The mob surrounding De Witt, now about 300, opens fire on the town. The Kirtland Camp arrives at Far West, and reaches Adam-ondi-Ahman two days later.

Oct. 4, 1838

The mob fires on the Saints in De Witt, some of whom decide to return the fire in self defense. General S.D. Lucas (an enemy of the Saints since the Jackson County expulsion in 1833) writes to Governor Boggs that "if a fight has actually taken place, of which I have no doubt, it will create excitement in the whole of upper Missouri, and those base and degraded beings will be exterminated from the face of the earth. If one of the citizens of Carroll should be killed, before five days I believe there will be from four to five thousand volunteers in the field against the Mormons, and nothing but their blood will satisfy them." (HC 3:150.)

Oct. 6, 1838

Joseph travels through back roads with several volunteers

119

and reaches De Witt. There he finds the Saints in desperate circumstances, with very few supplies left. He obtains several affidavits and sends an urgent plea for aid to Governor Boggs, asking for the protection of the state militia. On this same date a quarterly conference is held at Far West, Mo. John Taylor is sustained as one of the Twelve.

Oct. 9, 1838
Mr. Caldwell, who took the Saints' plea for help to the governor, returns with the governor's reply that because the quarrel is between the mob and the Mormons, they might "fight it out" on their own. Captain Samuel Bogart, a former mobber, is placed in control of the militia forces. Several of the Saints start to fight back against the mob.

Oct. 11, 1838
In a compromise move, the Saints agree to leave. They are never paid for their lands, and as they leave, they see many of their cattle killed and their homes burned; some Saints die during the journey.

Oct. 14, 1838
Seven are cut off from the Church in Preston, England. It is a time of pruning there; "the powers of darkness raged, and it seemed as though Satan was fully determined to make an end of the work in that kingdom." (HC 3:162.)

Oct. 15, 1838
The 70 wagons of the destitute De Witt Saints have, by now, reached and settled in Far West. Joseph organizes the Far West Saints into a company of 100 men, to operate as a legal unit of the state militia, under Lt. Colonel George M. Hinkle, who has been acting under orders of General Doniphan. They are very careful to be sure that all actions are in strict accordance with state law. Joseph addresses the Far West Saints in terrible anger, saying, "All are mobs; the governor is mob, the militia is mob, and the whole state is mob. . . . I am determined that we will not give another foot, and I care not how many come against us." (DH 231-32.)

Oct. 17-19, 1838
A snowstorm hits Missouri. Col. Hinkle and his 100 men march to Adam-ondi-Ahman to join forces with Lyman

Wight. There they hear that the nearby town of Millport has been attacked and several houses burned. General Parks of the state militia gives Lyman Wight official orders to disperse any mobs around Adam-ondi-Ahman and Millport. Lyman Wight and Captain David Patten each command a force of about 60 men, and Wight takes his and heads for Millport, while Patten heads for Gallatin. Patten's men find a cannon left by the mobs. Houses and stores are burned, the mobs blaming the Mormons and the Mormons saying the mobs burned their own houses in order to blame the Mormons.

Oct. 19, 1838

Joseph, having been accused of running away and cheating his creditors in Kirtland, receives a card stating that his agent in Kirtland, Oliver Granger, has done his best to be honest in satisfying old debts. Joseph happily records this rare positive note in his record. Samuel Bogart, William P. Peniston, and several others swear out affidavits accusing the Saints of terrible robbings, burnings, etc. Orson Hyde leaves Far West (on his way to apostasy).

Oct. 22, 1838

Joseph returns to Far West, where he learns that several of the brethren have been taken prisoner by the mobs.

Oct. 23, 1838

The Saints flock into Far West until it is full of destitute citizens.

Oct. 24, 1838

Thomas B. Marsh, formerly president of the Twelve, goes to Richmond to swear out an affidavit against Joseph Smith. He accuses Joseph of secretly backing the Danites in their many works of destruction, saying that Joseph claimed "he would be a second Mohammed to this generation, and that he would make it one gore of blood from the Rocky Mountains to the Atlantic ocean; that like Mohammed, whose motto in treating for peace was, 'the Alcoran or the Sword.' So should it be eventually with us, 'Joseph Smith or the sword.'" Orson Hyde, sick with fever, also signs the affidavit stating that he believes most of Marsh's accusations to be true. (HC 3:166-68; twenty years later, Marsh repents and tells of his apostasy in JD 5:206-10.)

Oct. 25, 1838
The Battle of Crooked River. Rumors spread throughout the state that the Mormons are fighting back in strength. Citizens organize a militia under Samuel Bogart, who rides to drive the Mormons from the southern part of Caldwell County. When Captain David Patten (known as Captain Fear-Naught) hears this, he assembles 70 elders and marches to Bogart's camp on the Crooked River. At dawn they attack and Bogart's men flee across the river. The Saints take the supplies left behind by the Missourians, but seven Saints are wounded and three eventually die, including Patten himself, the first martyred apostle. When Patten dies two days later, some of his last words are, "Whatever you do else, O! do not deny the faith!" (HC 3:169-72.)

Oct. 26, 1838
A mob of almost 2,000 begins to camp at Richmond, Mo.

Oct. 27, 1838
A funeral is held for David Patten. Joseph testifies, "There lies a man that has done just as he said he would—he has laid down his life for his friends." (HC 3:175.) Governor Boggs's exterminating order is issued. Hearing the many rumors of the destruction and insurrection of the Saints, Boggs orders that "the Mormons must be treated as enemies and *must be exterminated* or driven from the state, if necessary for the public good. Their outrages are beyond all description." (HC 3:175.)

Oct. 30, 1838
Haun's Mill Massacre. At about four P.M. approximately 240 men ride up to the small community of Haun's Mill (which has fewer than 15 buildings) and open fire on a flag of truce. Many of the Saints gather in the blacksmith's shop; guns are stuck through the cracks in the logs and fired until most in the building are dead. A few escape across the river into the hills. By the end of the massacre, 1600 rounds of ammunition have been fired at 40 people; 18 or 19 have been killed, and about 15 wounded. Among those killed are boys under 10 and men over 75 years old.

As soon as Governor Boggs's exterminating order is received, General Atchison withdraws from the army at Richmond, Mo. At evening a state militia force of about 2,000 approaches and surrounds the city of Far West. They are led by General Lucas. The Saints spend the night building up fortifications and preparing for a massive battle in the morning.

Oct. 31, 1838

Far West is surrounded by 2,000 troops, which are soon reinforced by 1500 more troops. The Saints are outnumbered by approximately five to one. However, neither side is eager to begin the battle, and the day is spent in a standoff, with each side trying to decide what to do. In the evening, Col. Hinkle goes out with a flag of truce to meet with the Missourians. Joseph, Sidney Rigdon, Parley P. Pratt, Lyman Wight, and George W. Robinson then go out to meet the flag and are taken prisoner. General Lucas marches them in front of the leering, screaming soldiers, who abuse them greatly. They are forced to sleep on the ground during a rainstorm while the guards mock them, asking Joseph to show them angels and miracles.

Nov. 1, 1838

Hyrum Smith and Amasa M. Lyman are added to the group of prisoners. A long court-martial is held, which lasts until midnight. During this time, the militia goes into various Mormon settlements, robbing, destroying, ransacking, and raping at will. After the court-martial, General Lucas orders Brigadier General Doniphan to "take Joseph Smith and the other prisoners into the public square of Far West, and shoot them at 9 o'clock tomorrow morning." Doniphan answers, "It is cold-blooded murder. I will not obey your order. . . . If you execute these men, I will hold you responsible before an earthly tribunal, so help me God." (HC 3:190-92. For details concerning General Doniphan and his heroic stand in defense of Joseph, see CHC 1:490-93; BYS, Su '73, 462-72.)

Nov. 2, 1838

Sampson Avard is captured and begins to testify that Daniteism is an order from the Church. Joseph and the other prisoners are taken into town to bid a quick goodbye to their wives and children. The Saints are ordered to surrender all arms and sign away all possessions. Hyrum, who is very sick, is forced to march with the other prisoners. General S.D. Lucas writes the details of the conquest to Gov. Boggs. Prisoners are then put in covered wagons for a 60-mile journey to Independence, where they are to be sentenced.

Nov. 3, 1838

Joseph prophesies to Parley P. Pratt: "The word of the Lord came to me last night that our lives should be given us, and that whatsoever we may suffer during this captivity, not one of our lives should be taken." (PPP 192.)

Nov. 4, 1838

General Clark arrives in Far West with 1600 men and 500 more on the way. (Six thousand men had thus visited Far West within a week, when it only had 500 men to defend it.) Clark forbids anyone to leave the city, and the starving Saints are forced to live on parched corn. Joseph and the other prisoners arrive in Independence. One lady asks which of the prisoners is the one the Saints worship as Lord and Savior. When Joseph replies that he is nothing but a man sent by Jesus Christ to preach the gospel, he is able to preach a sermon to the lady and the others, thus fulfilling his own prophecy of a few months previous that an elder would preach a sermon in Jackson County before the close of 1838.

Nov. 5, 1838

Joseph and the other prisoners are kept under a small guard. Parley P. Pratt escapes; but fearing reprisals against Joseph and the others, he decides to return voluntarily. General Clark arrives in Far West to arrest 56 additional prisoners.

Nov. 6, 1838

General Clark addresses the Saints in Far West, telling them that it is only out of kindness that he is allowing them to leave the state instead of murdering them, and that "as for your leaders, do not once think—do not imagine for a moment—do not let it enter your mind that they will be delivered, or that you will see their faces again, for their *fate is fixed—their die is cast—their doom is sealed."* He then takes the new prisoners from Far West and heads for Richmond under a large guard. (HC 3:202-4.)

Nov. 8, 1838

A snowstorm hits Missouri. General Wilson arrives at Adam-ondi-Ahman and surrounds the town with his guards so no one can leave or enter. A court of inquiry is instituted, with Adam Black a member of the bench (most of the problems began with him on Aug. 8, 1838). Joseph and the other prisoners are marched toward Richmond, but because there are so few guards it is feared that they will come under mob violence, and more guards are sent for.

Nov. 9, 1838

Joseph and the other prisoners reach Richmond, Ray County, where they are put in double chains. After much abuse they are forced to sleep on the floor in the cold and rain. Joseph meets General Clark.

Nov. 10, 1838

The other 56 prisoners are put in Richmond jail with Joseph and his fellow prisoners. Joseph learns that during the mobbings about 30 Saints were killed, many more were wounded, 100 are missing, and approximately 60 prisoners are waiting trial at Richmond for an unknown charge. In Adam-ondi-Ahman a three-day board of inquiry concludes, Adam Black having been judge, and all Saints are honorably acquitted. General Wilson orders every family out of Adam-ondi-Ahman within ten days. He gives them permission to go to Caldwell County until spring, but says they must leave the state by then or be exterminated.

Nov. 11-28, 1838

Over 50 Latter-day Saint prisoners are kept in the Richmond jail, chained together in an unroofed courthouse. Sidney Rigdon gets very sick from exposure and loses his powers of reasoning. One night during this time the guards blaspheme and boast about their treatment, rapings, and murder of the Saints, and Joseph arises in his chains and rebukes the guards with might and power, causing them to quail and beg before him. (For a list of prisoners, see HC 3:209.)

Nov. 12, 1838

Joseph writes a touching letter to Emma, thanking her for her letter and praying that he might see his "lovely family" once again. He lists the prisoners he is chained to, stating "and thus we are bound together in chains as well as the cords of everlasting love." He also tells her that the lawyers Doniphan and Rees will defend them. (DH 247.)

Nov. 13-28, 1838

The 13-day mock trial is held at Richmond with Judge Austin A. King presiding. On Nov. 28 most of the prisoners are released. Lyman Wight, Caleb Baldwin, Hyrum Smith, Alexander McRae, Sidney Rigdon, and Joseph Smith are sent to Liberty jail, while Parley P. Pratt and four others are sent to Richmond jail to await further trials. During the trial Joseph's lawyer states, "If a cohort of angels were to come down, and declare we were innocent, it would all be the same." (HC 3:209-13.) Shortly after Avard testifies against the Danites, the society that had been led by him dies out altogether, having existed less than five months.

Nov. 30, 1838

Joseph and the other prisoners begin their trip to the Liberty jail. During this time former apostle Wm. E. McLellin and others rob the homes of some of the Saints, including that of Sidney Rigdon. McLellin asks for the privilege of flogging Joseph, but the sheriff only agrees to a fair fight between the two, and McLellin backs down.

Dec. 1, 1838

Joseph begins his stay in Liberty jail, which lasts almost six months. The jail is 22 feet square, with walls four feet thick. The food is filthy, and at one time the guards boast that they have fed the prisoners human flesh. At another point the prisoners are fed poison. However, some exciting things also occur during their prison stay. Parley P. Pratt writes poetry and a history of his life; Lyman Wight is blessed several times by Joseph and learns many things "yet unknown to the Church." George A. Smith is called to the apostleship; Brigham Young and others receive instructions about moving the Saints to Illinois; Joseph reveals several of the most important sections of the D&C.

Dec. 16, 1838

Joseph writes to the Church from Liberty jail, comforting the Saints in their afflictions and cautioning them to beware of those like Sampson Avard who would teach false doctrines in the name of the First Presidency.

Dec. 19, 1838

John Corrill presents a petition to the state legislature signed by Edward Partridge, Brigham Young, Heber C. Kimball, and others, which explains the history of the conflict in Missouri. A Mr. Turner submits a bill calling for a full investigation of the troubles in Missouri. A huge debate develops over the problem, but eventually nothing happens. After the Saints have completely left Missouri, $2,000 in relief funds is approved for the 12,000 Saints, while $200,000 is voted to pay the state militia for the expenses in the Mormon war.

John Taylor and John E. Page are ordained apostles at Far West.

Dec. 25, 1838

Don Carlos Smith and George A. Smith return to Missouri from missions in Kentucky and Tennessee, 1500 miles away. They are chased by a mob, and almost freeze to death, but arrive safely.

Dec. 27, 1838

Anson Call returns to Ray County to sell some property and is taken by a mob and beaten for four hours, until he escapes.

1839

Jan. 1839

Sidney Rigdon, due to ill health, is allowed out of Liberty jail to stand an early trial. He defends himself in a room full of Mormon haters. His speech is so eloquent that his former enemies are moved to tears, and they collect $100 for his benefit.

Jan. 7, 1839

Anson Call returns to his farm to secure his property, and is again captured and beaten with a stick.

Jan. 16, 1839

Mr. Turner introduces in the Missouri state senate a bill to investigate the recent disturbances in Missouri. About this time, President Brigham Young begins to make plans to help the poor and other Saints leave Missouri.

Jan. 24, 1839

Joseph petitions the Missouri legislature for justice, claiming "it is not our object to complain—to asperse any one. All we ask is a fair and impartial trial. We ask the sympathies of no one. We ask sheer justice." (HC 3:247-49.)

Jan. 26, 1839

A meeting of Church leaders is held in Far West to discuss the best way out of the present emergency. A committee of seven is appointed to seek relief for the poor.

Jan. 29, 1839

The brethren again meet at Far West to discuss how to best help each other. Brigham Young moves that they make an oath to never desert the poor until they are free from the state of Missouri. This passes.

Jan. 31, 1839

Turner's bill calling for an investigation passes the senate. Joseph sends a $100 bill from jail to the poor brethren trying to leave the state.

Feb. 4, 1839

Mr. Turner's bill of Jan. 16 is tabled until July 4 (by which time all the Saints will be out of the state). The bill is never taken up again.

Feb. 6-15, 1839

Emma, having visited Joseph twice since his imprisonment, leaves Missouri with her children, with the help of Stephen Markham. They walk 150 miles across Missouri to the east toward Illinois. When Emma crosses the frozen Mississippi on Feb. 15, she has her four small children with her and two cotton bags full of Joseph's most sacred papers hidden under her full skirts (including his inspired revision of the Bible). She crosses the river and reaches Quincy, Illinois, on the other shore, where she stays until Joseph is freed from prison.

Feb. 8, 1839

Joseph and the others make their first prison escape attempt, which fails because six Saints come to visit in the middle of the effort.

Feb. 14, 1839

Brigham Young (acting president of the Quorum of the Twelve, since Thomas B. Marsh's apostasy and David W. Patten's death) leaves Far West for Illinois because of bitter persecution against him.

Feb. 25, 1839

The citizens of Quincy, Ill., approve a resolution offering aid to the destitute Latter-day Saints.

Feb. 26, 1839

Dr. Isaac Galland, an admitted thief, counterfeiter, and gang member, writes to a Church member stating that he has several farms and lands for sale in Illinois and the Iowa territory. About this time, Sidney Rigdon is allowed to escape from jail. He had been released in January by the decision of a judge; however, because of his fear of mobs he decided to stay in prison until it was safer to leave the area. At this time his sufferings became too great; he became sick and declared that "the sufferings of Jesus Christ were a fool to his." The sheriff allows him to escape. He is chased by a mob, but finally succeeds in reaching Quincy, Ill. (HC 3:264.)

Feb. 27, 1839

Citizens of Quincy, Ill., adopt a resolution denouncing the Missouri mobs and Missouri state officials. Soon Gov. Thomas Carlin of Illinois and Iowa Territorial Governor Robert Lucas invite the Saints to settle in those areas. The Saints have been debating whether to gather in one place again or to scatter throughout the area, but Brigham Young and Joseph continue to promote the idea of the gathering.

Mar. 1839

One hundred and thirty families camp on the bank of the Mississippi waiting for the ice to thaw so they can cross into Illinois. Soon after this time, approximately 5,000 Saints move into western Illinois.

Mar. 3, 1839

Joseph makes his second escape attempt from Liberty jail by digging through the wall. The tools break before the wall does, but he is pleased because, to fix the wall, he states, "cost the county a round sum." (HC 3:292.)

Mar. 5, 1839

Edward Partridge writes to Joseph advising him not to make a deal with Dr. Isaac Galland.

Mar. 8, 1839

Alanson Ripley brings news from Joseph in Liberty jail that the Saints should sell all lands in Missouri, including the lands that they own in Jackson County. They make about $2700 from these sales, which greatly helps the poorer Saints in moving from Far West to Illinois.

Mar. 15, 1839

Joseph writes a letter of encouragement and friendship to Mrs. Norman Bull (Buell) who had tried to visit him in Liberty jail.

Mar. 17, 1839

A conference is held at Quincy, Ill., and George Hinkle, Sampson Avard, John Corrill, Reed Peck, W.W. Phelps,

F.G. Williams, Thomas B. Marsh, Burr Riggs, and several others are excommunicated from the Church because they "left us in the time of our perils, persecutions and dangers, and were acting against the interests of the Church." (HC 3:283-84.) Parley P. Pratt's wife leaves the prison house, where she stayed with him voluntarily most of the winter.

Mar. 20-25, 1839
Between these dates Joseph writes a long letter to Bishop Edward Partridge in particular and the Saints in general. Parts of the letter are later extracted and form what is now D&C 121, 122, and 123. Besides these sections, the letter also encourages the Saints to have love, fellowship, and compassion on the orphans and the widows; expresses thanks for the letters he (the Prophet) has received; explains the reasons why the Lord tries his Saints; warns the Saints against pride; encourages the Saints to become friends with Isaac Galland; encourages abiding the law. (For the full text of the letter see HC 3:289-305 or TPJS 129-48.)

Apr. 4, 1839
Heber C. Kimball visits Joseph in Liberty jail. Joseph tells him to get the Saints away from Missouri as fast as possible. Joseph writes Emma from the jail describing his life "within the walls, grates, and screeking iron doors, of a lonesome, dark, dirty prison." He also advises Emma to be more gentle with the children: "don't be fractious to them, but listen to their wants." (ENS, Ap '77, 12.)

Apr. 5, 1839
A company of 50 men from Daviess County swear never to eat or drink again until they have murdered "Joe Smith."

Apr. 6, 1839
Having been in Liberty jail since Dec. 1, 1838, Joseph and the other prisoners leave the prison for Gallatin jail in Daviess County, a two-day walk.

Apr. 8, 1839
Joseph and the other prisoners arrive in Daviess County, where they will again be held for trial.

Apr. 9, 1839
Joseph's trial begins before a drunken grand jury. Judge

Morin visits him in Millport that evening and recommends that they escape to avoid enduring persecution.

Apr. 10, 1839

The trial continues without much progress. Sidney Rigdon writes a letter to Joseph from Quincy, Ill., stating that Governor Carlin and others are excited about Rigdon's plan to remove Missouri from the United States because she broke her constitutional duty to the Latter-day Saints.

Apr. 15, 1839

Joseph and others leave Daviess County for Boone County.

Apr. 16, 1839

Joseph's guard gets purposely intoxicated and tells Joseph he has been instructed never to reach Boone County with the prisoners. Three of the guards get drunk, while the fourth helps Joseph and the other prisoners saddle horses and escape. When the sheriff returns to Gallatin, the people become very angry, and ride the sheriff out of town on a rail. Joseph and the others head for Quincy, Ill.

Apr. 18, 1839

The last of the Saints in Missouri are harassed and threatened. They leave Far West within an hour.

Apr. 20, 1839

The last few Saints finally leave Far West.

Apr. 22, 1839

After a severe journey, Joseph crosses the Mississippi, and reaches Illinois, where he is reunited with Emma. He had paid lawyers in Missouri a total of $34,000 in cash and land for law fees there.

Apr. 24, 1839

Parley P. Pratt and others are brought before a grand jury at Richmond in Ray County. Two are released after six months in prison, so that only four prisoners are left alone in the state of Missouri. Joseph presides over a council meeting in Quincy, in which it is resolved that he and others will go to Iowa to look for a location for the gathering of the Saints.

Apr. 25, 1839

Joseph travels toward the head of the Des Moines River

rapids, where he determines that the land on both sides of the Mississippi—Commerce on the east and Montrose on the west—will be the future gathering sites for the Saints.

Apr. 26, 1839
Shortly after midnight, several of the Twelve ride back to the temple site in Far West, Mo., where they hold a meeting and officially set out on their missions across the ocean, despite threats that they would be murdered if they tried to leave from Far West. This fulfills Joseph's revelation—D&C 118:5. Five of the Twelve (Brigham Young, Heber C. Kimball, Orson Pratt, John E. Page, and John Taylor) meet with about 20 members and ordain two new men, Wilford Woodruff and George A. Smith, to the Quorum of the Twelve. After prayer and songs, one elder lays the cornerstone of the future temple. The Saints ride off 39 miles before daybreak.

May 1, 1839
Joseph, in connection with the Church committee, buys the first Church land in Commerce, a 135-acre farm from Hugh White for $5,000 and a farm from Dr. Isaac Galland for $9,000. About this time Joseph receives word from England stating that Isaac Russell, who had become a self-appointed prophet and apostatized, had led many of the Saints astray, but Elder Willard Richards was working hard to get the Saints back into the Church.

May 4-6, 1839
General conference is held near Quincy, Ill. Sidney Rigdon is called to take affidavits and grievances to Washington, D.C., to lay before the government officials concerning the Missouri persecutions.

May 8, 1839
Joseph prepares to move to Commerce, Ill.

May 10, 1839
Joseph and Emma move into a small log cabin on the riverbank in Commerce. When the Saints begin to move to the Iowa territory across the river from Commerce, they find that Dr. Isaac Galland, from whom they bought the land, did not have legal title to the half-breed lands. They are therefore eventually forced to move back across the river to Commerce.

May 13, 1839

Parley P. Pratt, still in jail after seven months, writes to Judge Austin A. King requesting permission to either leave the state or have an immediate trial.

May 22, 1839

Parley P. Pratt, King Follett, and two others are given a change of venue. They leave Richmond, Mo., in handcuffs and are taken to Columbia, Boone County, Mo.

May 26, 1839

Elder Pratt and the others reach Boone County and are thrown into another dirty prison.

June 4, 1839

Joseph writes up a "Bill of Damages Against the State of Missouri on Account of the Suffering and Losses Sustained Therein." (See HC 3:368-74.)

June 11, 1839

Joseph commences dictating his personal history to his clerk, James Mulholland. This document will eventually become the basis of Joseph's *History of the Church*. Elder Theodore Turley raises the first house in Commerce that is built by the Saints themselves. Joseph records his impressions of the land about Commerce, stating that "the land was mostly covered with trees and bushes, and much of it so wet that it was with the utmost difficulty a footman could get through, and totally impossible for teams. Commerce was so unhealthful, very few could live there; but believing that it might become a healthful place by the blessing of heaven to the Saints, and no more eligible place presenting itself, I considered it wisdom to make an attempt to build up a city." (HC 3:375.)

June 24, 1839

Isaac Galland sells the whole town of Nashville, Iowa, together with 13,000 other acres of half-breed land, to the Saints for over $38,000. Because Galland has no clear titles to many of these lands, which had originally been designated by the government for half-breeds, many of the Saints who move here end up losing their money and their lands.

June 27, 1839

A conference of the Twelve is held, at which time Orson

134

Hyde confesses his sins and is restored to his apostleship. Joseph gives detailed explanation about many doctrines, including faith, repentance, baptism, the gift of the Holy Ghost, tongues, resurrection and eternal Judgment, election, the two Comforters, and the spirit of revelation. (See HC 3:379-81.)

July 1839

The Saints, still mostly without homes, camp in tents along both sides of the river. The damp climate contributes to the spreading of malaria among thousands of them. Joseph's father is sick all summer. Joseph himself becomes sick and is finally healed with Emma's herbal remedies. Doctors Wiley and Pendleton go from bed to bed prescribing Sapinton's pills, a quinine compound. Many of the sick camp on Joseph's doorstep and stay in his house.

July 1, 1839

Parley P. Pratt is supposed to stand trial on this day, but since all his witnesses have been banished from the state, it is declared that he is not ready for trial and the trial is postponed until Sept. 23.

July 2, 1839

Joseph suggests naming the town in Iowa "Zarahemla." In the afternoon Joseph and Hyrum meet with the Twelve and counsel them before they leave on their foreign missions.

July 3, 1839

Joseph baptizes Isaac Galland and ordains him an elder.

July 4, 1839

Parley P. Pratt, King Follett, and Morris Phelps escape from Boone County prison after over seven months of imprisonment. King Follett is recaptured. Several days later, Pratt and Phelps arrive safely in Quincy, Ill.

July 7, 1839

Joseph holds a large farewell meeting with the Twelve before their departure to England.

July 8-10, 1839

Joseph spends much time with the Twelve, selecting hymns for a hymnbook. "About this time much sickness began to manifest itself among the brethren, as well as among the inhabitants of the place, so that this week and the following were generally spent in visiting the sick and administering to them; some had faith enough and were healed; others had not." (HC 4:3.)

July 22, 1839

Joseph records that "the sick were administered unto with great success, but many remain sick, and new cases are occurring daily." On this day he walks through the sick, healing almost everyone he touches. Wilford Woodruff borrows a silk bandana from Joseph and wipes it on the faces of sick twins, who are immediately healed. (For details of this miraculous day, see HC 4:3-5; IJB 439-40; CHC 2:18-22. For several diary accounts of this day, see NE, Mar '71, 16-18.)

July-Aug. 1839

Joseph spends most of these months recovering from sickness and visiting the sick. Dozens in Nauvoo die during the summer from disease.

Aug. 4, 1839

Joseph preaches at a Sunday meeting and the Church passes a resolution stating that the Twelve should leave for England as soon as possible.

Aug. 8, 1839

John Taylor and Wilford Woodruff are the first to leave for their missions to England. Both are terribly sick, and Wilford Woodruff says that "I feel and look more like a subject for the dissecting room than a missionary." (CHC 2:22-26.)

Aug. 12, 1839

The third purchase of land in and around Commerce is made. Joseph, Hyrum, and Sidney sign a bond of $113,500 to a Mr. Hotchkiss for 400 acres. On this same day, for $2500, another 80 acres are bought.

Aug. 29, 1839

Parley P. Pratt, Orson Pratt, and Hiram Clark leave Commerce for their missions to England. They are poverty stricken.

Aug. 30, 1839

The word *Nauvoo* appears officially in print, published on the city plat, for the first time. Some time previous to this the word had been chosen as the new name of Commerce.

Sept. 14, 1839

Brigham Young and Heber C. Kimball leave their sick families in Commerce for their missions to England.

Sept. 21, 1839

George A. Smith and others leave for their missions to England.

Oct. 5-8, 1839

A general conference is held in Nauvoo. The city is divided into three wards.

Oct. 10, 1839

Parley P. Pratt in Detroit, on his way to England, publishes his history of the Missouri persecutions. He had written this during his long imprisonment in the Richmond jail, and had smuggled part of it out of the jail through his wife.

Mid-Oct. 1839

King Follett, the last prisoner in Missouri, is finally freed.

Oct. 20, 1839

A high council meeting is held in Nauvoo and it is decided that the council will disfellowship any person who allows any animal to destroy crops; Joseph Smith, Jr., shall go to Washington D.C., to seek redress for the Missouri persecutions; Joseph Smith, Jr., will be treasurer for the Church; Henry G. Sherwood should sell town lots in Nauvoo for approximately $500 per lot.

Oct. 29, 1839

Joseph, Signey Rigdon, Judge Elias Higbee, and Orrin Porter Rockwell leave in a two-horse carriage for Washington, D.C., to lay grievances before Congress.

Nov. 15, 1839

The first issue of the *Times and Seasons* is published at Nauvoo.

Nov. 18, 1839

The roads are so bad and Sidney Rigdon's health is so

poor that when the group reaches Columbus, Joseph leaves Brothers Rockwell, Rigdon, and Foster in Columbus until Sidney can recover his health. Joseph and Judge Higbee continue toward Washington alone.

Nov. 27, 1839

While Brigham Young is on the steamer *Columbus* on Lake Erie, the winds become so bad that Brigham Young commands, in the name of Jesus, that the winds and waves cease. They obey him and he gives glory to God; he arrives safely in Buffalo in the morning. The horses of Joseph's coach take fright and charge down a hill full speed. Joseph climbs out the door and successfully stops the horses before anyone is hurt. Everyone praises Joseph until they learn his name and what he claims to be, at which point all gratitude ends.

Nov. 28, 1839

Joseph and Judge Higbee arrive in Washington with a list of petitions and grievances.

Nov. 29, 1839

Joseph and Judge Higbee meet President Martin Van Buren. The president patiently reads some of the petitions but then says, "What can I do? I can do nothing for you! If I do anything, I shall come in contact with the whole state of Missouri. . . . Gentlemen, your cause is just, but I can do nothing for you." (HC 4:40, 80.) He asks Joseph how his religion differs from others. Joseph says it differs in mode of baptism "and the gift of the Holy Ghost by the laying on of hands. We considered that all other considerations were contained in the gift of the Holy Ghost, and we deemed it unnecessary to make many words in preaching the Gospel to him." (HC 4:42.)

Dec. 5, 1839

Joseph spends several frustrating days in Washington trying to find allies. Henry Clay tells him, "You had better go to Oregon," and John C. Calhoun says, "It's a nice question—a critical question, but it will not do to agitate it." (HC 5:393.) He finally finds one sympathetic listener in Richard M. Young, a senator from Illinois. Joseph writes a letter to Hyrum, commenting on the hypocrisy of government officials in Washington, D.C. (See HC 4:39-42.)

Dec. 7, 1839

Richard M. Young speaks in favor of the Mormons to a room full of various delegates. It is decided that he should present the case of the Saints to Congress. The Saints ask for almost $2 million for losses in the state of Missouri. Missouri officials begin to gather affidavits claiming the Mormons had committed atrocities there.

Dec. 8, 1839

The high council in Nauvoo puts a notice in the *Times and Seasons,* advising the Saints not to move back to Kirtland, but adding, "We do not wish by this to take your agency from you." (HC 4:45.)

Dec. 21, 1839

Joseph decides to leave Washington, leaving Higbee there to try to continue the work of the Saints. He travels to and reaches Philadelphia, Pa., on this date, and preaches in Philadelphia until Dec. 30.

Dec. 29, 1839

The Nauvoo high council votes to print 10,000 copies of a new hymnbook and a new edition of the Book of Mormon.

Dec. 30, 1839

Joseph leaves Philadelphia with Orson Pratt to visit the Church in New Jersey for a few days.

1840

Jan. 4, 1840

The high council at Montrose votes to disfellowship any members who sue each other in law.

Jan. 9, 1840

Joseph returns to Philadelphia, where he continues to preach and visit among the members.

Jan. 13, 1840

John Taylor, Wilford Woodruff, and Theodore Turley reach Preston, England.

Jan. 14, 1840

Sidney Rigdon and Dr. Robert Foster reach Philadelphia and meet Joseph there.

Jan. 17, 1840

John Taylor and Wilford Woodruff hold a conference in Preston, England. It is decided that John Taylor and Joseph Fielding will return to Liverpool, where they convert 28 people by April 1840. Wilford Woodruff goes south to the county of Staffordshire, where he finds a branch of 66 Saints in the village of Burslen.

Jan. 30, 1840

About this time, Joseph leaves Philadelphia for Washington with Orrin Porter Rockwell, Judge Higbee, and Dr. Foster, having left Sidney Rigdon sick in Philadelphia. During his stay in Philadelphia, Joseph had met with some of the Twelve on their way to England, and had held a conference wherein he "arose like a lion about to roar; and being full of the Holy Ghost, spoke in great power. . . . The entire congregation were astounded; electrified, as it were, and overwhelmed with the sense of the truth and power by which he spoke, and the wonders which he related. . . . Multitudes were baptized in Philadelphia and in the regions around." (PPP 297-99.)

Feb. 5, 1840

Joseph preaches in Washington before a large congregation that includes several Congressmen. His sermon lasts over two hours. (For a detailed report of the sermon, see HC 4:77-80.) Shortly thereafter he decides that his remaining in Washington is useless, and he returns to Nauvoo, leaving Elias Higbee in Washington to pursue the interests of the Saints.

Feb. 20-26, 1840

Elias Higbee sends a series of letters to Joseph about progress in Washington. He relates his efforts in taking the Mormon case before the various congressional committees, and explains many of the opposing viewpoints and rumors he has run into (such as the Mormons had tried to take over the state, and the Mormons were the aggressors). His final letter states that "the decision is against us, or in other words unfavorable, that they believe redress can only be had in Missouri." (HC 4:81-88.)

Mar. 4, 1840

Wilford Woodruff arrives at the home of John Benbow, a member of the United Brethren religious organization, among whom he begins preaching with great success.

On this date Joseph arrives back in Nauvoo, having denounced the iniquity of Martin Van Buren on his trip home, and finally prophesying, "May he never be elected again to any office of trust or power, by which he may abuse the innocent and let the guilty go free." (HC 4:89.) On this date the Senate Judiciary Committee in the case of the Saints versus Missouri renders its judgment "that the case presented for their investigation is not such a one as will justify or authorize any interposition by this government." (HC 4:90-92.)

Mar. 6, 1840

Joseph attends a meeting of the Iowa high council, across the river from Nauvoo. He encourages them to stop trying to live the law of consecration.

In Herefordshire, England, John Benbow, his wife,

and four others are the first of the United Brethren to be baptized, having been converted by Wilford Woodruff. Within the next five weeks, Woodruff converts 158 people, including 48 lay preachers. By the time he completes his mission in southern England, he will have been responsible for more than 1800 baptisms. (For details of these dramatic successes in England, see BYS, Su '75, 499-526; A&L 145-51; IJB 453-67.)

Mar. 8, 1840

While Wilford Woodruff is preaching at John Benbow's Hill Farm to over 1,000 people, the local rector preaches to only 15. The rector sends a constable to arrest Elder Woodruff for preaching without a license. When the constable learns that he has a license, he sits and listens to the sermon and requests baptism at the end of the meeting. The next day the rector sends two more people to spy on Elder Woodruff's preachings, and both of them request baptism.

Mar. 9, 1840

Brigham Young, Parley P. Pratt, Heber C. Kimball, George A. Smith, and others sail from New York on the ship *Patrick Henry* and arrive in Liverpool on April 6, 1840.

Mar. 24, 1840

Elias Higbee writes Joseph from Washington City: "Our business is at last ended here. Yesterday a resolution passed the Senate, that the committee should be discharged; and that we might withdraw the accompanying papers, which I have done." (HC 4:98-99.)

Mar. 25, 1840

Howard Coray is baptized. He later becomes a clerk in Joseph's office and writes some very interesting descriptions of Joseph. (See BYS, Sp '77, 341-47.)

Apr. 6-8, 1840

A general conference of the Church is held in Nauvoo. A motion is passed that Orson Hyde be sent on a mission to the Jews. Elder John E. Page will go with him. A committee of five is appointed to draft a resolution to be sent to Washington, D.C., expressing disappointment concerning the treatment of the Saints by the Congress. Frederick G.

Williams humbly asks for forgiveness for his conduct in Missouri, and a motion is passed that Williams be accepted back into the Church.

Apr. 14, 1840
Willard Richards is ordained an apostle in England by the other Twelve who are there present.

Apr. 15, 1840
Orson Hyde leaves Nauvoo for Jerusalem.

Apr. 15-16, 1840
A general conference of the Church is held in Preston, England. There are now 1,686 members in England. The conference decides to publish a hymnbook and a monthly periodical. Brigham Young is chosen President of the Twelve. On April 16 Parley P. Pratt is appointed editor of a new paper to be called the *Latter-day Saints Millennial Star*.

May 1840
Don Carlos Smith and Robert Thompson, on missions to Philadelphia, report that there are no less than 400 Saints in Philadelphia (this area was opened by Joseph on his trip to Washington in December 1839).

June 1, 1840
By this time approximately 250 homes have been built in and around Nauvoo.

June 6, 1840
The first Saints from a foreign country leave to emigrate to America. Forty-one English Saints board the ship *Britannia* at Liverpool, with John Moon as the leader. Eventually more than 4700 will emigrate from England before the downfall of Nauvoo. (For John Moon's description of the crossing see BYS, Sp '77, 340-41.)

June 13, 1840
Don Carlos Smith is born to Emma and Joseph at Nauvoo.

June 14, 1840
Wilford Woodruff attends a meeting at the Gadfield Elm Chapel of the United Brethren, where they unanimously pass a resolution that henceforth they will be known as the Brand Green and Gadfield Elm Conference of the Church

of Jesus Christ of Latter-day Saints. Woodruff remains in this area until August, by which time he will have converted approximately 800 members.

June 18, 1840

Joseph asks the high council in Nauvoo to relieve him of his burdensome responsibility as chief land agent for the Church because he needs more time for the spiritual needs of the Church, such as his translation of the Bible and his translation of Egyptian.

June 29, 1840

W.W. Phelps writes a letter to Joseph humbly confessing his great errors in going against the Church in Missouri. Orson Hyde and John E. Page also write a letter to the presidency of the Church pleading in behalf of W.W. Phelps.

July 3, 1840

Joseph records that the Lord has begun to send plagues upon the nation because they are "guilty of murder, robbery and plunder, as a nation, because they have refused to protect their citizens, and execute justice according to their own Constitution." He goes on to list several hailstorms and other acts of God that are afflicting the nation at the present time. (HC 4:145.)

July 7, 1840

Four Saints are kidnapped from Hancock Co., Ill. and taken to prison in Missouri, where they are whipped and beaten. A group of Missourians had crossed the Mississippi in search of goods they claimed had been stolen from them, and having found a cache of them in the caves near the river bottoms on the Nauvoo side, they blamed the four Mormons, captured them, and beat confessions out of them. At this time there was a crime wave along the banks of the Mississippi, and many criminals would join the Church as a cover. When the four Mormons are kidnapped, Joseph protests loudly to Gov. Carlin about Gov. Boggs of Missouri. However, when the supposed theft is investigated, the cache of goods is found to be entirely too large to be the frame-up the Mormons had claimed it was, and Gov. Carlin begins to act less favorably toward the Saints. One of the Saints, Alanson Brown, is found guilty of the theft.

July 22, 1840

Joseph Smith writes a long letter to W.W. Phelps welcoming him back into the Church.

July 25, 1840

A Dr. John C. Bennett writes to the Saints stating his intention to move to Nauvoo and join the Saints. He will later become an influential member of the Church. He has the reputation of being both a genius and an imposter. In addition to being a professor, a preacher, a doctor, and a military leader, he is also claimed to be an abortionist, a wife deserter, and a traitor. When he gains Joseph's confidence, he helps draft the Nauvoo charter and push its passage through legislature, shows him how to drain the Nauvoo swamps, and administers quinine to the sick of Nauvoo, thus saving many lives. He later writes one of the most famous exposes against the Saints. In writing to Joseph a second time he states that "wealth is no material object with me. I desire to be happy." (HC 4:169-70.)

July 30, 1840

John C. Bennett writes to Joseph and Sidney Rigdon a third time, expressing his desire to join with the Saints and stating that his sympathies were with them during their bitter persecutions.

Aug. 1840

The number of Wilford Woodruff's converts in Herefordshire has, by now, reached 800. Heber C. Kimball, Elder Woodruff, and George A. Smith then open London to the gospel, although they are not as successful as in previous areas, due to troubles with local ministers.

In the state elections held this month, the Mormons generally vote for the Whig candidate, because Van Buren and Boggs were Democrats. To show they are nonpartisan, however, they decide to vote for one Democrat instead of one Whig. They choose a friendly Democrat named Ralston and vote for him instead of the bottom name on the Whig ballot. The one Whig the Saints do not vote for is Abraham Lincoln.

Aug. 8, 1840

Joseph answers John C. Bennett's letters, stating, "My general invitation is, Let all that will, come, and partake of the poverty of Nauvoo freely." (HC 4:177-79.)

Aug. 10, 1840

Col. Seymour Brunson dies in Nauvoo. During his funeral sermon Joseph makes the first public mention of the doctrine of baptism for the dead. (Some say this funeral was on Aug. 15—IJB 488; some say it was Aug. 10—JFS 252.) The idea of preaching to the dead had been given on Feb. 16, 1832. (D&C 76:73.)

Aug. 15, 1840

The first baptisms for the dead take place. Jane Neyman promptly asks Harvey Olmstead to baptize her in the Mississippi for her dead son Cyrus. When Joseph hears the words that were used he pronounces the ceremony valid, Vienna Jacques having been a witness.

Aug. 21, 1840

Noah Rogers and Benjamin Boyce escape from a Missouri prison, having been kidnapped on July 7, 1840. The other two who were kidnapped that same date, Alanson Brown and James Allred, had escaped previously. (For a record of the hardships and torture to which Boyce and Rogers were subjected, see HC 4:180-81.)

Aug. 30, 1840

Elders Kimball, Woodruff, and Smith are forbidden to preach in the streets of London.

Sept. 5, 1840

Joseph prefers charges against Elder Almon W. Babbitt, accusing him of having spread rumors about Joseph and others implying that they had been extravagant in their monetary affairs.

Sept. 14, 1840

Joseph's father, Joseph Smith, Sr., dies in Nauvoo. All of his family except one daughter had been able to gather around him before his death, and he gave them each a final patriarchal blessing. As with every family in disease-ridden Nauvoo at that time, many of the Smith family suffered disease and death in 1840 and 1841, including Joseph's uncle Silas, Joseph's sister-in-law Mary, Joseph's brother Don Carlos, Joseph's youngest son named after Don Carlos, Hyrum's seven-year-old son Hyrum, and many others.

Sept. 15, 1840

The funeral for Joseph Smith, Sr., is held. (HC 4:191-97 includes the full funeral sermon.)

Governor Boggs of Missouri, having renewed his vengeance against Joseph because of Joseph's accusations against Boggs in Washington, and also because of the recent scandal concerning the kidnappings and river bottom thefts, asks Governor Carlin of Illinois to turn over Joseph, Sidney Rigdon, Lyman Wight, Parley P. Pratt, Caleb Baldwin, and Alanson Brown to Missouri officials, claiming they are escaped convicts and fugitives from justice.

Oct. 1840

During this month Orson Pratt, in Scotland, publishes a 31-page pamphlet titled "An Interesting Account of Several Remarkable Visions, and of the Late Discovery of Ancient American Records." This is the first known time that Joseph Smith's first vision is put into print.

Oct. 3-5, 1840

A general conference is held in Nauvoo. The conference moves to send some brethren to preside over the building up of Kirtland as the gathering place of the eastern Saints. Joseph speaks on the necessity of building a house of the Lord in Nauvoo, the newly disclosed doctrine of baptism for the dead, the two priesthoods, the ordinances, Adam and the keys of the presidency, the mission of Enoch, a need for sacrifice, the mission of Elijah, and the restoration of all ordinances. (See HC 207-12.) The building of the temple is authorized and building committees are appointed.

Oct. 6, 1840

General conference is held in Manchester, England. There are over 3700 members in England at this time.

Oct. 17, 1840

A conference is held in Philadelphia, with Orson Hyde presiding, and 896 persons in attendance.

Oct. 19, 1840

Joseph and Hyrum write to the Saints in Kirtland, encouraging them to be unified in the gospel. Joseph writes to the Twelve in Great Britain about several spiritual and temporal concerns, especially referring to the doctrine of baptism for the dead. (See HC 4:226-32.)

Dec. 9, 1840

A bill to incorporate the city of Nauvoo is passed by the state senate. One senator jokingly tries to amend the bill title to "A Bill for the Encouragement of the Importation of Mormons." This proposal is withdrawn. (BYS, Su '75, 493.)

Dec. 12, 1840

The bill is passed by the Illinois House.

Dec. 17, 1840

The Council of Revision passes the Nauvoo charter. It will take effect on Feb. 1, 1841. The charter is then signed by Governor Carlin. It includes provisions for the city of Nauvoo, the Nauvoo Legion, the University of the City of Nauvoo, and all other municipal necessities. In addition to Governor Carlin, Stephen A. Douglas, Illinois secretary of state, signs it. The charter was written by Joseph Smith, John C. Bennett, and Robert B. Thompson. Once the charter was complete, Bennett took it to the state legislature and pushed it through in 21 days. (The complete charter appears in HC 4:239-48.)

1841

Jan. 1841

Brigham Young and Willard Richards publish a long article on election and reprobation in the *Millennial Star,* which Joseph calls "one of the sweetest pieces that has been written in these last days." (See HC 4:256-66.)

Jan. 8, 1841

The First Presidency publishes a proclamation to the Saints scattered abroad, explaining and expressing gratitude for the Nauvoo charter. They say the advantage of the Nauvoo Legion is that "it will enable us to show our attachment to the state and nation, as a people, whenever the public service requires our aid, thus proving ourselves obedient to the paramount laws of the land, and ready at all times to sustain and execute them." The University of Nauvoo is also praised. The Presidency asks the Saints coming into Nauvoo from abroad to have patience with the imperfections of man. (See HC 4:267-73.)

Jan. 15, 1841

Joseph writes in the *Times and Seasons* that the Lord is not pleased with Orson Hyde and John E. Page because they have delayed their missions.

Jan. 19, 1841

Joseph receives D&C 124.

Jan. 24, 1841

In accordance with D&C 124, Hyrum Smith is ordained a Patriarch to the Church and is called an assistant president in the First Presidency (a calling formerly held by Oliver Cowdery). William Law replaces Hyrum as second counselor.

Jan. 30, 1841

In a special conference Joseph is elected sole trustee-in-trust for the Church. As trustee-in-trust he is entitled to receive, acquire, manage, and convey property in behalf of the Church. He will hold this office for life, and the First Presidency would be the successor to this position.

Feb. 1, 1841

The Nauvoo charter, which was passed the previous December, goes into effect. The first election for mayor and members of the city council takes place. John C. Bennett is elected mayor, with Joseph Smith, Hyrum Smith, Sidney Rigdon, and several other leading Church officials elected to the city council. It is said that Joseph received less than $25 total pay for two years service as city councilman.

Feb. 3, 1841

Mayor John C. Bennett gives his inaugural address. The same day a bill officially organizing the University of the City of Nauvoo is passed. Another bill officially organizing the Nauvoo Legion is also passed. The Legion is divided into six companies, with Joseph Smith as the lieutenant-general.

Feb. 13, 1841

Orson Hyde, accompanied by George J. Adams, sails from New York to Liverpool, headed eventually for Jerusalem.

Feb. 15, 1841

Joseph, as chairman of the committee on vending of spirituous liquors, suggests a bill that would prohibit selling whiskey in smaller quantities than a gallon. After a long debate it is passed. Joseph says, "I spoke at great length on the use of liquors, and showed that they were unnecessary, and operate as a poison in the stomach, and that roots and herbs can be found to effect all necessary purposes." (HC 4:298-99.)

Mar. 1, 1841

Work on the temple begins. Joseph presents a bill ensuring equal toleration of all religions within Nauvoo.

Mar. 10, 1841

Gov. Thomas Carlin officially commissions Joseph as

lieutenant-general in the Nauvoo Legion.

Mar. 20, 1841

Upon inquiry by some local brothers, Joseph receives a revelation explaining the details for selling stock for the Nauvoo House. He also inquires about the will of the Lord concerning the Saints in Iowa, and receives D&C 125.

Apr. 6, 1841

In celebration of the twelfth anniversary of the Church, 16 companies of the Nauvoo Legion march in review before a huge crowd. Sidney Rigdon then gives a speech before those who have gathered to watch the parade. The southeast cornerstone of the temple, representing the First Presidency, is laid with great ceremony. (The basement of the temple was dug and walled before this time in readiness for the cornerstone.) The high priests then lay a second cornerstone; the high council lays the third cornerstone; and the bishops lay the fourth cornerstone.

Apr. 7-8, 1841

General conference is held in Nauvoo. Elder Lyman Wight is called to the Quorum of the Twelve, replacing David W. Patten. John C. Bennett is appointed as a temporary assistant president in the First Presidency during Sidney Rigdon's illness.

Apr. 21, 1841

Elders Young, Kimball, Orson Pratt, Richards, Woodruff, Smith, and Taylor sail from Liverpool with 130 Saints, arriving in New York on May 20, 1841. Parley P. Pratt remains behind in England to edit and publish the *Millennial Star.*

May 2, 1841

A teachers quorum is organized in Nauvoo. (For the history and evolution of the teachers quorum from its initial organization to its present-day functions, see BYS, Sp '76, 375-98.)

May 4, 1841

Joseph, still troubled about his Kirtland debts, writes to his agent, Oliver Granger, asking him to settle them as soon as possible. However, Granger dies in Kirtland on Aug. 25, 1841. Joseph exchanges a series of letters with

Stephen A. Douglas about the Nauvoo Legion. Douglas had come to Nauvoo to inspect the Legion to determine whether or not Legion members should be exempt from other military duty. Joseph justifies the Legion on the grounds that it is not exclusively a Mormon legion, and that it is merely for self-preservation.

May 16, 1841

Joseph gives a sermon on free agency, the first principles of the gospel, the possibility of redemption for murderers, and the doctrine of election. (See HC 4:358-60.)

May 23, 1841

At a Kirtland conference, preservation of the Kirtland Temple is discussed. There are 300 to 400 Saints still living in Kirtland.

May 24, 1841

The First Presidency calls on all Saints to gather to Hancock County, Ill., or Lee County, Iowa. All stakes outside these areas are discontinued.

June 1, 1841

Sidney Rigdon is ordained a prophet, seer, and revelator. Joseph accompanies Hyrum Smith and William Law as far as Quincy on their mission to the East.

June 4, 1841

Joseph calls at the home of Governor Carlin in Quincy, Ill. The governor shows him great courtesy, and doesn't mention that Missouri has asked him to turn Joseph over to them. Within a few hours of Joseph's leaving the governor's mansion, Carlin sends a posse of law officers to capture him and turn him over to the Missouri authorities.

June 5, 1841

While Joseph is staying in a hotel 28 miles from Nauvoo, Sheriff King and his posse arrest him. Joseph obtains a writ of habeas corpus and appears before Judge Stephen A. Douglas, who happens to be in town.

June 9, 1841

The trial is held to see if Illinois should send Joseph back to Missouri. The actions of the young prosecuting attorney are so outrageous that the judge is forced to silence him. By the time Joseph's attorney, Mr. Browning, finishes his sad tale of the Saints being driven from Missouri and walking on bloody bare feet across the snow to Illinois, Judge Douglas himself is in tears.

June 10, 1841

Judge Douglas orders Joseph to be liberated. The Prophet returns to Nauvoo the next day.

June 15, 1841

Joseph receives a letter from Orson Hyde recounting his travels on the way to Jerusalem. Hyrum Smith and William Law, on a mission in Pittsburgh, learn that John C. Bennett has an estranged wife and child (he had claimed to be unmarried). This is reported to Joseph. Soon afterward, Joseph confronts Bennett with these facts, and Bennett takes poison in an attempted suicide. However, many assume that because he is a doctor, he knows how much he can consume and stay alive. At any rate, he does survive the suicide attempt. Joseph accepts his dramatic show of repentance and allows him to remain in power in the Church and in the city.

July 1841

Heber C. Kimball writes Parley P. Pratt in England that although there were not more than 30 buildings in Nauvoo when the Twelve left two years ago, now there are about 1200 completed buildings and hundreds more in progress.

July 1, 1841

Brigham Young, Heber Kimball, and John Taylor reach Nauvoo from their missions to England. Joseph meets with them until late at night, explaining the law of plural marriage.

July 3, 1841

At the Independence Day celebration the Nauvoo Legion comes out in parade and Joseph gives a patriotic speech, closing with the words, "I would ask no greater boon, than to lay down my life for my country." (HC 4:382.)

July 9, 1841

Joseph receives D&C 126.

July 13, 1841

George A. Smith reaches Nauvoo from his mission in England.

July 15, 1841

Joseph mentions all the lies and falsehoods that are being published about him in various newspapers.

Aug. 7, 1841

Twenty-six-year-old Don Carlos Smith, Joseph's youngest brother, dies in Nauvoo. He was the editor of the *Times and Seasons* and became sick while printing in a damp cellar. He leaves three daughters.

Aug. 12, 1841

Joseph preaches to a good number of Sac and Fox Indians who have come to visit him in Nauvoo.

Aug. 15, 1841

Joseph's 14-month-old son, Don Carlos, dies in Nauvoo. Death is becoming so widespread at this time in and around Nauvoo that Sidney Rigdon begins preaching a "general" funeral sermon.

Aug. 16, 1841

Willard Richards arrives in Nauvoo from his mission to England. Ebenezer Robinson succeeds Don Carlos Smith as editor of the *Times and Seasons.* Joseph calls a special conference, although he is absent because of his son's death. In the afternoon he tells the Twelve that "the Twelve should be called upon to stand in their place next to the First Presidency, and attend to the settling of emigrants and the business of the Church at the stakes. . . ." (HC 4:402-4.)

Aug. 22, 1841

Joseph preaches on the wars and desolations that await nations.

Aug. 25, 1841

Joseph exchanges letters with Horace R. Hotchkiss concerning tardy payments for the Nauvoo lands. Apparently both Joseph and Hotchkiss assume that the Saints might get some financial compensation for their losses in Missouri, with which they might pay for the Nauvoo lands. When this does not come about, Hotchkiss begins to get quite anxious about the payment due him for his land. Joseph, of course, has little or no money of his own with which to pay for the lands.

Sept. 4, 1841

Col. Charles C. Rich is elected brigadier-general of the Nauvoo Legion to replace Don Carlos Smith.

Sept. 25, 1841

Hyrum Smith, the seven-year-old son of Hyrum and Jerusha Smith, dies in Nauvoo.

Sept. 30, 1841

Joseph draws up a bill of expenses caused by his trial in Monmouth in June 1841 and sends it to the deputy sheriff of Adams County because he officiated in the arrest initiated by Gov. Boggs. Joseph includes a note asking that the $685 be refunded to him as soon as possible.

Oct. 1, 1841

George M. Hinckle, an apostate who had robbed Joseph's home when Joseph was imprisoned in Missouri, is passing through the area. Joseph places a suit against him for his lost goods, but Hinckle manages to have the suit put off until spring.

Oct. 2, 1841

The original handwritten manuscript of the Book of Mormon is placed in the southeast cornerstone of the Nauvoo House. Construction of the Nauvoo House begins on this date, but most of the effort is put into the temple, and the Nauvoo House is never completed above the first floor.

Oct. 2-5, 1841

An important general conference is held in the Grove at Nauvoo. Joseph gives a sermon on baptisms for the dead. He announces that "there shall be no more baptisms for the dead, until the ordinance can be attended to in the Lord's House; and the Church cannot hold another General Conference, until they can meet in said house. *For thus saith the Lord!*" A motion is passed that the Twelve write an epistle abroad to encourage the Saints to exchange, purchase, or donate monies or lands to satisfy the Hotchkiss debt. (HC 4:423-29.)

Oct. 6, 1841

Wilford Woodruff arrives in Nauvoo from his British mission.

Oct. 9, 1841

Joseph has more correspondence concerning the Hotchkiss land troubles.

Oct. 15, 1841

Grandmaster Jonas grants permission to George Miller to open a lodge of Free Masons in Nauvoo.

Oct. 24, 1841

Orson Hyde has reached Jerusalem and makes an altar of stones on the Mount of Olives and on Mount Moriah. He gives a prayer dedicating the land of Palestine for the return and gathering of the Jews. (For the complete prayer see HC 4:456-59.)

Oct. 30, 1841

In obedience to an order from the mayor, Joseph calls out two companies of the Nauvoo Legion to remove a grog shop kept in town.

Oct. 31, 1841

Hyrum Smith writes to the Saints who still remain in Kirtland. He disapproves of their plans to build up that place, and prophesies that a scourge will fall upon Kirtland.

Nov. 1, 1841

A small shack that has deteriorated into a graffiti-covered brothel is declared a nuisance by the city council and torn down. The owner becomes angered and demands payment for the damages. Joseph argues vigorously against making any such payments.

Nov. 7, 1841

When William O. Clark preaches, rebuking the Saints for a lack of sanctity and holiness, Joseph preaches against him, calling him a Pharisee and a hypocrite. Joseph tells the Saints not to follow the adversary in accusing each other, and says, "If you do not accuse each other, God will not accuse you. . . . If you will not accuse me, I will not accuse you. If you will throw a cloak of charity over my sins, I will over yours—for charity covereth a multitude of sins. What many people call sin is not sin; I do many things to break down superstition, and I will break it down." (HC 4:455-46.)

Nov. 8, 1841

A temporary baptismal font is set up in the Nauvoo

Temple basement. The basement is dedicated by Brigham Young.

Nov. 21, 1841

Baptisms for the dead commence in the Nauvoo Temple. Brigham Young and others of the Twelve baptize 40 persons for the dead.

Nov. 28, 1841

Joseph spends the day with the Twelve at Brigham Young's house and says, "I told the Brethren that the Book of Mormon was the most correct of any book on earth, and the keystone of our religion, and a man would get nearer to God by abiding by its precepts, than by any other book." (HC 4:461.)

Nov. 29, 1841

Joseph runs a notice in the *Times and Seasons* denouncing thieves and robbers. At this time many gangs of criminals were hiding out in the caves along the Mississippi River where they could strike across stream to Missouri and return quickly. Because some of them joined the Church as a cover-up, the Saints were getting a bad reputation as protectors of thieves.

Dec. 1, 1841

A notice from the Twelve denouncing thievery and warning thieves appears in the *Times and Seasons*.

Dec. 2, 1841

Joseph receives a revelation for Nancy Marinda Hyde (Orson Hyde's wife), in which he is told that Ebenezer Robinson and his wife are to take in Nancy until Orson Hyde returns from his mission. Nancy is to hearken unto "the counsel of my servant Joseph in all things," and it shall be a blessing to her. (HC 4:467.)

Dec. 5, 1841

Joseph proofreads the Book of Mormon for a new edition.

Dec. 11, 1841

Joseph sits in his new store on Water Street. He records the difficulty he has keeping his journal and history up-to-date.

Dec. 13, 1841

Joseph records the history of an anti-Mormon society that

has caused troubles in Warsaw, Ill. The Twelve draw up an epistle concerning baptism for the dead.

Dec. 14, 1841
Joseph begins to set up his new store.

Dec. 18, 1841
Joseph attends a city council and draws up a resolution thanking James Gordon Bennett for his "very liberal and unprejudiced course towards us as a people, in giving us a fair hearing in his paper." (HC 4:477-78.)

Dec. 20, 1841
Joseph publishes an article in the *Times and Seasons* in which he backs Adam W. Snyder for governor of Illinois. The election takes place in August 1842. Joseph says that "Douglas is a master spirit," and that since "Snyder and Moore are his friends—they are ours. . . . We will never be justly charged with the sin of ingratitude—they have served us, and we will serve them." (HC 4:479-80.)

Dec. 22, 1841
Joseph receives two revelations. John Snyder is told to go on a mission to the eastern continent. Amos B. Fuller is told to preach the gospel wherever the Holy Ghost leads him.

Dec. 26, 1841
Joseph gives a sermon on the gift of tongues, stating its value in the Church.

Dec. 28, 1841
Joseph baptizes Sidney Rigdon for his dead parents.

Dec. 30, 1841
Joseph prophesies in the name of the Lord "that the first thing toward building up Warsaw was to break it down." (HC 4:486-87.) George Miller, having been granted an official dispensation by Grandmaster Jonas, on Oct. 15, to meet with other Masons in Nauvoo, holds the first Masonic gathering in Nauvoo on Dec. 29, at the office of Hyrum Smith. Temporary officers are elected and by-laws are drafted. On Dec. 30 the second meeting of the Nauvoo Lodge is held. By-laws are approved and a petition with a list of names applying for new membership is submitted. Included among the applicants are Joseph Smith, Willard

Richards, Brigham Young, Sidney Rigdon, Wilford Woodruff, John Taylor, and many other prominent Church leaders. No new members are actually admitted until the next formal installation on March 15, 1842.

1842

Jan. 5, 1842

Joseph opens his new store on Water Street. He works all day behind the counter serving the Saints. By March he ceases his active involvement in the store, but in his office on the second floor he translates, receives revelations, organizes the Relief Society, and introduces temple endowments.

Jan. 15, 1842

Joseph proofreads the Book of Mormon.

Jan. 18, 1842

Joseph revokes his power of attorney from Dr. Isaac Galland, who can now no longer transact business for the Church. Joseph rests in the afternoon, corrects the Book of Mormon, and debates John C. Bennett concerning the Lamanites and Negroes.

Jan. 19, 1842

Joseph writes Dr. Galland expressing his financial disagreements with him.

Jan. 25, 1842

The Nauvoo Legion parades in review before Lieutenant-General Joseph Smith. In the past year the Legion has grown from six companies to 26 companies, about 2,000 men.

Jan. 28, 1842

Joseph receives a revelation for the Twelve, which is printed in the *Times and Seasons;* the Twelve are to take over the editorial department of the *Times and Seasons.*

Feb. 3, 1842

A new national bankruptcy act becomes effective. Wilford Woodruff becomes superintendent of the printing office, and John Taylor is made editor of the *Times and Seasons.*

Feb. 4, 1842

In the evening Joseph attends one of the weekly debates being held in Nauvoo.

Feb. 6, 1842

A son is stillborn to Emma and Joseph in Nauvoo.

Feb. 10, 1842

Joseph is sick and stays in bed.

Feb. 15, 1842

Joseph's name appears as editor and publisher of the *Times and Seasons.* Ebenezer Robinson had been running the paper since Don Carlos Smith died in 1841, but now Joseph seems to have taken over, with John Taylor and Wilford Woodruff of the Twelve helping him.

Feb. 19-Mar. 18, 1842

According to some sources, Joseph translated the book of Abraham between these dates.

Feb. 28, 1842

A man sends Joseph a note stating that Joseph has been honest and fair in his financial dealings with the man. Joseph immediately publishes the rare but welcome compliment in the *Times and Seasons.*

Mar. 1, 1842

Joseph works in the printing office correcting the first plate or cut of the record of Abraham, in preparation for publishing it. The *Times and Seasons* carries facsimile No. 1 of the book of Abraham and Abraham 1:1—2:18. (It may have been published later than this date.) The famous Wentworth letter is also published on this date in the *Times and Seasons,* as a reply to the editor of the Chicago *Democrat.* It briefly explains the history and beliefs of the Latter-day Saints. This letter contains Joseph's recollection of his first vision, the history of the Church since then, and the Articles of Faith.

Mar. 4, 1842

Joseph exhibits the original book of Abraham to Reuben Hedlock so that he can prepare proper printing blocks for the *Times and Seasons.* Sarah M. Kimball and other women decide to make shirts for the men working on the temple. When they organize into a group, Joseph offers to help them. Eventually this small group will be organized as the Female Relief Society of Nauvoo.

Mar. 7, 1842

Joseph writes to John C. Bennett about slavery, stating that "it makes my blood boil within me to reflect upon the injustice, cruelty, and oppression of the rulers of the people." (HC 4:544-45, 548.)

Mar. 13, 1842

Joseph spends the day with his family.

Mar. 15, 1842

Joseph publicly announces that he is editor of the *Times and Seasons* and will be responsible for all material published in the paper from this day forward. The second half of the book of Abraham (2:19—5:21, and facsimile No. 2) is published in the March 15 *Times and Seasons* (which, like the previous issue, may have come out a few days late). The Masonic Lodge of Nauvoo has now grown to 33 members, and more than 50 others have made application to become Masons. (See Dec. 30, 1841.) The meeting on Feb. 17, 1842, decided upon this date as the formal installation date of all new Masons in Nauvoo. Abraham Jonas, "Grand Master of the Grand Lodge of the State of Illinois," comes to Nauvoo with several other prominent Masons from throughout the state. The Nauvoo Lodge of Free Masons is officially installed. Joseph Smith and Sidney Rigdon are installed as Apprentice Masons. Jonas gives special permission to confer the three degrees of Ancient York Masonry on Joseph and Sidney "as speedily as the nature of the case will admit." (DM 101-3.)

Mar. 16, 1842

In the morning Joseph and Sidney receive the second degree of masonry. At two P.M. they rise to the sublime degree. By May 6, 65 other prominent men have become

Masons, 54 having risen to the third degree. Other lists indicate as many as 145 or 250 other Saints may have become Masons around this time. (See DM 103-4.)

Mar. 17, 1842

The organization of the Female Relief Society of Nauvoo commences this day, and is completed on March 24, 1842. Joseph Smith, John Taylor, and Willard Richards meet with 18 women in the Masonic Hall. (Eight other women not present were also accepted as members on the first day.) Emma Smith is made president, with Elizabeth Ann Whitney and Sarah M. Cleveland as her counselors. Eliza R. Snow is made secretary. Joseph states, "I will organize the sisters under the priesthood after the pattern of the priesthood," and later adds, "[the] Church was never perfectly organized until the women were thus organized." (IJB 504-8.)

Mar. 20, 1842

On this Sunday Joseph preaches to a large congregation in the grove near the temple lot. After the sermon, he personally baptizes 80 people in the Mississippi River, including Emma Smith's nephew, the first of her family to embrace the gospel. Joseph then confirms about 50 of those people. While this is taking place, baptisms for the dead are being performed in the temple font.

Mar. 24, 1842

Joseph attends to the completion of the Female Relief Society of Nauvoo. He comments that a great number of sisters attend the meetings and that "they will fly to the relief of the stranger; they will pour in oil and wine to the wounded heart of the distressed; they will dry up the tears of the orphan and make the widow's heart to rejoice." (HC 4:567-68.) By September 1842, the membership of this society increases to 1,142; it increases 200 more during the following 18 months.

Mar. 27, 1842

After a sermon on baptism for the dead, Joseph baptizes 107 persons in the Mississippi River. On the same date 170 English Saints reach Nauvoo, and $3,000 worth of goods are donated for the building of the temple and Nauvoo House.

Mar. 30, 1842

Joseph addresses the Female Relief Society, commending them on their zeal but saying that "sometimes their zeal was not according to knowledge." (HC 4:570.)

Apr. 1842

Several eastern newspapers carry articles about Joseph's book of Abraham.

Apr. 1, 1842

Joseph publishes an editorial in the *Times and Seasons* titled "Try the Spirits," in which he talks about discerning of spirits by the power of the priesthood, the difference between the body and the spirit, various false prophets and false sects, and the manifestations of Satan. (See HC 4:571-81.)

Apr. 6-8, 1842

A special conference is held in Nauvoo, in which 275 brethren are ordained elders. According to the Council of Fifty minutes of 1880, on Apr. 7, 1842, Joseph received a revelation outlining how the kingdom of God would eventually have political power. (For further developments of this idea, see Mar. 11, 1844.)

Apr. 9, 1842

Joseph gives a funeral sermon for Ephraim Marks, son of stake president William Marks.

Apr. 10, 1842

Sunday. Joseph preaches in the grove against adulterers and fornicators and "those who have made use of my name to carry on their iniquitous designs." He says, "If you wish to go where God is, you must be like God . . . for if we are not drawing towards God in principle, we are going from Him and drawing towards the devil. Yes, I am standing in the midst of all kinds of people. Search your hearts, and see if you are like God. I have searched mine, and feel to repent of all my sins. . . . A man is saved no faster than he gets knowledge . . . hence it needs revelation to assist us, and give us knowledge of the things of God." (HC 4:587-88. His reference to people using his name to carry on their own unvirtuous activities probably refers to his growing disenchantment with John C. Bennett, which will be made manifest in May 1842.)

Apr. 14, 1842

Calvin A. Warren is hired by Joseph to explain and investigate the technicalities of the Federal Bankruptcy Law, which had gone into effect on Feb. 1, 1842. Joseph records, "The justice or injustice of such a principle in law, I leave for them who made it, the United States. Suffice it to say, the law was as good for the Saints as for the Gentiles, and whether I would or not, I was forced into the measure by having been robbed, mobbed, plundered, and wasted of all my property, time after time, in various places, by the very ones who made the law, namely, the people of the United States." (HC 4:594-95.)

Apr. 16, 1842

The *Wasp*, edited by Joseph's brother William, is published for the first time in Nauvoo as a miscellaneous weekly newspaper. Subscription price is $1.50 per year.

Apr. 18, 1842

Joseph, Hyrum Smith, and Samuel Smith go to Carthage to declare bankruptcy before the county commissioner's court. Other leading Latter-day Saints file similar papers at the same time. According to the law, Joseph's goods, except for a $300 exemption, would then be turned over to pay old debts. However, before a person is declared bankrupt, a long investigation must take place. Seven months later, in December, Joseph is still waiting the approval of his declaration of bankruptcy. He never does record whether he is awarded the bankruptcy judgment or not.

Apr. 20, 1842

Joseph, suspecting betrayal by John C. Bennett, records that he feels there is a conspiracy against the peace of his household.

May 2, 1842

An editorial in the *Times and Seasons* encourages the rapid building of the temple.

May 4, 1842

Joseph teaches the full endowment ceremony for the first time. He meets with James Adams, Hyrum Smith, Newel K. Whitney, George Miller, Brigham Young, Heber C. Kimball, and Willard Richards to instruct them "in the principles and order of the Priesthood, attending to washings, anointings, endowments, and the communication of keys pertaining to the Aaronic Priesthood, and so on to the highest order of the Melchizedek Priesthood." (HC 5:1-2.) He and Hyrum give the endowments to the other six men, and on the next day they receive the endowment from the others (except James Adams, who had returned to Springfield).

May 6, 1842

In Missouri ex-Governor Lilburn W. Boggs is shot in the head by an unknown assassin. He lingers on the edge of death but finally recovers from the wound. A man named Tompkins is charged with the shooting at first, but is later released. When Boggs learns that Orrin Porter Rockwell has recently been in Missouri with his pregnant wife, he begins to suspect that Rockwell has been sent there to shoot him under orders from Joseph Smith. He therefore begins to press charges.

May 7, 1842

Twenty-six companies and 2,000 men of the Nauvoo Legion march in review and fight a sham battle. John C. Bennett urges Joseph to take his place on a horse in a prominent place among the troops, and Joseph thinks that Bennett plans to use a real bullet to assassinate him during the proceedings. Stephen A. Douglas and Gov. Carlin are both in Nauvoo on this date. Joseph records, "If General Bennett's true feelings toward me are not made manifest to the world in a very short time, then it may be possible that the gentle breathings of that Spirit, which whispered me on parade, that there was mischief concealed in that sham battle, were false; a short time will determine the point." (HC 5:3-5.)

May 10, 1842

An unknown delegation of Saints in Washington, D.C., presents a petition to the House Judiciary Committee, setting forth grievances about the Missouri persecutions.

May 11, 1842

John C. Bennett is disfellowshipped from the Church for immorality, among other things.

May 14, 1842

Joseph attends a city council meeting in which he advocates suppressing all "houses and acts of infamy in the city." This act is passed and published in the *Wasp*. (HC 5:8.)

May 16, 1842
Joseph publishes facsimile No. 3 from the Book of Abraham on the front page of the *Times and Seasons*.

May 17, 1842
John C. Bennett swears an affidavit before Alderman Daniel H. Wells stating that Joseph Smith never authorized or taught John C. Bennett either in public or in private that "an illegal, illicit intercourse with females, was under any circumstances justifiable, and that I never knew him to so teach others." (Bennett then resigns from the office of mayor of Nauvoo.) (HC 5:11-12.)

May 19, 1842
John C. Bennett, having spread immorality supposedly with Joseph's authorization, testifies before the city council of Joseph's uprightness and swears that he (Bennett) was never taught anything immoral by the Prophet. After Bennett's resignation, Joseph is elected mayor of Nauvoo by the city council, and Hyrum Smith is elected vice-mayor. During the election Joseph receives a revelation stating that Hiram Kimball has been insinuating evil about Joseph and the Lord will punish him if he continues. Joseph writes down the revelation and hands it to Kimball, one of the councilors. Joseph speaks about the evil reports that are spreading throughout the city concerning him and asks for a night watch, which is approved.

May 22, 1842
Joseph publishes an article in the *Wasp*, addressed to the editor of the *Quincy Whig*, refuting the claim that Joseph had prophesied Bogg's death by violent means the previous year.

May 25, 1842
John C. Bennett is officially notified that fellowship has been withdrawn from him. Upon Bennett's urgent request that the matter not be published, "for his mother's sake," the notice is not published in the paper as had been intended. (HC 5:18.)

May 26, 1842
John C. Bennett confesses his guilt before 100 Masons in the Masonic Lodge in Nauvoo. Joseph addresses the Female Relief Society and tells them not to be too zealous or rigid, to have the spirit of forgiveness, and to guard against the spreading of rumors.

May 27, 1842
Joseph is sick and stays in bed, taking medicine.

May 28, 1842
Joseph speaks to the Female Relief Society and tells the sisters how they can have the blessings and gifts of the priesthood, such as healing the sick and casting out of devils. The *Wasp,* published by Joseph's brother William, prints the news that "Boggs is undoubtedly killed according to a report but Who did the Noble Deed remains to be found out." (HC 5:xxii.)

June 1, 1842
A conference is held in England presided over by Parley P. Pratt. There are now over 7500 members there.

June 3, 1842
Joseph sells one lot of property and goes on a horseback ride with Emma and others.

June 9, 1842
Joseph speaks to the Female Relief Society in the grove. He tells the sisters that they must be more particular in accepting new members and should accept no one unless they present a petition signed by at least two or three other members. Joseph tells the sisters that they need better fellowship, more mercy and compassion, and less self-righteousness (which is a principle of the devil), and that there must be no strife among them.

June 14, 1842
Joseph buys three-quarters of a section of land from Hiram Kimball.

June 15, 1842
Joseph publishes an editorial on the gift of the Holy Ghost. (See HC 5:26-32.)

June 16, 1842
The Masonic Lodge publishes a bulletin confirming that

John C. Bennett is an expelled Mason.

June 17, 1842

William Law publishes a defense of the morality of the Saints in Nauvoo. Joseph comments on it, saying, "There is no city . . . that can compare with the city of Nauvoo. You may live in our city for a month, and not hear an oath sworn; you may be here as long and not see one person intoxicated. So notorious are we for sobriety, that at the time the Washington convention passed through our city a meeting was called for them, but they expressed themselves at a loss what to say, as there were no drunkards to speak to." (HC 5:32-34.)

June 18, 1842

Joseph begins speaking and publishing rebuttals to the lies being spread abroad by John C. Bennett.

June 23, 1842

Joseph publishes an order of excommunication against John C. Bennett, which had been drawn up on May 11.

June 24, 1842

Joseph sends a letter to Gov. Carlin explaining the controversy with John C. Bennett.

June 28, 1842

Joseph visits Sidney Rigdon's family, who have had unpleasant feelings because of the lies spread by John C. Bennett.

June 29, 1842

Joseph is married to Eliza R. Snow. Eliza records her lonely and unsure feelings on this day. (See BYS, Su '75, 392-395.)

June 30, 1842

Gov. Carlin writes back to Joseph Smith, stating the reasons for his uncertain feelings in regard to the Mormons.

July 2, 1842

The *Wasp* publishes Joseph Smith's phrenology chart, which purports to describe Joseph's character according to the bumps in his head.

July 3, 1842

This Sunday Joseph preaches to 8,000 in the grove.

July 4, 1842

A grand parade of the Nauvoo Legion is led by Wilson Law. Two are fined $10.25 for selling whiskey.

July 8, 1842

John C. Bennett publishes the first of his anti-Mormon articles in the *Sangamon Journal,* stating that he will expose the Prophet and the Saints. "I write you now from the Mormon Zion, where I am threatened with death by the Holy Joe, and his Danite band of murderers." Elsewhere in this Springfield paper it is stated: "The Mormons are so constituted that in these temperate times, the world will be divided between the Pope and the Catholics on one side and Joseph Smith and the Mormons on the other. The oyster is opening and will soon be equally divided. There are now approximately 30,000 of these war-like fanatics." Bennett's letters appear intermittently for the next three months, after which he publishes a book on the same subject. His most famous accusation is that the Saints have an elaborate "spiritual wife" system of plural marriage. (FMG 293; DM 131-32.)

July 15, 1842

The *Times and Seasons* publishes an article on the government of God, stating that it differs from the government of man mostly because it promotes peace and not war.

July 17, 1842

Brigham Young writes to Parley P. Pratt about Orson Pratt's recent troubles. He writes that Orson believes the word of Mrs. Pratt and John C. Bennett over that of Joseph. Brigham writes that "we will not let Br. Orson go away from us. He is too good a man to have a woman destroy him." (OPJ 561-62.)

July 22, 1842

The Council of the Twelve meets to draw up a letter stating that John C. Bennett is lying about Joseph Smith's character. Orson Pratt opposes the action, but when asked if he has any knowledge about Joseph's immorality, he says he has none.

Aug. 1842

Gubernatorial elections are held in Illinois. Snyder, the pro-Mormon Democratic candidate, died suddenly in

May 1842. His more neutral successor, Thomas Ford, defeats the anti-Mormon Whig candidate, Joseph Duncan. (For details on the involvement of the Saints in these political events, see Dec. 8, 1842, the date of Ford's inauguration.)

Aug. 6, 1842

Joseph prophesies that "the Saints would continue to suffer much affliction and would be driven to the Rocky Mountains, many would apostatize, others would be put to death by our persecutors or lose their lives in consequence of exposure or disease, and some of you will live to go and assist in making settlements and build cities and see the Saints become a mighty people in the midst of the Rocky Mountains." (HC 5:85-86.)

Aug. 8, 1842

After working diligently with Orson Pratt for 12 days, the Twelve decide to cut him off from the Church for believing his wife and John C. Bennett over Joseph Smith. The action officially takes place August 20.

A deputy sheriff of Adams County and two assistants arrest Joseph in Nauvoo. They have a warrant from Gov. Carlin that is based upon a requisition from Gov. Reynolds of Missouri, which, in turn, was based upon an affidavit of ex-Governor Boggs. Boggs accused Joseph of ordering Orrin P. Rockwell to shoot Boggs. A Nauvoo court, under Hyrum Smith, issues a writ of habeas corpus allowing the prisoners to be released temporarily. This begins approximately four months of arrest attempts against Joseph, in which he spends much of his time hiding out. It is reported that anywhere from $200 to $1300 is offered as a reward for Joseph's arrest. Joseph, knowing that Gov. Carlin would allow him to be extradited to Missouri (and knowing he would never return alive if he were ever taken to Missouri), refuses to submit to the law. On this date the city of Nauvoo passes a special ordinance that would quash all writs based upon religious prejudice. This seems like special legal maneuvering and arouses more opposition to the Saints.

Aug. 10, 1842

Deputies return to arrest Joseph and Rockwell, but they

are in hiding. The sheriffs threaten Emma and others. Joseph is across the river in Zarahemla, Iowa, in the house of his uncle John Smith.

Aug. 11, 1842

After dark, Joseph meets with Emma and several of the brethren on an island in the middle of the Mississippi River. After much discussion it is decided that Joseph should go upriver in a skiff, which he does. He then stays at the home of Edward Sayers.

Aug. 12-16, 1842

Joseph hides out and moves from place to place, visiting Emma and his friends whenever possible. An article on persecution appears in the *Times and Seasons.*

Aug. 16, 1842

Joseph writes a tender love note to Emma. He records his affection and gratitude and love for Emma, Hyrum, Newel K. Whitney, and others. James Arlington Bennett writes to Joseph from New York, stating that most people are being convinced by John C. Bennett's articles against the Prophet. Bennett also suggests that the newspaper, the *Wasp,* be given a milder title.

Aug. 19, 1842

Joseph returns home at night.

Aug. 20, 1842

The Twelve carry out their decision of August 8 and excommunicate Orson Pratt and his wife. Amasa M. Lyman is ordained to the apostleship in Pratt's place. John C. Bennett is officially deposed as chancellor of the University of the City of Nauvoo. (Pratt will be reinstated into the Twelve on Jan. 20, 1843.) The high council of Nauvoo decides to divide the city into ten wards with a bishop over each. (This does not take place until Dec. 4, 1842.)

Aug. 21, 1842

Sunday. Sidney Rigdon preaches in the grove. He has begun to oppose Joseph bitterly. However, his daughter, Eliza, whom doctors had pronounced dead, has risen up in bed and said to her elder sister Nancy, "It is in your heart to deny this work; and if you do, the Lord says it will be the damnation of your soul." Because of this miraculous healing, Rigdon announces that rather than denounce the faith and call Joseph a fallen prophet, as many have been saying Rigdon believes, he wants instead to testify to the miracle of God and restate that his faith in Joseph is still strong. The Saints, having heard so many recent negative things about Joseph, are greatly rejuvenated in spirit by Sidney's testimony. (HC 5:121-23.)

Aug. 22, 1842

Joseph, still in hiding, records his love for the Joseph Knight family, Orrin Porter Rockwell, and his own family.

Aug. 27, 1842

Joseph prepares affidavits for the press, including an article on happiness, which states, "God said, 'Thou shalt not kill'; at another time He said, 'Thou shalt utterly destroy.' This is a principle on which the government of heaven is conducted—by revelation adapted to the circumstances in which the children of the kingdom are placed. Whatever God requires is right, no matter what it is, although we may not see the reason thereof till long after the events transpire." (HC 5:134-36.) A footnote on HC 5:134 states, "It is very likely that the article was written with a view of applying the principles here expounded to the conditions created by introducing said [plural] marriage system."

Aug. 29, 1842

A special conference is held wherein Joseph speaks publicly for the first time after three weeks of hiding out. Three hundred and eighty elders volunteer to go on missions to refute the lies of John C. Bennett. Orson Pratt again disappears, and many people fear he will attempt suicide.

Aug. 31, 1842

Joseph speaks to the Female Relief Society, stating that the Church will prevail against all enemies, and that "although I do wrong, I do not the wrong that I am charged with doing." He also remarks that a recorder must be an eyewitness to all baptisms for the dead. (HC 5:139-41.)

Sept. 1, 1842

Joseph writes an epistle concerning baptism for the dead, which is now D&C 127.

Sept. 3, 1842

Joseph, still in hiding, comes to see Emma, who has been sick (she had been baptized in the Mississippi River several times for recovery). Joseph invites John F. Boynton, an apostate apostle, to dinner. While dining, Deputy Sheriff Pitman arrives to arrest the Prophet. Boynton detains Pitman in the front room while Joseph runs out the back through a corn patch and hides in Bishop Whitney's home. Pitman rips the house apart looking for Joseph.

Sept. 6, 1842

Joseph writes another epistle concerning baptism for the dead, which later becomes D&C 128.

Sept. 7-12, 1842

Joseph returns home at times, undetected, and corresponds with various people concerning his legal problems.

Sept. 25, 1842

Sunday. Joseph preaches in the grove for more than two hours on the subject of persecution.

Sept. 29, 1842

Joseph stays with Emma, who is sick all day. The Female Relief Society holds its seventeenth and last meeting of the year in the grove. By this time the membership has grown to 1,189.

Oct. 1, 1842

Orson Pratt publishes a letter in the *Wasp*, refuting John C. Bennett's claim that the Pratts would be leaving the Church. Orson further states that he and his wife "intend to make Nauvoo our residence, and Mormonism our motto." (HC 5:167.)

Oct. 2, 1842

The *Quincy Whig* publishes notices that Gov. Carlin of Illinois and Gov. Reynolds of Missouri have offered $200 and $300 rewards for Joseph and Orrin Porter Rockwell. The non-Mormon Masons of Illinois, hearing of the rapid growth of the Masonic lodge in Nauvoo, meet on this day to discuss this growth. The original dispensation granted by Grandmaster Jonas the previous October (which was to last only one year) is not renewed, and the Nauvoo lodge is placed under suspension until further investigation can be made. When the investigative committee reports its findings in October of 1843, the Saints are accused of advancing new Masons too rapidly, nominating and advancing a whole group of men without any indication of individual worthiness. Joseph Smith is also accused of copying Masonic ritual in the temple ordinances, and when the endowments are given to women, he is accused of initiating women into Masonry. Joseph's comment concerning this is that "free masonry was the apostate religion." In October 1844 the Grandmaster decides that the Nauvoo Lodge has still not reformed; therefore, all official fellowship is cut off with the Nauvoo lodges. Thus, when Joseph is murdered by a mob, some of whom were certainly Masons, Joseph has been cut off from all official Masonic vows of fellowship and loyalty. (DM 104-5.)

Oct. 5, 1842
Emma, very sick, is rebaptized twice in the river for her health. (BYS, W '78, 226-32, explains the practice of rebaptism in Nauvoo.)

Oct. 7-20, 1842
Joseph is again in hiding, coming to see Emma when possible, sneaking in and out after dark. Emma is very ill at this time, and at one point he fears she might die.

Oct. 10, 1842
Frederick G. Williams dies in Quincy, Ill., of a hemorrhage of the lungs.

October 13, 1842
Several brethren return from the pineries in Wisconsin with 90,000 feet of boards and 24,000 cubic feet of timber to be used in building the temple and the Nauvoo House.

Oct. 15, 1842
The *Times and Seasons* announces that the Book of Mormon and hymnbook have just been published and are for sale.

Oct. 28, 1842
The temporary floor and seats of the temple are completed. About this time a 37-page pamphlet titled "An Israelite, and a Shepherd of Israel. An Extract from a Manuscript entitled The Peace Maker, or the Doctrines of

the Millennium" is published in Nauvoo by "J. Smith, printer." The pamphlet uses the scriptures to defend the practice of polygamy, and is published about a month after John C. Bennett's exposé of Mormonism (with its lurid tales of "spiritual wifery") has been published. The author of the pamphlet, Udney Hay Jacob, is a non-member. When there is a negative uproar about the contents of the pamphlet, Joseph Smith, on Dec. 1, 1842, denies that he knew the content of the pamphlet before publication, but defends the author's right to publish his opinions.

Nov. 1842
Joseph spends time with Emma, who is sick; watches the construction of the temple; preaches; meets with visitors, including several Indian dignitaries; and visits sick members.

Nov. 1, 1842
While on a carriage ride with his family, Joseph's carriage overturns. He hurries to see if any of his children have been killed, but F.G.W. Smith has only been bruised on his cheeks, and all the others are safe.

Nov. 15, 1842
Joseph publishes a valedictory notice in the *Times and Seasons* as John Taylor takes over as editor.

Nov. 21, 1842
The Council of the Twelve votes to suspend until further notice printing of the *Millennial Star* and other publications in England.

Dec. 1, 1842
Orrin P. Rockwell writes Joseph a letter from Philadelphia, where he has gone to escape the law officers who were seeking his arrest. Rockwell, sad and lonely, asks Joseph to write him as soon as it is safe for him to return.

Dec. 7, 1842
Orson Hyde arrives in Nauvoo from his mission to Palestine and dines with Joseph Smith.

Dec. 8, 1842
Thomas Ford is inaugurated as governor of Illinois, replacing Gov. Carlin. During the elections the previous

summer, the Whig candidate, Joseph Duncan, ran on a furiously anti-Mormon campaign, urging repeal of the Nauvoo charter and the Nauvoo Legion. Because of John C. Bennett's articles against Joseph Smith, the anti-Mormon feeling in the state had been rising. It was thought that the Democratic nominee, Adam Snyder, who had been friendly to the Saints, would lose the election. When Snyder died suddenly, the Democrats took the opportunity to choose a candidate from northern Illinois, Thomas Ford, who could honestly claim he was neither for nor against them. The Saints voted overwhelmingly for Thomas Ford and he was elected, although he made no special concessions to the Mormons. Ford's basic campaign promise was to improve the miserable economy of the state. During these elections the Saints were often accused of voting as a bloc, but as they saw it, when one candidate was devoutly against Mormonism, they had no choice.

Dec. 9, 1842

Joseph chops wood all day. His brother Hyrum is still working on their application for bankruptcy. Joseph's brother William, having been elected as a representative of Hancock County, Ill., speaks in the state legislature in defense of the Nauvoo Charter.

Dec. 10, 1842

William Smith resigns as editor of the *Wasp,* and John Taylor takes over.

Dec. 14, 1842

Joseph sends a delegation to Springfield. They call on Gov. Ford to present an affidavit from Joseph. Ford, who interprets the law much more literally than his predecessor, Gov. Carlin, states that in his interpretation the writ against Joseph by Carlin is illegal. Joseph, feeling he can trust Ford not to extradite him (as Carlin had tried to do), now feels free to come out of hiding.

Dec. 17, 1842

Gov. Ford writes to Joseph, advising him to submit to the laws and have a court in Springfield decide if the writ of extradition to Missouri is legal or not. Ford assures Joseph that it is his duty to ensure Joseph's safety.

Dec. 21, 1842
Williard Richards is appointed Church historian.

Dec. 26, 1842
Joseph, having been assured of safety by Gov. Ford, allows himself to be arrested on the requisition from Missouri by General Wilson Law of the Nauvoo Legion. This ends the period of Joseph's hiding from law officers. Before going to Springfield, Joseph visits a Sister Morey, who is ill, and prescribes lobelia for her, which he recommends as an excellent remedy.

Dec. 27, 1842
With several other brethren, Joseph leaves for trial in Springfield, Ill.

Dec. 30, 1842
Joseph reaches Springfield, having traveled from Nauvoo with 40 brethren. On the journey, when the brethren cannot find a place to stay in Paris, Ill., Joseph becomes angry and tells the local townspeople, "We will stay; but no thanks to you. I have men enough to take the town; and if we must freeze, we will freeze by the burning of these houses." With many apologies the taverns are then opened up hospitably. (HC 5:209-12.) In Springfield Joseph explains to Judge Adams that during the millennium Christ and the resurrected Saints "will not probably dwell upon the earth but will visit it when they please, or when it is necessary to govern it. There will be wicked men on the earth during the thousand years." (HC 5:212.)

Dec. 31, 1842
Joseph meets in Springfield with Justin Butterfield, the attorney who will defend him. After discussing legal matters, they visit Gov. Ford. During dinner, Mr. Butterfield tells Joseph that he (Butterfield) is no religionist. Joseph replies, "I told him I had no creed to circumscribe my mind; therefore, the people did not like me." (HC 5:213-14.) Joseph also meets with James Collins Brewster, a teenage boy, who shows him a book of revelations he has been writing. Joseph replies, "If God ever called me, or spake by my mouth, or gave me a revelation, he never gave revelations to that Brewster boy or any of the Brewster race." (HC 5:214.) (The Brewsters had been

disfellowshipped on charges of receiving false revelations on Nov. 20, 1837.)

Sometime in 1842

During this year Charles Dickens publishes his first comments about Mormons. In *A Child's History of England and American Notes* he suggests an insane lady should be committed to an asylum, and suggests it would be just as good "to shut up a few false prophets of these latter times," beginning with "a Mormonist or two." (Twenty years later when Dickens actually boards an emigrant ship filled with Mormons "to bear testimony against them if they deserved it, as I fully believed they would; to my great astonishment they did not deserve it. . . . I went over the Amazon's side, feeling it impossible to deny that, so far, some remarkable influence had produced a remarkable result, which better known influences have often missed." (See BYS, Sp '68, 325-34.)

1843

Jan. 1, 1843

Joseph meets with Mr. Butterfield, Judge Stephen A. Douglas, and others and explains that the difference "between the Latter-day Saints and Sectarians was, that the latter were all circumscribed by some peculiar creed, which deprived its members the privilege of believing anything not contained therein, whereas the Latter-day Saints have no creed, but are ready to believe all true principles that exist, as they are made manifest from time to time." He also explains that he professes to be a prophet because "the testimony of Jesus is the spirit of prophecy." (HC 5:215.)

Jan. 2, 1843

Orson Hyde asks Joseph about the situation of the Negro. The Prophet replies, "Change their situation with the whites and they would be like them. They have souls, and are subjects of salvation. . . . The slaves in Washington are more refined than many in high places, and the black boys will take the shine off many of those they brush and wait on." He also explains, "If I raised you to be my equal, and then attempted to oppress you, would you not be indignant and try to rise above me?" He says he would "confine them by strict law to their own species and put them on a national equalization." He also prophesies, "In the name of the Lord, that I should not go to Missouri dead or alive." (HC 5:216-18.)

Jan. 4, 1843

Joseph stands trial in Springfield, accused of being an accessory to the shooting of ex-Governor Boggs. Judge Pope comes in the courtroom accompanied by several ladies. (Some say that this was the judge's joke about the rumors of polygamy.) Mr. Butterfield, Joseph's attorney, jokingly announces, "It is a momentous occasion in my life to appear before the Pope, in defense of a prophet of God, in the presence of all these angels." The case boils down to whether or not Joseph can be taken from Illinois to Missouri to be tried for a crime that, if committed, was committed in Illinois. The judge rules that it is illegal, and Joseph is freed. (DH 321-22.)

Jan. 6, 1843

Gov. Ford gives Joseph some advice, telling him that he "should refrain from all political electioneering." Joseph says he always acts upon that principle. (HC 5:232.)

Jan. 7-10, 1843

Joseph travels back to Nauvoo after his trial. The axle on the carriage breaks and they all agree that Gov. Boggs should pay the damage. Many friends assemble to greet Joseph back in Nauvoo.

Jan. 17, 1843

This day is set apart as a day of humility, praise, fasting, prayer, and thanksgiving for Joseph's deliverance from the courts of law.

Jan. 18, 1843

Joseph talks with Orson Pratt and Sidney Rigdon about a letter of Jan. 10, written to them by John C. Bennett. In the letter Bennett had tried to conspire with them to get Joseph back to Missouri, where he would be executed on the Boggs's shooting charge. Because Orson Pratt had delivered the letter to Joseph in the first place, Joseph trusts Orson but suspects Sidney Rigdon (because he did not show the letter to Joseph).

Jan. 20, 1843

Orson Pratt goes into the Mississippi River, "from the ice," to be baptized with his wife by Joseph Smith. Joseph then reordains Orson Pratt into the Quorum of the Twelve. He tells the Twelve to reinstate Pratt into the Quorum, and that he (Joseph) will take Amasa Lyman (who had replaced Pratt) into the First Presidency. He also prophesies that once the temple is built, "we will have means to gather the Saints by thousands and tens of thousands." (HC 5:255-56.)

Jan. 22, 1843

Joseph preaches at the temple on the kingdom of God, stating that "where there is a Prophet, a priest, or a righteous man unto whom God gives His oracles, there is the Kingdom of God; and where the oracles of God are not, there the Kingdom of God is not." (HC 5:256-59.)

Jan. 23, 1843

Joseph publishes in the *Wasp* that he is revolted by the idea of having anything to do with politics, and that he wishes only to be left alone to attend to the spiritual affairs of the Church.

Jan. 28, 1843

Joseph plays ball with the brethren. The city council approves paying him $500 a year as mayor and $3 a day when he sits as justice of the municipal court.

Jan. 29, 1843

Sunday. Joseph preaches, explaining why the Savior considered John the Baptist to be the greatest prophet.

Late Jan. 1843

A group of young people gather at Heber C. Kimball's home. Their "loose style of morals" was made evident because they wasted time with "too frequent attendance at balls, parties, etc." Elder Kimball offers to give them some instruction. Soon they begin meeting regularly. This leads to the formation of the "Young Gentlemen and Ladies Relief Society," a forerunner of future Church youth organizations. (HC 5:320-22; BYS, Su '75, 469.)

Feb. 1, 1843

In the *Times and Seasons,* John Taylor announces that he expects to print "further extracts from the Book of Abraham" by Joseph Smith. (This never happens.)

Feb. 3, 1843

Joseph studies and reads German and proofreads the Doctrine and Covenants.

Feb. 6, 1843

City elections are held and Joseph is elected mayor by a unanimous vote.

Feb. 8, 1843

Joseph studies German and tells a visiting couple from Michigan "that a prophet was a prophet only when he was acting as such." In the afternoon he goes sliding on the ice with his son. (HC 5:265.)

Feb. 9, 1843

Joseph receives D&C 129.

Feb. 10, 1843

In mayor's court, Joseph sentences a man who claimed to have been visited by the "Ancient of Days" several times; he is charged with having stolen some goods from a store. He is sent to Carthage jail because he cannot pay the $5,000 bail.

Feb. 11, 1843

Joseph interviews the Sidney Rigdon family and finds that good feelings prevail.

Feb. 12, 1843

Joseph answers several inquiries concerning the end of the world in the coming spring as predicted by William Miller. The Prophet says that Millerism is false because the prophecies that must precede Christ have not all yet been fulfilled.

Feb. 14, 1843

Joseph proofreads the Doctrine and Covenants with W.W. Phelps, studies German, and sells Willard Richards a cow.

Feb. 15, 1843

Joseph publishes the parable "The Lions of the Press," satirizing the various publishers and writers who constantly treat Mormonism. Some writers are symbolized by lions and other animals

Feb. 18, 1843

At dinner Joseph tells his family that "when the earth was sanctified and became like a sea of glass, it would be one great urim and thummim, and the Saints could look in it and see as they are seen." This is the first mention of this doctrine, which will be given in more detail in D&C 130. (HC 5:279.)

Feb. 20, 1843

Seventy brethren help Joseph chop, split, and pile logs in

his yard. He studies German. He sees two boys fighting with clubs and stops the fight. He lectures the onlookers for not stopping the fight immediately and tells them that "nobody was allowed to fight in Nauvoo but myself." (HC 5:282-83.)

Feb. 21, 1843

Joseph addresses the 300 workmen who are constructing the temple. He encourages them to continue the work, and says, "It is our duty to concentrate all our influence to make popular that which is sound and good, and unpopular that which is unsound. 'Tis right, politically, for a man who has influence to use it, as well as for a man who has no influence to use his. From henceforth I will maintain all the influence I can get. In relation to politics, I will speak as a man; but in relation to religion I will speak in authority." (HC 5:284-87.)

Mar. 1, 1843

Joseph loans Orson Hyde his horse, "Joe Duncan," for a ride. Brigham Young, speaking for the Twelve, writes a letter to the Saints at Ramus, Ill., asking the Saints to donate food and other supplies to Joseph Smith so he can dedicate more time to "the bringing forth of revelations, translations, and history . . . one or two good new milch [sic] cows are much needed also." (HC 5:292-93.)

Mar. 3, 1843

The Illinois legislature passes a bill to repeal part of the Nauvoo Charter.

Mar. 4, 1843

Joseph speaks to the city council encouraging them to accept only hard cash, gold, or silver, and not paper money. George A. Smith debates about capital punishment, stating that imprisonment is better than hanging. Joseph replies that he too is opposed to hanging, but advises shooting or decapitation so that the man's blood will be spilled. Joseph notes later that the battle of Gog and Magog will be after the millennium.

Orrin Porter Rockwell, having been hiding out in Philadelphia, returns to Nauvoo by way of St. Louis. He gets off the steamboat in St. Louis, and while there is recognized and captured. This begins a Missouri prison stay lasting over nine months. During his imprisonment he tries to escape by stripping off his clothes and squeezing up a narrow stovepipe into an unlocked cell on the upper floor. Although he does reach the upper cell, he is so weak that he is unable to open the unlocked door. He climbs back down into the lower cell to regain his strength. When he again attempts this escape method, he passes out in the upper cell and is discovered. He will finally be tried in December of 1843, be sentenced to five minutes in prison (which will last five hours), and then be freed to walk back to Illinois. He reaches Nauvoo, having walked the skin off his feet, on Christmas night, 1843.

Mar. 10, 1843
Joseph and others see wondrous lights in the heavens.

Mar. 13, 1843
Joseph wrestles with William Wall, the best wrestler in Ramus, and throws him. That evening he blesses 19 children and records, "Virtue went out of me, and my strength left me, when I gave up the meeting to the brethren." The next day he explains the reason for this virtue going out of him. He states that he saw the influence of Lucifer and strove with all his might to protect the children against it. For this reason he becomes weak and has still not recovered by the next day. (HC 5:303.)

Mar. 15, 1843
Joseph prophesies "in the name of the Lord Jesus Christ, that Orrin Porter Rockwell would get away honorably from the Missourians." (HC 5:305.) The name of the *Wasp* is changed to the *Nauvoo Neighbor,* and a prospectus is published.

Mar. 18, 1843
Joseph writes, "About noon, I lay down on the writing table, with my head on a pile of law books, saying, . . . 'I am going to study law, and this is the way I study it'; and then fell asleep." (HC 5:307.)

Mar. 21, 1843
"Young Gentlemen and Ladies Relief Society of Nauvoo" is officially organized and a charter of 12 rules is drawn up. "If the youth throughout our land would follow this good example and form themselves into such societies,

there would be much less sin, iniquity, misery, and degradation among the young people than there is at the present day." (*Times and Seasons,* Apr. 1, 1843.)

Mar. 25, 1843

Joseph, as mayor, issues a proclamation against the secret gangs of thieves who are hiding out along the Mississippi River. He promises protection to anyone who will volunteer the names of the criminals.

Mar. 27, 1843

Joseph writes a letter to Sidney Rigdon stating that he believes that Rigdon had conspired with John C. Bennett against Joseph. Sidney immediately sends a return letter, denying the charge.

Apr. 2, 1843

Sunday. Orson Hyde preaches on the coming of the Savior, stating that "he will appear on a white horse as a warrior. . . . Our God is a warrior. It is our privilege to have the Father and Son dwelling in our hearts. . . ." Joseph waits until dinnertime to correct Orson's mistaken comments. (HC 5:323.) These instructions are recorded as D&C 130. Later, Joseph explains the beast in the book of Revelation of John, and explains that John's record is very different from Daniel's prophecy: one refers to things in heaven, and the other to a figure of things on earth.

Apr. 3, 1843

This is the day William Miller had predicted the world would end. As the supposed last day of the world, Joseph comments that the day "is too pleasant for false prophets." (HC 5:326, 272.)

Apr. 6, 1843

Joseph records in his personal journal, "If I had not actually got into this work, and been called of God, I would back out. But I cannot back out, I have no doubt of the truth." (DH 344.)

Apr. 6-9, 1843

General conference is held on the unfinished temple floor in Nauvoo.

Apr. 10, 1843

A special conference is called in Nauvoo in which 115

elders are called on missions and given instructions by the Twelve.

Apr. 13, 1843

Joseph preaches at the temple to 250 Saints who arrived the previous day from England. He tells them which part of the town is the most healthy for them to settle. He explains the reason he has sold some lots at a profit, saying, "Suppose I sell you land for ten dollars an acre, and I gave three, four or five dollars per acre; then some persons may cry out, 'You are speculating.' Yes. I will tell how: I buy other lands and give them to the widow and the fatherless. If the speculators run against me, they run against the buckler of Jehovah." (HC 5:354-57.)

Apr. 16, 1843

Joseph receives a letter supposedly by the order of John Tyler, the president of the United States, which accuses him of high treason. It turns out to be a farce. He preaches on the death of Lorenzo D. Barnes. He explains the importance of burial, some details about the resurrection, and forbids anyone from leaving a meeting just before it closes: "I don't care who does it, even if it were the king of England. I forbid it." (HC 5:360-63.)

Apr. 19, 1843

Joseph meets with the Twelve and calls most of them on missions to the eastern states; he says, "Take Jacob Zundall and Frederick Moeser, and tell them never to drink a drop of ale, wine, or any spirit, only that which flows right out from the presence of God; and send them to Germany; and when you meet with an Arab, send him to Arabia; when you find an Italian, send him to Italy. . . . Send them to the different places where they belong . . . to all Spanish America; and don't let a single corner of the earth go without a mission. Write to Oliver Cowdery and ask him if he has not eaten husks long enough? If he is not almost ready to return . . . ?" (HC 5:366-68.)

Apr. 23, 1843

Six brass plates are found near Kinderhook, Pike County, Ill., by a Robert Wiley and others. They are given to Joseph to see if he can translate them. He says, "I have translated a portion of them, and find they contain the his-

187

tory of the person with whom they were found. He was a descendant of Ham, through the loins of Pharaoh, king of Egypt, and that he received his kingdom from the Ruler of heaven and earth." Joseph never publishes a record of the plates, but the facsimile of the plates themselves is published in the *Times and Seasons* in April 1843. (HC 5:372-79.

Apr. 25, 1843
Lyman Wight and Justin Brooks go to Pittsburgh to buy a steamboat with which to transport the Kirtland Saints to Nauvoo.

May 3, 1843
The *Nauvoo Neighbor* (formerly the *Wasp*) is first issued. John Taylor and Wilford Woodruff are editors.

May 9, 1843
Joseph and 100 others go aboard the steamboat *Maid of Iowa,* take a trip up to Fort Madison, Wisconsin, and return in the evening.

May 11, 1843
Joseph rebaptizes Louisa Beaman, Sarah Alley, and others. He meets with the Twelve and calls Capt. Dan Jones on a mission to Wales, James Sloan to Ireland, and other elders to other parts of Great Britain. Elders Addison Pratt, Noah Rogers, Benjamin F. Grouard, and Knowlton F. Hanks are called on missions to the Pacific Isles (Society Islands).

May 12, 1843
Joseph purchases half ownership in the steamer *Maid of Iowa,* and Capt. Dan Jones begins renting her as a ferryboat between Nauvoo and Montrose, Iowa.

May 13, 1843
John Taylor publishes an article in the *Nauvoo Neighbor* encouraging the building of a pottery factory in Nauvoo.

May 14, 1843
Sunday. At Yelrome, Joseph preaches on salvation through knowledge. He explains the meaning of salvation, states that there can be no salvation except through a physical tabernacle, and explains the doctrine of the "more sure word of prophecy," or "calling and election made sure," as explained in 2 Peter. He also advises that

in times of trouble it is best to counsel with "wise men, experienced and aged men." He adds that "handsome men are not apt to be wise and strong-minded men; but the strength of a strong-minded man will generally create coarse features." (HC 5:387-90.)

May 16-17, 1843

Joseph travels toward Carthage, Ill., with George Miller, William Clayton, Eliza and Lydia Partridge, and others. They stop at Ramus, and Joseph gives instruction to Brother and Sister Benjamin F. Johnson, explaining the necessity of being married in the everlasting covenant. The next morning he preaches about 2 Peter and states, "Paul saw the third heavens and I more. Peter penned the most sublime language of any of the apostles." (HC 5:391-92.) Other instructions given on these two days are found in D&C 131.

May 18, 1843

Joseph dines with 30-year-old Judge Stephen A. Douglas in Carthage and relates the details of his trip to Washington to gain redress for the Missouri persecutions. He says, "I prophesy in the name of the Lord God of Israel, unless the United States redress the wrongs committed upon the Saints in the state of Missouri . . . the government will be utterly overthrown and wasted, and there will not be so much as a potsherd left. . . . Judge, you will aspire to the presidency of the United States; and if ever you turn your hand against me or the Latter-day Saints, you will feel the weight of the hand of Almighty upon you; and you will live to see and know that I have testified the truth to you; for the conversation of this day will stick to you through life." (HC 5:393-94. For the outcome of this prophecy, see IJB 581-82; CHC 2:183-92; HC 5:393-98.)

May 20, 1843

Joseph writes an article for the *Times and Seasons* on the derivation of the word *Mormon.* "The word Mormon, means literally, more good." (HC 5:399-400.)

May 21, 1843

Sunday. Joseph preaches at the temple to a large crowd. He gives his famous sermon on 2 Peter, explaining three keys with which to understand chapter one. (See HC 5:401-3.)

May 24, 1843

The *Boston Bee* carries a detailed article describing Joseph. It surprises him that a newspaper would actually publish something about him that is not slanderous. Thomas Rancliff complains to Joseph that he (Rancliff) has been swindled by William and Wilson Law and Dr. Robert Foster.

May 28, 1843

Joseph meets with six associates "to attend to ordinances and counseling." He prays that Orrin Porter Rockwell might be delivered from prison and James Adams might be delivered from his enemies. He says that of the original Twelve Apostles, "there have been but two but what have lifted their heel against me—namely Brigham Young and Heber C. Kimball." (HC 5:412.)

June 2, 1843

Joseph closes the contract whereby he becomes half-owner of the steamboat *Maid of Iowa* for $1,375. This will serve as the ferryboat across the Mississippi.

June 8, 1843

Elias Higbee dies unexpectedly in Nauvoo. Joseph records his affection for him. Emma Smith is ill.

June 10, 1843

Gov. Ford of Illinois receives a letter from Missouri stating that upon the urgings of John C. Bennett, Gov. Reynolds of Missouri will soon be asking Gov. Ford to arrest Joseph Smith and send him back to Missouri to stand trial for the 1838 charge of treason.

June 11, 1843

Sunday. Joseph preaches on various topics.

June 13, 1843

Joseph, Emma, and their four children leave Nauvoo on a much-needed vacation. They begin traveling toward the home of Emma's sister, Mrs. Wasson, who lives near Dixon, Lee County, over 200 miles north of Nauvoo.

June 16, 1843

At night, Judge James Adams of Springfield sends an urgent message to Nauvoo that Gov. Ford plans to issue a writ to take Joseph back to Missouri, based on the requisition from the Missouri governor.

June 18, 1843

Hyrum Smith receives the message from James Adams and immediately sends William Clayton and Stephen Markham to warn Joseph.

June 19-21, 1843

Leaving at midnight, Clayton and Markham ride at a furious pace and cover 212 miles in 66 hours; they reach the Wasson home in the afternoon of June 21. Learning that Joseph has gone to Dixon, they follow, catch him, and return with him to the Wassons'.

June 23, 1843

Meanwhile, Joseph H. Reynolds, the Jackson County sheriff, and law officer Harmon T. Wilson of Carthage reach that area to arrest Joseph. Joseph sends Clayton to the town of Dixon to get information. Halfway there, Clayton runs into Reynolds and Wilson. Clayton fails to recognize them, as they are disguised as Mormon elders. In Dixon, Reynolds and Wilson learn of Joseph's whereabouts and ride to the Wasson home. They capture Joseph, arresting him illegally at gunpoint. Brutal jabbings with their guns cause Joseph's chest to turn black and blue with an 18-inch bruise. They swear and threaten to shoot him. Joseph tells them to go ahead, but says he is willing to submit to any legal papers they may have. When they throw him in a wagon, Stephen Markham attempts to hold the horses. They level their guns at Markham, threatening to kill him. Markham lets go of the horses. They ride off just as Emma throws Joseph his hat and coat. Markham rides to Dixon immediately to report the kidnapping. When Reynolds and Wilson reach the town, eight miles away, they lock Joseph in a room while they change horses on the wagon. Joseph yells out the window for help from a lawyer and a writ of habeas corpus. When a few lawyers arrive, Reynolds claims he plans to take Joseph to Missouri without interference and threatens to shoot anyone who tries to stop him. However, as the crowd grows, Reynolds compromises, agreeing to allow 30 minutes for the writ of habeas corpus. Joseph sends messages to several lawyers, including Cyrus H. Walker, a Whig candidate for Congress, who has been electioneering nearby. During this time, Markham swears out a writ against Reynolds and Wilson for threatening his life. The two are then arrested on two counts: for threatening Markham's life and for illegally arresting and threatening Joseph. Reynolds and Wilson as well as Joseph are all locked up overnight so that the complications can be sorted out the next morning.

June 24, 1843

Joseph sends William Clayton on an early morning steamer back to Nauvoo. Cyrus Walker arrives and tells Joseph he will help him in exchange for Joseph's vote in the upcoming election. When Joseph promises, Walker says to Stephen Markham, "I am now sure of my election, as Joseph Smith has promised me his vote, and I am going to defend him." Reynolds and Wilson are again arrested on charges of false imprisonment, but getting a writ of habeas corpus for themselves, they are freed into the custody of the Lee County sheriff. Reynolds and Wilson then take Joseph to Pawpaw Grove, 32 miles away. Cyrus Walker sends Lee County Sheriff Campbell to stay the night with Joseph and protect him from abuse by Reynolds and Wilson.

June 25, 1843

In the morning, crowds gather and threaten to harm Reynolds and Wilson if they harm Joseph. Joseph is allowed to speak in public. He preaches for an hour and a half on marriage. Emma and the children begin their return to Nauvoo at this time. The Ottawa judge is out of town, so they are unable to serve the writ of habeas corpus. They return to Dixon for another writ. Stephen Markham has the writ worded so that trial can be held at the nearest tribunal. Joseph and his lawyers and friends decide to take the writ to the court of Judge Stephen A. Douglas at Quincy, 260 miles away. They plan to set out in the morning by stagecoach. Joseph also sends Markham to arrange a meeting place with Gen. Wilson Law, hoping that Law will bring dozens of men with him.

At this time in Nauvoo, the cornerstone for the proposed Masonic temple is laid by "Worshipful Master Hyrum Smith." Several Pottawatamie Indians also call at the Nauvoo House and temple, but can't communicate well. William Clayton arrives in Nauvoo with the news of Joseph's capture. Three hundred men set out at once to rescue him. Seventy-five go upriver on the steamboat

Maid of Iowa. One hundred seventy-five ride out with Gen. Wilson Law and his brother William, taking different routes.

June 26, 1843
Joseph, with his lawyers and friends, sets out under guard of Reynolds and Wilson, heading south toward Quincy.

June 27, 1843
In the afternoon Joseph meets the first of the men on horseback from Nauvoo. Letting his tears go, Joseph cries, "I am not going to Missouri this time. These are my boys." These men have all been riding frantically from Nauvoo, sometimes forcing whiskey down their horses' throats just to keep them going. Emma and the children reach Nauvoo at night. (HC 5:451-52; DH 328.)

June 28, 1843
By this time dozens of men have joined Joseph and his captors on their ride to Nauvoo (having decided that the Nauvoo court is closer than the Quincy court). Reynolds and Wilson think they will never leave Nauvoo alive if forced to go there, and as more and more men surround them, they become increasingly nervous. They draw their guns on Stephen Markham as a hostage, but are convinced by Sheriff Campbell that such action is foolish. They surrender their arms and ride toward Nauvoo.

June 30, 1843
Joseph and the company arrive in Nauvoo triumphantly about noon. The whole town turns out to give them a hero's welcome, including a brass band, cannon fire, a line of decorated carriages, and streets lined with cheering people. Joseph has a feast at his home with fifty friends. He seats Reynolds and Wilson at the head of the table. The Nauvoo Municipal Court convenes that afternoon, and Reynolds is forced to turn over his prisoner, Joseph, to the city marshal. At 5 P.M., 10,000 people assemble at the grove to listen to Joseph's tale of the adventure. Joseph exuberantly states, "I feel as strong as a giant. I pulled sticks with men coming along, and I pulled up with one hand the strongest man that could be found. Then two men tried, but they could not pull me up, and I continued to pull mentally, until I pulled Missouri to Nauvoo. . . . Thank God, I am now a prisoner in the hands of the mu-

nicipal court of Nauvoo, and not in the hands of Missourians. . . . But before I will bear this unhallowed persecution any longer—before I will be dragged away again among my enemies for trial, I will spill the last drop of blood in my veins, and will see all my enemies in hell! To bear it any longer would be a sin." He claims that the Nauvoo court has power to free him, and while he is speaking, Reynolds and Wilson leave for Carthage, threatening to raise a militia to again arrest him. (HC 5:458-73.)

July 1, 1843

Joseph is tried before the Nauvoo Municipal Court on the writ of habeas corpus and is discharged from the previous arrest warrant. Despite the fact that the previous arrest was made illegally, the warrant has still been issued by the governor of the state. Thus, the city of Nauvoo has, in effect, overruled an order by the state. This will have future unfortunate implications as Gov. Ford and other once friendly neighbors begin to distrust the political power of Nauvoo. Heber C. Kimball and Orson Pratt start on missions to the East (the rest of the Twelve are to meet them in Pittsburgh).

July 2, 1843

Joseph petitions the governor not to issue any more writs, and has the petition signed by 150 citizens. He has an interview with the Pottawatamie chiefs who have come to visit him while he was away. He explains the gospel, kills an ox for them, and gives them some horses. The *Maid of Iowa* returns with the men who had gone to look for Joseph. He greets them, welcoming them home.

July 3, 1843

Joseph meets with the Twelve to call about 100 elders to go on special missions throughout Illinois to counteract the widespread negative feelings resulting from Joseph's escaping his arrest. Charles C. Rich and 25 others return to Nauvoo having traveled 500 miles in seven days looking for Joseph during his kidnapping.

July 4, 1843

A huge Fourth of July celebration is held. Steamers from as far away as St. Louis arrive in Nauvoo, bringing about 1,000 visitors for the day. 15,000 people assemble in the grove in the afternoon to listen to sermons by Joseph and others.

July 6, 1843

Gov. Ford writes to Joseph H. Reynolds that he should not make any attempts to rearrest Joseph Smith until Ford's representative in Nauvoo can report on the rumors of a Mormon military force in Nauvoo.

July 7, 1843

Ford's agent in Nauvoo, Mr. Brayman, meets with the Saints to get affidavits about the recent arrest, escape, and rescue by a military force. While Governor Ford is trying to decide whether or not to use a militia to rearrest Joseph, a heated congressional campaign is occurring between the Whig, Cyrus Walker (to whom Joseph had promised his vote), and the Democrat Joseph Hoge. The two most influential Church leaders other than Joseph, Hyrum Smith and William Law, are in disagreement about the candidates. The Democrats try to convince the Mormons that Gov. Ford will send out the militia against Joseph if the Mormons vote for the Whigs.

July 8, 1843

Brigham Young, Wilford Woodruff, George A. Smith, and others start on eastern missions to hold conferences and collect funds for building the temple and Nauvoo House. Most of the Twelve had been called on eastern missions April 19, 1843.

July 9, 1843

Sunday. Joseph speaks in the grove on the subject of love and toleration.

July 13, 1843

The Prophet writes: "I was in conversation with Emma most of the day." (HC 5:509.)

July 14, 1843

"Spent the day at home." (HC 5:509.)

July 15, 1843

"Spent the day at home." (HC 5:510.)

July 16, 1843

Sunday. Joseph preaches in the grove, stating that "the same spirit that crucified Jesus is in the breast of some who profess to be Saints in Nauvoo. I have secret enemies in the city intermingling with the Saints, etc. Said I would not prophesy any more, and proposed Hyrum to hold the office Prophet to the Church, as it was his birthright." (HC 5:510.)

July 18, 1843
"I was making hay on my farm." (HC 5:511.)

July 19, 1843
The *Nauvoo Neighbor* publishes a recent article from the *Illinois State Register* titled "Was the Arrest of the Prophet a Political Trick?" This article claims that Joseph's arrest may have been a Whig conspiracy to make the Democratic Governor Ford look bad by having to extradite Joseph Smith at election time. This would hopefully cause the massive Mormon vote to go for the Whigs. The Saints apparently give some credence to this accusation against the Whigs, because in the election they vote Democratic in spite of Joseph's promise to give his vote to the Whig candidate, Cyrus Walker.

July 23, 1843
Sunday. Joseph preaches on the burdens of his calling: "It has gone abroad that I proclaimed myself no longer a prophet. I said it last Sabbath ironically. . . . It was not that I would renounce the idea of being a prophet, but that I had no disposition to proclaim myself such. . . . I only said it to try your faith; and it is strange, brethren, that you have been in the Church so long, and not yet understand the Melchizedek Priesthood." Joseph rejoices at his friends who would sacrifice their lives for him and comments that "the burdens which roll upon me are very great. My persecutors allow me no rest, and I find that in the midst of business and care the spirit is willing, but the flesh is weak. . . . I am subject to like passions as other men, like the prophets of olden times. Notwithstanding my weaknesses, I am under the necessity of bearing the infirmities of others . . . but when I am in trouble, few of them sympathize with me. . . . I see no faults in the Church, and therefore let me be resurrected with the Saints, whether I ascend to heaven or descend to hell, or go to any other place. And if we go to hell, we will turn the devils out of doors and make a heaven of it." He also speaks on friendship as one of the "grand fundamental

principles of 'Mormonism,' " which will "revolutionize and civilize the world." (HC 5:516-18.)

July 24, 1843

Joseph meets with Mr. Hoge, the Democratic candidate for Congress. He also receives some money owed him by William and Wilson Law.

July 25-30, 1843

Joseph is sick all week, his "lungs oppressed and over-heated through preaching last Sunday." Hyrum Smith, William Law, and Willard Richards administer to him, and many others of the Twelve visit him.

July 31, 1843

Joseph's health improves, and he sells 100 acres of prairie land.

Aug. 1, 1843

Joseph is sick again in the morning. Candidates Hoge and Walker each give long speeches for the upcoming election. Joseph has an argument with Walter Bagby, a tax collector. Bagby throws a stone at Joseph, "which so enraged me that I followed him a few steps, and struck him two or three times." After the fight is broken up, Joseph gladly pays the assault fine. Bagby hereafter becomes a relentless enemy of Joseph, inspiring Carthage meetings and stirring up other old enemies against him. (HC 5:523-24.)

Aug. 5, 1843

Several thousand persons attend a meeting in which Hyrum Smith and William Law speak on the upcoming election. Hyrum says that the Mormons must support the Democrat, Hoge, because God has revealed it to him. William Law says that this is impossible because Joseph has promised his vote to the Whig, Cyrus Walker.

Aug. 6, 1843

Sunday. Joseph makes some comments about the election; he says, "The Lord has not given me a revelation concerning politics. I have not asked Him for one. I am a third party, and stand independent and alone." Joseph then says that Cyrus Walker is a good man and that he will vote for him, as promised. However, he also states, "Brother Hyrum tells me this morning that he has had a testimony to the effect it would be better for this people to vote for Hoge; and I never knew Hyrum to say he ever had a revelation and it failed. Let God speak and all men hold their peace. I never authorized Brother Law to tell my private feelings, and I utterly forbid these political demagogues from using my name henceforth and for ever." (HC 5:526.)

Aug. 7, 1843

The state elections are held. The Saints accept Joseph's word that, although he is voting for Walker, they should follow Hyrum's example and vote for Hoge. Hoge gets 2,000 Nauvoo votes and wins by only 700 statewide. It is thus the Nauvoo vote that elects Hoge, and the Saints as well as their enemies begin to realize that they can have enormous influence in state politics. Walker and the Whigs are, of course, furious with Joseph, having presumed that when he promised his own vote he would also deliver the whole Mormon vote. The Democrats also become suspicious of the Mormon strength in Illinois. Enemies outside Nauvoo begin to realize that something must be done about the Mormons.

Aug. 12, 1843

Emma returns to Nauvoo from St. Louis. (She had gone there on business on Aug. 6.) Robert D. Foster, having been elected school commissioner in the recent election, goes to Carthage to take the oath of office. He is met by 12 to 15 armed men who want to stop him from taking office. They are terribly angry over the election results and give notice of an anti-Mormon meeting to be held in one week.

Aug. 13, 1843

Joseph preaches on the death of Judge Elias Higbee. He praises the great man and gives important details about the spirit after death and the doctrine of election and sealing.

Aug. 14, 1843

Former Illinois Gov. Thomas Ford writes to Missouri Governor Thomas Reynolds explaining why he has decided not to call out the militia or to try to rearrest Joseph.

Aug. 19, 1843

The anti-Mormon meeting is held in Carthage. Walter Bagby and others address the group. A committee of six is appointed to draw up articles against Joseph Smith.

Aug. 26, 1843

Jonathon Dunham returns to Nauvoo after having been sent to explore the western areas of Iowa, 800 miles west of Nauvoo. This is the first example of Joseph's sending out scouts to explore routes to the West for a possible removal of the Church to those parts.

Aug. 27, 1843

The Quorum of the Twelve meets with the Saints in New York in conference.

Sunday. Joseph states that two weeks earlier a vote had been taken to disfellowship Sidney Rigdon. And although Gov. Carlin now denies any conspiracy with Rigdon, Joseph still believes there has been such a conspiracy. After these comments, Joseph gives a doctrinal sermon. Rigdon then takes the stand to defend himself, stating that he has seen Gov. Carlin only three times in his life and has never talked to a soul about the subject of a conspiracy to arrest Joseph. Sidney asks pardon for doing anything that would make Joseph come to this conclusion.

Aug. 31, 1843

Joseph begins moving into the Nauvoo Mansion. Up until this time the Smiths (Joseph, Emma, and four children) have been living in the same log house Joseph purchased from Hugh White in 1839. The mansion is a 22-room L-shaped building. The Smith family takes over six rooms and the rest are for entertaining visitors to Nauvoo. Fifteen days after moving into the mansion, Joseph gives notice that he is no longer able to provide free facilities, but thereafter the mansion will operate as a hotel. Joseph lives at the mansion until his death. At this time the men in Nauvoo are donating one day out of ten to work on the temple and Nauvoo House. The sisters are donating 1 percent of their weekly money for those structures.

Sept. 2, 1843

A "Notice of Expulsion" appears in the *Lee County Democrat* at Ford Madison, Wis., announcing a meeting that was held in Hancock County in which the citizens "declared the Mormons shall either peaceably leave the state or they will forcibly be driven away. It is said that the notices to that effect have been posted in public places in the county." (PHC 316.)

Sept. 4, 1843
The New York *Sun* carries a description of Joseph Smith. "This Joe Smith must be set down as an extraordinary character, a prophet-hero, as Carlyle might call him. He is one of the great men of this age, and in future history will rank with those who, in one way or another, have stamped their impress strongly on society." The article ends by stating, "That his followers are deceived, we all believe. . . . A great military despotism is growing up in the fertile West, increasing faster in proportion, than the surrounding population, spreading its influence around, and marshalling multitudes under its banners, causing serious alarm to every patriot." (HC 6:3.)

Sept. 6, 1843
An anti-Mormon meeting is held at Carthage. A preamble and ten resolutions are drawn up and approved that state generally that the signers of this resolution will stick together in opposing the Latter-day Saints. "We are therefore forced to the conclusion that the time is not far distant when the citizens of this county will be compelled to assert their rights in some way. . . . We pledge ourselves in the most solemn manner to resist all the wrongs which may be hereafter attempted to be imposed on this community by the Mormons, to the utmost of our ability,— peaceably, if we can, but forcibly, if we must." They pledge to oppose any candidates sympathetic to Mormons, to aid any law officers attempting to remove Joseph Smith to Missouri. (HC 6:4-8.)

Sept. 13-14, 1843
Joseph attends two lectures in the grove by Mr. John Finch, a socialist from England. After Finch's speeches, Joseph makes a few remarks in which he recalls the actual inequality that existed in the supposed equal communitarian societies once set up by Alexander Campbell and Sidney Rigdon and reveals, concerning socialism, "I said I did not believe the doctrine." (HC 6:32-33.)

Sept. 15, 1843
Joseph puts up a sign in front of the Nauvoo Mansion

stating that because of "cruel and untiring persecution," he is no longer able to provide free room and board to so many visitors, as he has been doing in the mansion. "I have been reduced to the necessity of opening 'The Mansion' as a hotel. I have provided the best table accommodations in the city; and the Mansion, being large and convenient, renders travelers more comfortable than any other place on the Upper Mississippi." The mansion also has a 75-horse stable. (HC 6:33.)

Sept. 24, 1843

Sunday. Joseph preaches on the second chapter of Acts, "designing to show the folly of common stock. In Nauvoo everyone is steward over his own." (HC 6:37-38.)

Sept. 28, 1843

Joseph meets in the upper room of his store and, later, in the front upper room of the mansion with ten or twelve brethren. "By the common consent and unanimous voice of the council, I was chosen president of the special council." He prays that he might live long enough to fulfill his mission, that his household, the Church, and the world will be blessed, and that he might have dominion over his enemies. (HC 6:39.) (Because three days after the meeting of this "special council" the *Times and Seasons* ran an article entitled "Who Shall Be Our Next President?," some have surmised that Joseph may have first discussed running for president of the United States during this Sept. 28 meeting. See KJH 59, 74. It is unclear exactly what this "special council" is, but it may have been a forerunner of the "Council of Fifty," which would be officially organized on March 11, 1844, for the administering of the political kingdom of God on earth. DH 367.)

Oct. 3, 1843

A gala dinner party is held at the grand opening of the Nauvoo Mansion. One hundred couples attend. The guests unanimously approve a series of resolutions made at the party, including tributes to "General Joseph Smith, whether we view him as a Prophet at the head of the Church, a General at the head of the Legion, a Mayor at the head of the City Council, or as a landlord at the head of his table, if he has equals, he has no superiors." Toasts are also made to the 15,000 citizens of Nauvoo, the

Nauvoo Legion, the Nauvoo Charter, and Gov. Thomas Ford. (HC 6:42-43.)

Oct. 7-9, 1843

A special conference is held in Nauvoo. Joseph addresses the congregation to try to convince them that he is dissatisfied with Sidney Rigdon as counselor, and that he thinks Sidney has done a poor job in the management of the post office, has had secret connections with John C. Bennett, and conspired with ex-Gov. Carlin when Joseph was arrested and almost taken back to Missouri on June 23. Joseph says the rift between himself and Sidney has grown too wide, and he does not want him as his counselor anymore. Sidney Rigdon then stands and pleads his case in a highly emotional manner, claiming that he is innocent of any ill feelings toward Joseph, and has never conspired with either John C. Bennett or Gov. Carlin. The weather deteriorates and the meeting is adjourned until the next day, Oct. 8, when Rigdon continues his appeal, listing the many sufferings and trying experiences he and Joseph have gone through together throughout the history of the Church. Elder Almon W. Babbitt and Joseph's second counselor, William Law, each speak in defense of Rigdon. Hyrum Smith also asks for mercy for Rigdon. Hyrum Smith seconds a motion by stake president William Marks that Sidney Rigdon be retained as counselor in the First Presidency. It is passed in spite of Joseph's objections. Joseph rises and says, "I have thrown him off my shoulders, and you have again put him on me. You may carry him, but I will not." (HC 6:47-49. For the history of Joseph's growing distrust of Sidney, see FMM 115-24.)

Oct. 9, 1843

At the final session of conference Joseph speaks in commemoration of the late Gen. James Adams, praising him, describing the glory his spirit must now be in, and urging the Saints to work with all possible diligence on the building of the temple. Joseph says, "Could you gaze into heaven five minutes, you would know more than you would by reading all that ever was written on the subject." (HC 6:50-52.)

Oct. 13, 1843

Joseph allows a phrenologist to examine the bumps on his head for an hour.

Oct. 14, 1843

Joseph has a long discussion with a physiologist and a mesmeriser.

Oct. 15, 1843

Sunday. Joseph preaches at the temple on the Constitution, the Bible, and finances.

Oct. 22, 1843

Brigham Young, Heber C. Kimball, and George A. Smith return to Nauvoo from their missions to the East, after nearly four months' absence. "I was very glad to see them," Joseph writes. (HC 6:60.)

Nov. 2, 1843

Joseph sits in council with Hyrum, Brigham Young, Heber C. Kimball, Willard Richards, John Taylor, William Law, and William Clayton. They decide to write letters to five candidates for the presidency of the United States to find out what the candidates might do for the Mormons in regard to the rights that were denied them in Missouri.

Nov. 4, 1843

Joseph carries out his decision of Nov. 2, 1843, and writes letters to John C. Calhoun, Henry Clay, Martin Van Buren, Richard M. Johnson, and Lewis Cass.

Nov. 13, 1843

Joseph replies to a letter of James Arlington Bennett written on Oct. 24, 1843, which suggested a secret deal between them that might put Bennett in the governor's chair of Illinois. Bennett calls his recent baptism by Brigham Young "a glorious frolic in the clear blue ocean," and says, "I am capable of being the most *undeviating friend,* without being governed by the smallest religious influence . . . my mind is of so mathematical and philosophical a cast, that the divinity of Moses makes no impression on me, and you will not be offended when I say that I rate you higher as a legislator than I do Moses . . . go ahead: you have my good wishes. You know Mahomet had his *'right hand man.'* . . . In short, I expect to be yet, through your influence, governor of the State of Illinois." Joseph is not terribly impressed with Bennett's bravado, and answers him, "The *boldness of my plans and measures* can readily be tested by the touchstone of all schemes, . . . *truth*; for truth is a matter of fact; and the fact is, that by the power of God I translated the Book of Mormon from hieroglyphics, the knowledge of which was lost to the world, in which wonderful event I stood alone, an unlearned youth, to combat the worldly wisdom and multiplied ignorance of eighteen centuries, with a new revelation. . . . Your good wishes to go ahead, coupled with Mohamet and a right hand man, are rather more vain than virtuous. Why, sir, Caesar had his right hand Brutus, who was his left hand assassin—not, however, applying the allusion to you. . . . I combat the errors of ages; I meet the violence of mobs; I cope with illegal proceedings from executive authority; I cut the gordian knot of powers, and I solve mathematical problems of universities, *with truth—diamond truth; and God is my 'right hand man.'* "

In spite of this fascinating, if somewhat hostile, exchange of letters, Joseph suggests on Mar. 4, 1844, that James Arlington Bennett become his vice-presidential candidate. Bennett, however, having been born in Ireland, is ineligible. (These letters appear in HC 6:71-78, with abridgements. NC 7-14 carries the complete versions.)

Nov. 15, 1843
Willard Richards suggests to Joseph the idea of preparing an Egyptian grammar.

Nov. 23, 1843
Joseph inspects the river shore and suggests the idea of petitioning Congress for money to either make a canal or a dam, in order to divert the water so it will be more useful for mills and other machinery. (This is finally done in 1877. See HC 6:80.)

Nov. 25, 1843
In a Church court, a man is accused of seduction, which he claims he learned from Joseph Smith. The charge is

not sustained. Joseph speaks to this charge, "exhorting them to practice virtue and holiness before the Lord; told them that the Church had not received any permission from me to commit fornication, adultery, or any corrupt action; but my every word and action has been to the contrary. If a man commit adultery, he cannot receive the celestial kingdom of God. Even if he is saved in any kingdom, it cannot be the celestial kingdom. . . . I condemned such action *in toto*, and warned the people present against committing such evils." (HC 6:81.)

Nov. 26, 1843

Joseph, Hyrum, and the Twelve, among others, meet with Col. Frierson concerning sending a petition to Congress for the redress of grievances and losses in Missouri. Frierson is a representative of John C. Calhoun, who is suddenly interested in helping the Mormons now that he (Calhoun) is running for U.S. President.

Nov. 29, 1843

A meeting is held over Joseph Smith's store to discuss the petitions to be given to Frierson and to discuss the grievances concerning Missouri in general. Joseph has prepared an appeal to his home state of Vermont, a pamphlet titled "An Appeal to the Freemen of the State of Vermont, the 'Brave Green Mountain Boys,' and Honest Men," in which Joseph remembers his birth in Vermont, relates the persecutions in Missouri, remarks on the lack of protection from the government, relates his imprisonment in Missouri, "where they tried to feed us with human flesh," and ends with an appeal for understanding from the "Green Mountain Boys" of his native state. (HC 6:88-93; unabridged version in NC 15-20.) The other brethren then become overly enthusiastic about the past wrongs they have suffered. Parley P. Pratt confesses that "he was wrong in one thing in Missouri; that is, he left alive, and left them alive; and asked forgiveness, and promised never to do so again." Brigham Young, John Taylor, Joseph Smith, and others each ask forgiveness for having been so merciful and restrained in Missouri. Joseph moves that every man write a similar pamphlet to his home state. (HC 6:88-97.)

Dec. 2, 1843

A prayer meeting is held in the assembly room over Joseph's store. Orson Hyde, Parley P. Pratt, Wilford Woodruff, George A. Smith, and Orson Spencer receive their endowments, with 35 people present. About this time some women receive their endowments also. Bathsheba W. Smith, wife of George A. Smith, receives her anointings in a room in Emma's house. Emma is the first female ordinance worker, and Elizabeth Ann Whitney is the second.

Daniel Avery and his son, Philander, who live in Warsaw, Ill., are kidnapped by Levi Williams of Warsaw, John Elliott, and others, and are taken across the Mississippi to Missouri. They are imprisoned in Clark County while a Joseph McCoy looks for witnesses to prove that Daniel Avery had stolen a mare from him. Philander escapes and returns to Illinois, but his father remains a prisoner and suffers great cruelty in Missouri. He too is finally released on a writ of habeas corpus. Violent acts like this seem to be increasing between the Mormons and the non-Mormons in Hancock County at this time. Gov. Ford is notified of all acts of violence, but remains unconvinced that there is any real danger, refusing to order out any militia for protection.

Dec. 7, 1843

The citizens of Nauvoo meet to draw up petitions against the Missouri kidnappings of the two Avery men and others.

Dec. 8, 1843

The Nauvoo City council passes a law stating that any officer bringing a writ against Joseph Smith based on a Missouri charge will be subject to life imprisonment, "which convict or convicts can only be pardoned by the Governor, with the consent of the Mayor of said city." (Joseph Smith himself is, of course, the mayor.) The Nauvoo Legion is also ordered to be ready to protect the rights of Nauvoo citizens. Affidavits are drawn up in protest of the recent kidnappings. (HC 6:103-7.)

Dec. 13, 1843

In Missouri, Orrin Porter Rockwell has been in prison for over nine months, never having had a trial. Recently, however, his mother visited him and gave him $100, with which he could afford to hire Mr. Doniphan as counsel. Within two weeks Doniphan got him into court. There being no evidence that could convict Rockwell on the charge of shooting Boggs, he was charged with breaking the Independence jail. In spite of the fact that the Missouri law states that in order to break a jail, "a man must break a lock, a door, or a wall" (and all Porter had done was to walk out when the door was open), Judge King nevertheless orders that Porter has broken jail. He is sentenced to five minutes in the county jail. He is kept there five hours while the Missouri lawmen try to bring another charge against him. Failing to do so, they finally free him at 8 P.M. on Dec. 13, 1843. Doniphan warns him not to walk in daylight or on any known road. Rockwell, having only ragged clothes and shoes, walks three or four days toward Illinois. His feet become so raw that at times he pays people 50 cents or 75 cents to carry him on their backs for several miles. After riding on horseback or walking the 150 miles, he finds a small boat in which he can cross the Mississippi to Nauvoo. (HC 6:135-42.)

Dec. 14, 1843

Joseph receives a letter from Governor Ford stating that he will not call out the state militia for the general protection of Nauvoo, except on rare and very specifically defined occasions. He tells Joseph not to worry about past offenses by the state of Missouri, and says, concerning any affidavits about their wrongs in Missouri given to him by the Mormons the previous August, "I have not yet read them and probably never will." Joseph records his personal anger at Ford's letter. (HC 6:113-15.)

Dec. 16, 1843

Joseph meets with several others to officially sign the memorial to Congress for the redresses of the losses in Missouri. In discussion, Joseph prophesies "by virtue of the holy Priesthood vested in me, and in the name of the Lord Jesus Christ, that, if Congress will not hear our petition and grant us protection, they shall be broken up as a government." (HC 6:116.)

Dec. 18, 1843

A constable, King Follett, returns to Nauvoo, having gone

with ten men to arrest John Elliott, a schoolmaster, on the charge of kidnapping Avery and his son. Elliott is put under a $3,000 bond. Joseph, however, pleads in Elliott's behalf for a reduction in the amount of bail. In spite of Joseph's emotional and eloquent speech, Elliott threatens Joseph's life, and Joseph charges Elliott with making threats. At this time, rumors of a warlike force gathering in Warsaw hit Nauvoo, and Joseph orders out a 100-man detachment of the Nauvoo Legion for military purposes.

Dec. 19, 1843
The 100-man detachment of the Nauvoo Legion parades near the temple for inspection in readiness against the mob possibly forming in Warsaw. One man is wounded when his own gun accidentally discharges. Josiah Stowell, the man who had originally hired Joseph as a "money digger" in 1825, writes Joseph from New York, stating "his faith is still good concerning the work." (BYS, Sp '70, 377.)

Dec. 21, 1843
The city council sends to the Congress of the United States a petition that explains the abuses suffered by the Saints in Missouri and the unwillingness of the state of Illinois to protect the Saints. They therefore ask Congress to make the City of Nauvoo an independent sovereign territory, free from the control of the state of Illinois, to be governed as the Congress governs any other territory. Joseph instructs the police force to clean the streets of carrion, to stop boys from fighting in the streets, to keep children from floating on ice, and to correct anything else out of order; he also offers to build the city jail.

Dec. 22, 1843
A member's house is burned at Ramus, Ill. Foul play is suspected.

Dec. 25, 1843
At one o'clock on Christmas morning, a family of English converts sings Christmas carols under Joseph's window. Joseph's family and boarders in the Mansion House are awake and listen to the music. Joseph blesses the singers. In the afternoon Joseph has 50 couples over for Christmas dinner. During the evening a long-haired man breaks in and acts "like a Missourian." The police are called, but

when Joseph sees the man, he realizes, to his "great surprise and joy untold," it is Orrin Porter Rockwell, just returned to Nauvoo from his Missouri imprisonment. (HC 6:134-42.) Rockwell then eats and drinks and relates his Missouri experiences, after which Joseph blesses him, saying, "I prophesy, in the name of the Lord, that you—Orrin Porter Rockwell—so long as you shall remain loyal and true to thy faith, need fear no enemy. Cut not thy hair and no bullet or blade can harm thee!" (HC 6:134-42; HS 108-9.) Daniel Avery, who had been kidnapped and taken to Missouri, is released by habeas corpus. The First Presidency sanctions a plan that the sisters will donate one cent or a half-penny per week for the building of the temple.

Dec. 29, 1843

W.W. Phelps gives Joseph and others a lesson on eloquence. Joseph relates his early revelations to Dr. Bernhisel and John H. Jackson (a man who recently became a close friend, but will soon turn against Joseph). Jackson states he is almost persuaded to join the Church. Joseph, as mayor, calls 40 extra policemen to be on guard throughout the city. Relating his fear that there are Saints in Nauvoo working against him, he tells the policemen, "My life is more in danger from some little dough-head of a fool in this city than from all my numerous and inveterate enemies abroad. I am exposed to far greater danger from traitors among ourselves than from enemies without. . . . I can live as Caesar might have lived, were it not for a right-hand Brutus. . . . Judas was one of the Twelve . . . *and we have a Judas in our midst.*" (HC 6: 149-52.)

Dec. 31, 1843

Joseph writes: "At midnight, about 50 musicians and singers sang Phelps' New Year's Hymn under my window." (HC 6:153.)

1844

Jan. 1, 1844

A large party and New Year's supper is held at Joseph's house, with music and dancing till morning.

Jan. 2, 1844

Joseph writes a "strong" letter to John C. Calhoun. (He had written Calhoun on Nov. 4, 1843, and Calhoun had answered on Dec. 2, 1843, stating that the redress of the Saints "does not come within the jurisdiction of the Federal Government.") Joseph tells Calhoun, "If the Latter-day Saints are not restored to all their rights and paid for all their losses . . . God will come out of His hiding place, and vex this nation with a sore vexation: yea the consuming wrath of an offended God shall smoke through the nation. . . ." (HC 6:155-60.)

Jan. 3, 1844

The city council holds a trial most of the day. William Law, Joseph's second counselor, said that some policemen told him Joseph had called Law a "Judas," and that "he must be taken care of." Law believes that Joseph has threatened his life. The policemen who told him this, and several others, testify throughout the day as to the source of this story. Law realizes that the policemen had only supposed that Law was the "Judas" of whom Joseph had spoken. Law promises to stand by Joseph to the death. (HC 6:162-65.)

Jan. 4, 1844

Joseph dines with Emma and W.W. Phelps. When Joseph praises Emma for cooking in great quantities, Phelps says that Joseph should do as Bonaparte did and just have a small table. Emma says, "Mr. Smith is a bigger man than Bonaparte; he can never eat without his friends." Joseph says, "That is the wisest thing I ever heard you say." (HC 6:165-66.)

Jan. 5, 1844

Joseph dreams of "2 serpents swallowing each other tail foremost." During the cold night some people had built a fire on the shore opposite Stake President William Marks's house. Marks swears before the city council that the fire was a warning against his life. It is charged that Joseph's statement about a "Judas" was a signal to the forty special policemen to take certain action against traitorist brothers. Thirty policemen swear that they were never given any special or private instructions. After many testimonies, Wilson Law says, "I am Joseph's friend: he has no better friend in the world: I am ready to lay down my life for him." Joseph records his own thoughts: "What can be the matter with these men? Is is that . . . hit pigeons always flutter, that drowning men catch at straws, or that Presidents Law and Marks are absolutely traitors to the Church, that my remarks should produce such an excitement in their minds. Can it be possible that the traitor whom Porter Rockwell reports to me as being in correspondence with my Missouri enemies, is one of my quorum?" (HC 6:166-70.)

Jan. 10, 1844

Joseph ordains his uncle John Smith as a patriarch. Francis M. Higbee sends Joseph a letter charging him with slandering his (Higbee's) character. He does not deny the supposed charges Joseph made against him.

Jan. 13, 1844

The ten policemen who were not present on Jan. 5 to swear in the supposed threats against William Marks and William Law testify that they have never received any private instructions from Joseph Smith against any of his supposed enemies.

Jan. 16, 1844

Francis M. Higbee is tried before the municipal court for "slanderous and abusive language." During the trial Higbee and Joseph are reconciled, and Higbee states that the difficulties between him and Joseph are buried and that they are friends forever. An "Ordinance concerning the Sale of Spirituous Liquors" is also passed by the city council. (HC 6:178-79.)

Jan. 21, 1844

Sunday. Joseph preaches on the sealing power of the priesthood and the mission of Elijah.

Jan. 23, 1844

Joseph leases the Mansion House (except for three rooms reserved for his own family and stables) for $1,000 a year to Ebenezer Robinson. He also sells his printing office to John Taylor.

Jan. 28, 1844

A *Millennial Star* editorial advises all elders to keep journals.

Jan. 29, 1844

Joseph meets with the Twelve and others to consider whom to support for the presidency of the United States. Henry Clay (who had told the Saints, "You had better go to Oregon for redress") and Martin Van Buren are the only candidates. It is decided that "it is morally impossible for this people . . . to vote for either candidate." Willard Richards moves that Joseph Smith be a candidate for president on an independent ticket. The motion is carried unanimously. Joseph suggests that missionaries be sent throughout the country to advocate his candidacy. He says, "Tell the people we have had Whig and Democratic Presidents long enough; we want a President of the United States. If I ever get into the presidential chair, I will protect the people in their rights and liberties. . . . The Whigs are striving for a king under the garb of democracy. There is oratory enough in the Church to carry me into the presidential chair the first slide." He works on his political platform with W.W. Phelps. (HC 6:187-89).

Gov. Ford sends a letter to the people of Hancock County, stating that he has been called upon to intervene in the increasing problems in the county, but refusing to either aid the Mormons or take away the arms from the Nauvoo Legion. "I believe that there has been nothing like war among you . . . let a state of war ensue, and I will be compelled to interfere with executive power . . . against those who shall be the first transgressors." (HC 6:189-90.)

Jan. 31, 1844

Joseph contributes over three dozen volumes of personal books to the Nauvoo Library and Literary Institute (a group of at least 74 members organized earlier in the month). (For a list of the books Joseph donated, see BYS, Sp '74, 386-89.)

Feb. 4, 1844

Joseph comments on the 144,000 mentioned by John the Revelator, "showing that the selection of persons to form that number had already commenced." (HC 6:196.)

Feb. 5, 1844

William Weeks, the architect of the temple, argues with Joseph about the possibility of putting round windows in the temple. "I told him I would have the circles, if he had to make the temple ten feet higher than it was originally calculated; that one light at the centre of each circular window would be sufficient to light the whole room; that when the whole building was thus illuminated, the effect would be remarkably grand. 'I wish you could carry out *my* designs. I have seen in vision the splendid appearance of that building illuminated.'" (HC 6:196-97.) Joseph works on his political platform with W.W. Phelps and John M. Bernhisel.

Feb. 7, 1844

Joseph meets with the Twelve and completes and signs his "views of the powers and policy of the government of the United States." In this platform policy he reviews American leaders from Benjamin Franklin to John Tyler. He then makes eight propositions:

1. Reduce Congress by two-thirds. Pay them $2 a day: "That is more than the farmer gets, and he lives honestly."
2. Turn penitentiaries into "seminaries of learning" and pardon all convicts except murderers.
3. Abolish slavery by 1850 by paying slave holders a fair price with money from the sale of public lands.
4. Abolish court-martials for desertion from the armed forces.
5. Work for more government economy and fewer taxes.
6. Establish a national bank.
7. Give the president power to suppress mobs.
8. "When we have the Red Man's consent," let the

Union spread from coast to coast, inviting Oregon, Texas, Mexico, and Canada to join the Union if they so desire. (HC 6:197-209.)

(DLG, Au '68, 17-27 compares Joseph's platform with other platforms of the day, calling it "an intriguing blend of *ante bellum* political rhetoric, Whig economic doctrines, Democratic expansionism, abolitionism, and the original and wide-range constitutional and political ideas of Joseph Smith himself." See also DLG, Sp '70, 23-36; DM 137-39; A&L 187-90.)

Feb. 8, 1844

Mayor's court is held. In the evening W.W. Phelps reads Joseph's political platform, and Joseph comments, "I would not have suffered my name to have been used . . . as President of the United States . . . if I and my friends could have had the privilege of enjoying our religious and civil rights as American citizens. . . . I feel it to be my right and privilege to obtain what influence and power I can, lawfully, in the United States, for protection of injured innocence; and if I lose my life in a good cause I am willing to be sacrificed on the altar of virtue." (HC 6:210.)

Feb. 9, 1844

Gov. Reynolds of Missouri shoots himself through the head, having written that although he has tried to carry out his duties, he has not been able to escape "the slanders and abuse of my enemies, which has rendered my life a burden to me." Many assume that Reynolds is referring to criticisms of him because he had not been able to return Joseph Smith to Missouri for trial. (BYS, Sp '71, 292.)

Feb. 17, 1844

Anti-Mormons hold a convention in Carthage and draw up various resolutions, one of which is to declare March 9, 1844, as a day of fasting and prayer for the downfall of Joseph Smith.

Feb. 20, 1844

Joseph meets with the Twelve and tells them to send out delegations to California and Oregon to "hunt out a good location, where we can remove to after the temple is completed, and where we can build a city in a day, and have a government of our own, get up into the mountains, where the devil cannot dig us out." (HC 6:222.)

Feb. 21, 1844

Another meeting is held for "selecting a company to explore Oregon and California, and select a site for a new city for the Saints." Four men volunteer to go West, and four more are called to go West. (HC 6:223.) An anti-Mormon meeting is held in Warsaw, in which the people resolve to drive the Mormons from Hancock County.

Feb. 23, 1844

Joseph meets with Hyrum, Sidney Rigdon, and the Twelve to further discuss the exploration of the West by at least twenty-five men.

Feb. 25, 1844

Sunday. Joseph prophesies "that within 5 years we should be out of the power of our old enemies, whether they were apostates or of the world." (HC 6:225.)

Feb. 27, 1844

Joseph mails his political platform, "Views of Powers and Policy . . ." to all national elected officials, newspapers, postmasters, etc.

Mar. 1, 1844

Times and Seasons publishes Joseph's name publicly for the first time as candidate for the United States presidency.

Mar. 4, 1844

Joseph proposes James Arlington Bennett of Long Island, N.Y., as candidate for vice-president. It is also decided to let the Nauvoo House remain unfinished until the temple is completed, "as we need the temple more than anything else." (HC 6:230-33.)

Mar. 7, 1844

Joseph and the Twelve meet at the temple with about 8,000 Saints for a special meeting. Joseph speaks about his candidacy: "We have as good a right to make a political party to gain power to defend ourselves, as for demagogues to make use of our religion to get power to destroy us. . . . When I get hold of the Eastern papers, and see how popular I am, I am afraid myself that I shall be elected." (HC 6:236-44.)

Mar. 8, 1844

Joseph writes an article titled "A Friendly Hint to

Missouri." He learns that James Arlington Bennett, having been born in Ireland, is ineligible for the vice-presidency. He then suggests that Colonel Solomon Copeland of Tennessee should be approached as candidate for vice-president.

Mar. 9, 1844

King Follett dies. While working on a well, a rope breaks and a bucket of rocks falls on him.

Mar. 10, 1844

Joseph preaches on the mission of Elijah, Elias, and the coming of the Savior. He talks about the impossibility of murderers receiving forgiveness without going through hell, and states, "The Lord once told me that what I asked for I should have. I have been afraid to ask God to kill my enemies, lest some of them should, peradventure, repent." He also prophesies the Lord will not come in forty years. (HC 6:249, 253.) He receives a letter from Lyman Wight and his expedition company, which suggests that the south and southwestern area of the United States, as well as Texas, Mexico, and Brazil, be opened to the gospel.

Mar. 11, 1844

Joseph meets in the lodge room over Henry Miller's house with 23 brethren "whom I organized into a special council" to consider the recent letters by Lyman Wight concerning a place in the West where the Saints might establish a permanent home. This council continues to meet at intervals, and comes to be known as the Council of Fifty, because of its approximate number. Its name and purpose, however, are kept secret, and one member writes the letters backwards—YTFIF—in an attempt to camouflage the name. Although most of the leading brethren of the Church attend (some such as Rigdon, Law, and Marks are not invited at first), it is not primarily a Church council. Set up to have nonmembers also participate, it is formed for the purpose of setting up and controlling the political kingdom of God on earth. The immediate purpose of the council is to help elect Joseph Smith as U.S. president, but if that fails it will help organize the reestablishment of the Saints in the West, where they might be safe from their enemies and have a government of their own. However, the council's ultimate goal is to politically rule the world in preparation for Christ's return and reign on earth. Reports eventually spread that Joseph has been ordained a king and the Saints are planning a political as well as a religious takeover. Hostility against the Saints from nearby areas begins to increase rapidly.

Mar. 12-15, 1844
On these days and every few days for the next several weeks, Joseph meets in his "special council." (HC 6:262-64.)

Mar. 16, 1844
A meeting of the Female Relief Society of Nauvoo is held. This turns out to be their last meeting in Nauvoo. The membership has, by this time, reached 1,341.

Mar. 20, 1844
Articles begin to appear in several newspapers commenting on Joseph's candidacy for the U.S. Presidency.

Mar. 24, 1844
Sunday. Joseph preaches at the temple, accusing several people by name of conspiracy against him—especially Dr. Robert D. Foster, Joseph H. Jackson, William and Wilson Law, and Chauncey L. Higbee. Sidney Rigdon also preaches, and then Joseph concludes: "Did I ever exercise any compulsion over any man? Did I not give him the liberty of disbelieving any doctrine I have preached, if he saw fit? Why do not my enemies strike a blow at the doctrine? They cannot do it: It is truth, and I defy all men to upset it. . . . Henceforth the ax is laid unto the root of the tree; and every tree that bringeth not forth good fruit, God Almighty (and not Joe Smith) shall hew it down and cast it into the fire." (HC 6:272-74.)

Mar. 26, 1844
Joseph, having recently become aware that President Tyler has asked Congress to establish military posts to protect pioneers going on the Oregon Trail, petitions Congress to empower him as a military officer to raise 100,000 volunteer troups to open up the unsettled sections of the American West and to protect American borders. On Mar. 30, 1844, Joseph sends a similar petition to Pres. Tyler. Orson Hyde takes both petitions to Washington. On

May 25, 1844, John Wentworth of Chicago tries to present the bill to Congress, but Wentworth's motion to suspend certain rules so that the petition might be read is defeated.

Mar. 27, 1844

Several affidavits are filed that testify that secret meetings were held about March 15 for the purpose of formulating an opposition to Joseph Smith.

Apr. 1, 1844

Several minor lawsuits are held concerning the Higbees, Foster, and others.

Apr. 4, 1844

Orson Hyde leaves Nauvoo for Washington in order to assist Orson Pratt and John E. Page in interesting President Tyler in Joseph's offer to raise 100,000 volunteers to control national boundaries.

Apr. 5, 1844

The Masonic Temple is dedicated, with 550 Masons from various parts of the world attending. The Nauvoo Brass Band parades from Henry Miller's house to the hall. Worshipful Master Hyrum Smith dedicates the building; Erastus Snow, Dr. Goforth, and Joseph Smith also address the assembly.

Apr. 6, 1844

General conference begins. Joseph states that he will not speak until the next day "in consequence of the weakness of my lungs." Sidney Rigdon and John Taylor speak. (HC 6:287-97.)

Apr. 7, 1844

Sunday. Sidney Rigdon, having stopped in the middle of his sermon yesterday due to lack of lung power, completes his sermon this morning. During intermission 35 people are baptized. Hyrum Smith speaks, encouraging the rapid building of the temple, and says, "It is better not to have so much faith, than to have so much as to believe all the lies." (HC 6:297-301.)

Joseph Smith delivers the King Follett funeral sermon before 20,000 people. It is one of his greatest sermons. He goes back to the beginning, stating that "God himself was once as we are now, and is an exalted man, and sits enthroned in yonder heavens!" He says the Saints must understand how God came to be God. He once dwelt on an earth, the same as the Savior, because the Bible says that the Son has done only what he has seen the Father do. (John 5:19.) "You have got to learn how to be gods yourselves, and to be kings and priests to God, the same as all gods have done before you, namely, by going from one small degree to another." (See HC 6:302-17.)

Apr. 8, 1844

Conference continues. Joseph wants to continue his sermon, but "it is just as impossible, for me to continue the subject of yesterday as to raise the dead. My lungs are worn out." He does, however, state that "the whole of America is Zion itself from north to south." He also speaks on the "washings and anointings, and . . . those last and more impressive ordinances." He urges the completion of the temple, but is physically unable to speak any longer. Another elder preaches for three hours, then Hyrum Smith speaks. (HC 6:318-21.)

Apr. 9, 1844

Conference continues. Brigham Young, Hyrum Smith, and Heber C. Kimball speak.

Apr. 13, 1844

Joseph is in municipal court with Dr. Robert D. Foster. He asks Foster to tell him of any wrongs he (Joseph) has committed against Foster so that he might ask Foster's forgiveness, but Foster refuses to make any testimony. Joseph therefore swears out a complaint against Foster "for unchristianlike conduct in general, for abusing my character privily, for throwing out slanderous insinuations against my peace and safety, for conspiring against my life." (HC 6:332-33.)

Apr. 14, 1844

Sunday. Because it is raining, the normal meeting is canceled, and Joseph preaches on board the *Maid of Iowa.*

Apr. 15, 1844

The Twelve draw up a list of upcoming conferences throughout the East and appoint over 300 missionaries to go on political missions throughout those states electioneering for Joseph. By this date, Dr. Foster is told that he will be tried in a Church court on the charges made by

Joseph on April 13. The trial is to take place April 20, 1844. Foster begins gathering witnesses to testify in his behalf.

Apr. 18, 1844

Joseph meets with 32 leading Church brethren (22 of whom belong to the Council of Fifty) to make a ruling about certain Church dissidents. Robert D. Foster, Wilson Law, William Law, Jane Law, and Howard Smith are excommunicated for "unchristianlike conduct." These men did not reject Mormonism, but regarded Joseph as a fallen, not a false, prophet, and planned to set up their own church. They made various charges against Joseph's character. William Law accused Joseph of propositioning Law's wife. Joseph claimed that when he told Jane Law that her husband, William, was unworthy of celestial sealing due to admitted adultery, she then begged to be sealed to Joseph. Several months later Jesse Price would testify that on April 18, 1844, William Law had gone out with pistols determined to blow Joseph's "infernal brains out," saying that he was determined to kill Joseph at first opportunity. (HC 7:227.)

Apr. 20, 1844

Emma starts for St. Louis to purchase some goods. Joseph and Dr. Bernhisel ride through the green prairie with Joseph's sons, Frederick and Alexander. According to Robert D. Foster, as he was gathering 41 witnesses to testify in the Church court, which was supposed to be held on this date, he received notification that he had been excommunicated two days earlier.

Apr. 25, 1844

Emma returns from St. Louis. During rainstorms, the Mississippi River rises higher than at any time within memory. The Council of Fifty adjourns to disperse throughout the United States to campaign for Joseph's presidency.

Apr. 26, 1844

When Augustine Spencer assaults his brother Orson, Joseph, as mayor, orders Augustine arrested. Augustine refuses to go with Joseph, Orrin Porter Rockwell, and Marshal J.P. Greene. Joseph tells Greene to get some other citizens to help. Greene asks help from the first people he sees—Chauncey L. Higbee and Charles and Robert Foster. When they refuse, Joseph orders them arrested. A fight follows and Charles Foster pulls a gun on Joseph, swearing and threatening. Rockwell wrests the gun away, and several other policemen arrive to arrest the three. They are fined $100 each, which they appeal. Robert D. Foster accuses Willard Richards of trying to seduce his (Foster's) wife.

Apr. 27, 1844

Robert Foster's trial begins in the municipal court. Joseph tries to make a peaceful settlement with Foster, but Foster refuses. Joseph announces that he will no longer make overtures toward Foster: "The skirts of my garments were free from his (Foster's) blood; I have made the last overtures of peace to him; and then delivered him into the hands of God, and shook my garments against him as a testimony thereof." (HC 6:345.)

Apr. 28, 1844

While Hyrum Smith is preaching that "there were prophets before, but Joseph has the spirit and power of all the prophets," William and Wilson Law, Higbee, Foster, and others meet at Wilson Law's home to begin a new, "reformed" church. Calling Joseph a fallen prophet, they choose a replacement. William Law is made president of the new church, Austin Cowles and Wilson Law are made counselors, and a Council of the Twelve is called. They decide to order a press to publish their own views (HC 6:346-47.) They have about 200 followers.

Apr. 29, 1844

Robert D. Foster comes up for trial. He objects to the jurisdiction of the court, the informality of the writ, and several other items. Major-General Wilson Law is suspended, awaiting a court-martial by the Nauvoo Legion, and Charles C. Rich replaces him temporarily. Orson Hyde writes to Joseph from Washington stating that settling in Texas, which acts as a buffer between Mexico and the United States, could put the Saints in a very dangerous position.

Apr. 30, 1844

Joseph attends several plays, including *Pizarro*, at the Masonic Hall, which is decorated nicely.

May 3, 1844

Lucien Woodworth returns to Nauvoo from Texas to report to the Council of Fifty about a possible settling place for the Saints in Texas. (According to one report, the purpose of this expedition was to find a place where the Saints could settle in case Joseph did not win the U.S. presidency.)

May 6, 1844

The Council of Fifty votes to send Almon W. Babbitt on a mission to France and Lucien Woodworth back to Texas. Sidney Rigdon is nominated as Joseph's vice-presidential candidate. Francis M. Higbee swears out a warrant for Joseph's arrest, asking $5,000 damages, but does not state the charge. Joseph receives a writ of habeas corpus and is released.

May 8, 1844

Joseph is tried before the municipal court on Higbee's charge. He is acquitted, and Higbee pays the court costs.

May 9, 1844

Court-martial is held for the trial of Major-General Wilson Law. The charge is sustained and Wilson Law is released. Joseph attends the theater in the evening. Joseph blesses Wilford Woodruff and George A. Smith, who are starting for their missions to Illinois, Indiana, and Michigan, electioneering for Joseph. They will travel with Elders Jedediah M. Grant and Ezra Thayre.

May 10, 1844

The prospectus of the *Nauvoo Expositor* is distributed by the press of the reformed church among Nauvoo residents. Their prospectus advocates "Disobedience to Political Revelations," and denounces moral imperfection in all people, even in a "Self-Constituted Monarch."

May 12, 1844

Sunday. Joseph preaches on various topics, then says, "The Savior has the words of eternal life. Nothing else can profit us. . . . My enemies say that I *have* been a true prophet. Why, I had rather be a fallen true prophet than a false prophet. . . . False prophets always arise to oppose the true prophets and they will prophesy so very near the truth but they will deceive almost the very chosen ones. . . . I calculate to be one of the instruments of setting up the kingdom of Daniel by the word of the Lord, and I intend to lay a foundation that will revolutionize the whole world. . . . It will not be by sword or gun that this kingdom will roll on; . . . it may be that the Saints will have to beat their ploughs into swords, for it will not do for men to sit down patiently and see their children destroyed." (HC 6:363-67.)

May 13, 1844

Joseph receives a letter from Orson Hyde in Washington and discusses it in general council. Orson Hyde writes that Joseph's proposal that he be empowered to raise 100,000 volunteers will probably not be passed. However, Orson Hyde does have several discussions with prominent legislators who give him good advice about the possibility of moving to Oregon or Texas, or even California. Unfortunately, however, since many Missourians are moving to Oregon, Hyde says that the move, if it is to be made, must be made at once. Hyde also describes his meeting with President Tyler, whom he describes as a "very plain, home spun, familiar, farmer-like man." Stephen A. Douglas recommends Oregon and says "he would resign his seat in Congress if he could command the force that Mr. Smith could, and would be on the march to the country in a month." Elder Hyde also hints of the probable coming war with Mexico, if Texas is admitted into the Union, and says that Orson Pratt and Elder Hyde himself submitted a bill asking for $2 million in relief for the sufferings in Missouri. (HC 6:369-76.)

On this date Joseph answers Henry Clay's reply of Nov. 15, 1843. Joseph once again meets a noncommittal answer with a strong rebuke: "Honest men of every clime, and the innocent, poor and oppressed, as well as heathens, pagans and Indians, everywhere, who could but hope that the tree of liberty would yield some precious fruit . . . have long since given up all hopes of equal rights, of justice and judgment, and of truth and virtue, when such polluted, vain, heaven-daring, bogus patriots, are forced or flung into the front rank of government." (NC, "The Voice of Truth," 51-59.)

May 15, 1844

Two prominent Bostonians, Josiah Quincy (who will become mayor of Boston the next year) and Charles Francis Adams (who will become Lincoln's Minister to England in the Civil War), visit Joseph Smith all day during a rainstorm in Nauvoo. In 1883, Quincy will describe this visit, beginning with the oft-quoted, "It is by no means improbable that some future textbook . . . will contain a question something like this: What historical American of the nineteenth century has exerted the most powerful influence upon the destinies of his countrymen? And it is by no means impossible that the answer . . . may be thus written: *Joseph Smith, the Mormon Prophet."* Quincy describes Joseph's appearance: "A hearty, athletic fellow, with blue eyes standing prominently out upon his light complexion, a long nose, and a retreating forehead. He wore striped pantaloons, a linen jacket, which had not recently seen the wash tub, and a beard of some three days' growth." (WMRM 131-42.)

May 23, 1844

Joseph's clerk tells him that an officer is coming to arrest him; William Law has accused him of adultery. When Joseph hears of another false charge that is being brought against him, he sends Aaron Johnson and Orrin Porter Rockwell to Carthage to swear out a complaint of perjury against Dr. Foster, who had made the false charge.

May 24, 1844

Joseph H. Jackson also swears out a writ against Joseph. Rockwell and Johnson reach Carthage to find that a jury has already been called for Joseph's case, and it is too late to change the warrant.

May 25, 1844

Joseph learns that two indictments have been sworn out against him. William Law has charged Joseph with polygamy; Robert D. Foster and Joseph H. Jackson have charged him with false swearing. The high council in Nauvoo begins its counterattack against those attacking the character of Joseph Smith. They publish the sworn testimony of four Nauvoo women who claim that "Chauncey L. Higbee had brought about their ruin by deceit" by seducing them with the supposed approval and authorization of Joseph Smith. "The character of Chauncey L. Higbee is so infamous, and his exertions such as to destroy every principle of righteousness, that forbearance is no longer a virtue." (HC 6:407.)

Sidney Rigdon resigns the office of postmaster of Nauvoo and recommends Joseph Smith as his successor. (Apparently Joseph had been pressuring Sidney to resign ever since their disagreement the previous year in which Joseph charged him with corresponding and conspiring with John C. Bennett against Joseph. He had also suspected Sidney, as postmaster, of reading—and not delivering—some of Joseph's personal mail.)

May 26, 1844

Joseph speaks out against the apostates and recounts his many trials and persecutions. "I should be like a fish out of water, if I were out of persecutions. Perhaps my brethren think it requires all this to keep me humble. The Lord has constituted me so curiously that I glory in persecution. . . . When facts are proved, truth and innocence will prevail at last." Joseph then counterpoints each charge and each apostate—Mr. Simpson, Dr. Foster, Chauncey Higbee, William Law, Joseph Jackson, and Wilson Law. Joseph concludes, "I am the same man, and as innocent as I was fourteen years ago. . . . As I grow older, my heart grows tenderer for you. I am at all times willing to give up everything that is wrong, for I wish this people to have a virtuous leader." (HC 6:408-12.)

May 27, 1844

Joseph starts out toward Carthage on horseback with several friends to meet the indictments head on. Soon after the Prophet reaches Hamilton's hotel, Charles A. Foster catches up with him, telling him there is a conspiracy against his life. He decides to leave for home as soon as he gets his bail. Samuel H. Smith of Montebello, hearing that Joseph is being held prisoner in Carthage, rides there immediately with twenty-five men. Joseph arrives home the next day.

June 5, 1844

Joseph rides out to the prairie to show some land. It is 94½ degrees in the shade. He receives a book titled *An Original History of the Religious Denominations at Present*

Existing in the United States, for which he wrote the article on Mormonism.

June 6, 1844

Dimick B. Huntington comes to Joseph saying that Robert D. Foster wants to repent and return to the Church. Joseph says that if Foster truly withdraws all his suits against the Saints, he can be restored. Joseph also runs a notice warning Saints not to pass the old "Kirtland Safety Society" paper bills.

June 7, 1844

Robert D. Foster calls on Joseph and says he wants to talk to him in private. Joseph does not trust a private interview with any of the apostates, and says he will only meet with him in the presence of several other people. Their proposed meeting and settlement dissolves.

The first and only issue of the *Nauvoo Expositor* is published; Sylvester Emmons is editor. The four-page paper contains a short story, some poetry, some advertisements, and some national news. However, the vast majority of the paper is a direct attack on Joseph Smith and Mormonism. The attack has three bases: (1) religion (the Church was true once, but since introducing such doctrines as plurality of wives, plurality of gods, and unconditional sealings into eternal life, Joseph has become a fallen prophet); (2) politics (Joseph had combined Church and state, abused the right of habeas corpus, overstepped his bounds with his "views on the powers and policy" and his candidacy for U.S. president); (3) morality (Joseph had "taught secretly and denied openly" the doctrine of polygamy by which young, foreign girls were brought thousands of miles to America, and then told to submit their own will to God's for the gratification of the Prophet and his devotees). The newspaper does not deny the possibility of using force against the Mormons, "if it is necessary to make show of force, to execute legal process, it will create no sympathy in that case to cry out, we are mobbed." The paper also promises to be unrestrained in the future publications: "We intend to tell the whole tale and by all honorable means to bring to light and justice, those who have long fed and fattened upon the purse, the property, and the character of injured innocence." (ULR, Winter 1965, pp. 868-73.)

June 8, 1844

From 10 A.M. to 1 P.M. and from 3 P.M. to 6:30 P.M., Joseph discusses with the city council what to do about the *Nauvoo Expositor.* They first discuss the men behind the *Expositor,* stating that they were immoral, were diseased, had sued Joseph when he was in prison, and had hired a man to kill Joseph. In the afternoon Joseph suggests that the council pass an ordinance against libelous publications. He rails against R.D. Foster again, remembering his several immoralities and his threats against Joseph's life. Joseph says such papers "are calculated to destroy the peace of the city, and it is not safe that such things should exist, on account of the mob spirit which they tend to produce." After discussing the conspiracy of these men, the council adjourns until Monday morning. (HC 6:430-31, 434-43, 470, 7:62-63.)

June 9, 1844

Sunday. The Prophet writes: "My health not very good, in consequence of my lungs being impaired by so much public speaking. My brother Hyrum preached at the Stand." (HC 6:431.)

June 10, 1844

The city council meets again for over six hours to discuss the *Nauvoo Expositor.* Joseph reads from the *Expositor* and asks, "Is it not treasonable against all chartered rights and privileges, and against the peace and happiness of the city?" John Taylor says no city on earth would allow such a thing, that it is a threat to the security of the city. Councilor Stiles reads Blackstone and says that a nuisance is anything that disturbs the peace of the community. Hyrum Smith suggests smashing the press and scattering the type. Councilor Warrington, a nonmember, suggests fining the paper $3,000 for every case of libel, but Joseph answers that in order to take a man to court for libel, he would have to go to Carthage. The last time Joseph went to Carthage, he was almost killed. Therefore, the Saints have no legal recourse. (One historian states that there were 16 instances of violence between 1832 and 1867 to presses or editors who had expressed highly controversial views contrary to the public consensus, including one murder of an antislavery editor. Therefore, destroying a press at this time was not unusual.)

227

An ordinance concerning libelous publications is passed. The city council unanimously resolves that "the printing-office from whence issues the *Nauvoo Expositor* is a public nuisance and also all of said *Nauvoo Expositors* which may be or exist in said establishment." These ordinances are passed about 6:30 P.M. Joseph then orders City Marshal John P. Greene to carry out the order. Greene summons troops under Jonathan Dunham, acting major-general of the Nauvoo Legion. By 8 P.M. they destroy the press, scatter the type throughout the streets, and burn all the copies of the second issue. (HC 6:444-48; 7:61-64.)

June 11, 1844

Joseph issues a proclamation stating that he has destroyed the *Nauvoo Expositor,* which he considered a nuisance (and therefore had the legal right to destroy, just as he would any nuisance).

News of the action against the press travels quickly. A mass meeting of anti-Mormons assembles in Carthage. A resolution is adopted, stating, "We hold ourselves at all times in readiness to cooperate with our fellow citizens in this state, Missouri, and Iowa to *exterminate*—UTTERLY EXTERMINATE, the wicked and abominable Mormon leaders, the authors of our troubles. . . . A WAR OF EXTERMINATION SHOULD BE WAGED, to the entire destruction if necessary for our protection, of his adherents." (DLG, Su '69, 47.)

June 12, 1844

Thomas Sharp begins publishing in the *Warsaw Signal* violent calls for anti-Mormon action: "DIABOLICAL OUTRAGE—EXPOSITOR AFFAIR . . . war and extermination is inevitable. Citizens, Arise, One and All! ! Can you stand by and suffer such Infernal Devils! to rob men of their property and rights, without avenging them? We have no time to comment: every man will make his own. *Let it be made with powder and ball! ! !*" (CHC 2:236.) Joseph and seventeen brethren are arrested by Constable Bettisworth and charged with committing "a riot" by breaking and destroying the *Nauvoo Expositor* press. Joseph notices that the writ of arrest contains the words "before me or some other justice of the peace of said county." He therefore refuses to go to Carthage, but volunteers to go to the Nauvoo justice of the peace. Constable Bettisworth becomes furious. Joseph takes out a writ of habeas corpus, appearing before Aaron Johnson. The court decides that he "acted under proper authority in destroying the establishment of the *Nauvoo Expositor,*" and he is released. (HC 6:453-58.) At this time William Law is claiming that his store was completely gutted, with losses of $30,000. When Bettisworth returns to Governor Ford without Joseph as prisoner, most people in the surrounding area become infuriated.

June 13, 1844

The several brethren who were arrested by Bettisworth with Joseph take out writs of habeas corpus and are released. In the evening Joseph relates a dream in the Seventies Hall in which his enemies, Foster and Higbee, are symbolized as two large snakes who are locked together so tightly that they cannot get any power over Joseph. The dream also refers to the plans of William and Wilson Law being overcome.

The *Warsaw Signal* carries a story about an anti-Mormon meeting held on the night of June 13 in which several resolutions are drawn up to immediately drive any sympathizers of the Saints from the state. The *Signal's* editor, Thomas C. Sharp, accuses Hyrum Smith of planning to destroy the *Signal* press and of threatening his own life. A committee is drawn up to "notify all persons in our township suspected of being the tools of the prophet to leave immediately on pain of instant vengeance." (HC 6:462-66.)

June 14, 1844

Joseph Smith, John M. Bernhisel, Sidney Rigdon, and others write letters to Governor Ford explaining their reasons for destroying the *Nauvoo Expositor* press. Joseph explains that the city council had declared the press a nuisance and had carried out the order to destroy it "without riot, noise, tumult, or confusion." He asks the governor to be aware of the many slanderous stories going around about " 'mob at Nauvoo,' . . . 'blood and thunder,' . . . 'two men were killed.' " Joseph reaffirms his willingness to report before Judge Pope or any other legal tribunal at Springfield. (HC 6:466-71.)

June 15, 1844

Rumors reach Joseph that men and arms are being gathered at Carthage and Warsaw. He tells the brethren that "when they gave up their arms, to give up their lives with them as dearly as possible." (HC 6:471-72.)

June 16, 1844

Sunday. Joseph preaches, but is interrupted by a severe rainstorm. He explains the doctrine of the plurality of the Gods, stating, "It is all over the face of the Bible. . . . I say there are Gods many and Lords many, but to us only one, and we are to be in subjection to that one, and no man can limit the bounds or the eternal existence of eternal time." He also testifies, "I have reason to think that the Church is being purged. I saw Satan fall from heaven." (HC 6:473-79.)

Joseph meets with forty men from Madison who have come to inquire about the *Nauvoo Expositor* episode. He explains it and they are satisfied; then he asks them to go throughout the area to explain the truth of the situation to their neighbors. Joseph writes Governor Ford, citing the rumors of mobs of 1500 men gathering at Carthage to attack Nauvoo. He states that the Nauvoo Legion is at Ford's service if he needs it. Joseph exchanges letters with Saints who are living outside of Nauvoo and have been troubled by mobs recently. He calls a couple of dozen men throughout the area to go on missions to calm the public concerning the Mormons. He also issues a proclamation stating, "If, then, our charter gives us the power to decide what shall be a nuisance, and cause it to be removed, where is the offense? What law is violated?" (HC 6:479-85.)

June 17, 1844

Hyrum Smith writes to Brigham Young and explains the recent great excitement around Nauvoo with the mass meetings by mobs drawing up resolutions to "utterly exterminate the Saints." He recommends that the Twelve return without delay and advises, "A word to the wise is sufficient; and a little powder, lead and a good rifle can be packed in your luggage very easy without creating any suspicion." (HC 6:486-87.)

Joseph and 15 others are arrested on this day on the charge of "riot." They appear before Daniel H. Wells (who will later be baptized) and are discharged. Stephen Markham brings warning that mobs are joining together all around Nauvoo in preparation to attack. Joseph notifies both the police and the Nauvoo Legion to be prepared. He hears a rumor that the Law brothers will try to burn the *Nauvoo Neighbor* office this night, so a strong police force is placed on the premise.

June 18, 1844

Joseph proclaims martial law in the city of Nauvoo. The Legion and the police force are ordered out, and the 5,000 men of the Nauvoo Legion line up close to the Mansion House. Joseph stands on the top of the frame of the building in full uniform to address them, which he does for an hour and a half. This is his last public oration. He notes that the Saints are innocent of the charges that are being put against them. But he says that as American citizens, it is time to stand up for their rights. He draws his sword and raises it to heaven and says, "I call God and angels to witness that I have unsheathed my sword with a firm and unalterable determination that this people shall have their legal rights, and be protected from mob violence, or my blood shall be spilt upon the ground like water, and my body consigned to the silent tomb. . . . I do not regard my own life. I am ready to be offered a sacrifice for this people; for what can our enemies do? Only kill the body, and their power is then at an end. Stand firm, my friends; never flinch. Do not seek to save our lives, for he that is afraid to die for the truth, will lose eternal life." (HC 6:498-500.)

June 19, 1844

With a posse, David Bettisworth travels toward Nauvoo to arrest Joseph again. As he tries to pick up men on his way, they refuse to go with him, saying his orders are forgeries. Joseph orders General Dunham to put guards completely around the city and on all roads leading out of town. All powder and lead are readied for use by the legion. Joseph estimates that there are approximately 600 men surrounding Nauvoo at this time.

June 20, 1844

At daybreak Joseph inspects the city with Major-General Dunham to plan out the strongest areas of defense. He writes a letter to President Tyler of the United States noting that in a situation like this—of "insurrection and rebellion"—he has constitutional powers to interfere and stop the slaughter. Several Saints file petitions that Aaron Johnson, a supposed justice of the peace, has been trying to recruit them as well as everyone else to join his mob. At this time only two of the apostles are in Nauvoo—John Taylor and Willard Richards. Joseph writes to the others of the Twelve, who are on missions in the East, telling them to come home immediately. Theodore Turley asks Joseph if he should set up an ammunition supply in one of the buildings. Joseph answers, "I told him in confidence that there would not be a gun fired on our part during the fuss." He also tells his brother Hyrum to take his family to Cincinnati. Hyrum answers, "Joseph, I can't leave you." Joseph says, "I wish I could get Hyrum out of the way, so that he may live to avenge my blood." (HC 6:507-20.)

Willard Richards writes James Arlington Bennett on behalf of Joseph, asking for his help, stating, "All the horrors of Missouri's murders are crowding thick upon us. . . . [We] invite you to come to our assistance with as many volunteers as you can bring. . . . Will you come? . . . If you do not, your turn may come next; and where will it cease?" (DH 398.)

June 21, 1844

Gov. Ford finally arrives in Carthage to get a closer look at the situation. Ford realizes the violent anti-Mormon feeling around and says that even the non-Mormons who wanted to compromise, called "Jack Mormons," have been threatened by the anti-Mormon mobs. Ford writes to Joseph, stating that he needs more information. Joseph immediately assembles several affidavits to send to Gov. Ford, and expresses his wish that Ford come to Nauvoo.

June 22, 1844

Joseph sends a letter to Gov. Ford containing all the affidavits showing the Saints' side of the conflict. The Nauvoo Legion continues to prepare to defend Nauvoo, digging ditches, pitching tents, and setting up camp. Late the night before, John Taylor and Dr. John M. Bernhisel had gone to Carthage to meet with Ford, and had spent a terrified night, as the town was full of anti-Mormon rejoicing and celebration. Early on the morning of June 22, Taylor and Bernhisel meet with Ford, but find him surrounded by William and Wilson Law, the Higbees, the Fosters, etc. Whenever Taylor or Bernhisel try to explain their side of the *Expositor* story, they are immediately contradicted, and communication is almost totally blocked. After a five-hour wait, they receive a letter from Gov. Ford to take to Joseph Smith. It states that Joseph has committed one illegality after another and should plan to come to Carthage at once. Ford says, "I will also guarantee the safety of all such persons as may thus be brought to this place from Nauvoo either for trial or as witnesses for the accused." Joseph begins to write a reply to Ford, having decided that only the United States president, John Tyler, could truly decide the legality in a matter like this. He ends his letter to Ford with the statement, "We again say, if anything wrong has been done on our part, and we know of nothing, we will make all things right if the Government will give us the opportunity. Disperse the mob, and secure to us our constitutional privileges, that our lives may not be endangered when on trial." However, the more Joseph thinks about Ford's reply, the more he realizes, "There is no mercy—no mercy here." Hyrum adds, "No; just as sure as we fall into their hands we are dead men."

Unsure of what to do, Joseph gets a sudden idea. "It is clear to my mind what to do. All they want is Hyrum and myself. . . . Let them search; they will not harm you in person or property, and not even a hair of your head. We will cross the river tonight, and go away to the West." Joseph prepares to cross the river, and as his final recorded quote in his personal life's record, he writes, "I told Stephen Markham that if I and Hyrum were ever taken again we should be massacred, or I was not a prophet of God. I want Hyrum to live to avenge my blood, but he is determined not to leave me." (HC 6:525-46. HC 6:546 and PHC xiii-xvi state that, in regard to Joseph's final quotes, Hyrum was to be ordained to succeed Joseph as prophet, if he had not insisted on dying with him.)

The Prophet prepares to flee to the West, and to put his and Hyrum's families on the *Maid of Iowa*. Joseph, Hyrum, and Willard Richards wait on the banks of the Mississippi and as they do, they instruct W.W. Phelps to take their families to Cincinnati, and from there to petition the president of the United States. At midnight, Joseph, Hyrum, Willard Richards, and Orrin Porter Rockwell get in the boat, and at 2 A.M. Rockwell rows them across the Mississippi in a leaky skiff. Hyrum and Joseph bail water all the way.

June 23, 1844

Sunday. They reach the Iowa side at daybreak. Joseph immediately writes Emma a note asking her to let him know her whereabouts. They send Rockwell back across the river. He finds Nauvoo full of confusion, with people unsure whether to defend or flee the city. A posse arrives to arrest Joseph, but they cannot find him. When the news that he has fled fills the town, many who had thought themselves in great danger now consider him a coward. (Gov. Ford later says that he thought Joseph had taken the best solution.) Dr. Bernhisel and Reynolds Cahoon cross the river to see Joseph. At 1 P.M. Emma sends Porter Rockwell back across the river to beg Joseph to return to Nauvoo. Reynolds Cahoon and others accuse Joseph of cowardice, holding that, inasmuch as Gov. Ford has promised him a fair trial, he has nothing to worry about. When Joseph hears that he is considered a coward, he says, "If my life is of no value to my friends it is of none to myself. . . . What shall I do?" Rockwell says, "You are the oldest and ought to know best; and as you make your bed, I will lie with you." Joseph asks Hyrum for advice. Hyrum says, "Let us go back and give ourselves up, and see the thing out." After a few moments, Joseph says, "If you go back I will go with you, but we shall be butchered." Hyrum says, "No, no; let us go back and put our trust in God, and we shall not be harmed. The Lord is in it. If we live or have to die, we will be reconciled to our fate." Joseph writes a letter to Ford stating that he will give himself up. They head back in the afternoon, but Joseph says, "It is of no use to hurry, for we are going back to be slaughtered." He desires to speak to his people one more time, and Rockwell offers to get them out by starlight, but when Joseph sees his family, he decides to spend the evening with them. (HC 6:548-52.)

June 24, 1844

Monday. Sidney Rigdon, having prophesied that Joseph would die and that Nauvoo would fall, leaves for Pittsburgh with his family.

4:00 A.M. Jedediah M. Grant and Theodore Turley reach Nauvoo from Carthage with a message from an angry Gov. Ford that Joseph must be in Carthage by 10:00 A.M., and that he would not be given an escort by the state to protect him.

6:30 A.M. Joseph and the seventeen others named on the arrest warrant (charged with riot) ride from Nauvoo with several others. As they pass the temple, Joseph says, "This is the loveliest place and the best people under the heavens; little do they know the trials that await them." Joseph tells Daniel H. Wells, "I wish you to cherish my memory, and not think me the worst man in the world either." (HC 6:554.)

9:50 A.M. They are met by Captain Dunn and a militia of 60, four miles west of Carthage. Joseph says, "Do not be alarmed. . . . They can only kill the body." Dunn brings an order from Ford that all state arms of the Nauvoo Legion are to be turned over. Joseph sends one of his men to carry out the order. He then says, "I am going like a lamb to the slaughter, but I am calm as a summer's morning. I have a conscience void of offense toward God and toward all men. If they take my life I shall die an innocent man, and my blood shall cry from the ground for vengeance, and it shall be said of me 'He was murdered in cold blood!' " Captain Dunn then requests that Joseph return to Nauvoo and aid in the surrendering of the arms. (HC 6:554-55.)

2:30 P.M. Joseph and his men reach Nauvoo and help in gathering the arms at the Masonic Hall. The Nauvoo citizens are frightened and respond very unwillingly.

6:00 P.M. Three cannons and 200 firearms (although rumors claim 30 cannons and 600 firearms) are collected. Joseph goes twice to bid farewell to his family. Before he leaves Emma the last time, she requests a blessing from him. He tells her to write the best one she can think of and he will sign it. In her long handwritten letter, she requests a "fruitful, active mind," "the spirit of discernment," "wisdom to bring up all the children . . . in such a manner that they will be useful ornaments in the kingdom of God," "prudence that I may not through ambition abuse my body and cause it to become old and care-worn, but that I may wear a cheerful countenance," and several other things. Tradition says that after this Emma did not see Joseph again. (More complete versions are in BYS, W '74, 216; and DH 350.) Joseph finally leaves for Carthage. At the Masonic Hall, he says, "Boys, if I don't come back, take care of yourselves; I am going like a lamb to the slaughter." When he passes his farm he says, "If some of you had got such a farm and knew you would not see it any more, you would want to take a good look at it for the last time." He later tells Hyrum, privately, "Do not go another foot, for they say they will kill you, if you go to Carthage." When the others ride up, they continue their ride to Carthage. (HC 6:558.)

9:00 P.M. They stop at a house four miles west of Carthage for 30 minutes and eat.

11:55 P.M. They reach Carthage and go to Hamilton's tavern. The town is full of more than 1400 drinking, celebrating, excited militia troops from nearby towns, including 30 Carthage Greys. They shout curses and threats at the Mormons, until Gov. Ford leans out the window and says, "I know your great anxiety to see Mr. Smith. . . . You shall have that privilege tomorrow morning, as I will cause him to pass before the troops upon the square." The Laws, Higbee, and others are also at Hamilton's tavern. (HC 6:559-60.)

June 25, 1844   Tuesday

8:00 A.M. Joseph and Hyrum are arrested for treason by Constable David Bettisworth.

8:30 A.M.	The troops fall in line in the public square to listen to an excited speech by Gov. Ford.
9:15 A.M.	Gov. Ford marches Joseph in front of a line of soldiers.
9:53 A.M.	Joseph, Hyrum, Elders Richards, Taylor, and Phelps, and Gen. Deming march in front of the Carthage Greys and the other soldiers. Deming introduces Joseph and Hyrum as "general," at which time the soldiers break into shouting and throwing their hats and swords. Gov. Ford tells the soldiers that they shall have "full satisfaction." (HC 6:564.)
10:30 A.M.	News reaches the hotel that the Carthage Greys have revolted and have been put under guard by Gen. Deming.
10:50 A.M.	The Greys are restored to order.
11:15 A.M.	News arrives that the Warsaw militia has marched to Carthage.
12:48 P.M.	Joseph tells Gov. Ford that he wants Nauvoo to be protected; he has heard rumors that the apostates are going there to plunder.
1:30 P.M.	Mark Aldrich visits Joseph.
2:30 P.M.	Gov. Ford tells Joseph he has sent a man to protect Nauvoo. Joseph writes Emma expressing hope of an early release. He also writes Orrin Porter Rockwell, warning him to stay away from Carthage and not allow himself to be arrested.
3:00 P.M.	Joseph asks several military officers if they think he looks like a desperate character. They answer that they cannot see into his heart. He replies, "Very true, gentlemen, you cannot see what is in my heart, and you are therefore unable to judge me. . . . I can see what is in your hearts, and will tell you what I see. I can see that you thirst for blood, and nothing but my blood will satisfy you. It is not for crime of any description that I and my brethren are thus continually persecuted. . . . You and the people thirst for blood. I prophesy, in the

name of the Lord, that you shall witness scenes of blood and sorrow to your entire satisfaction. Your souls shall be perfectly satiated with blood, and many of you who are now present shall have an opportunity to face the cannon's mouth from sources you think not of. . . . They shall seek for peace, and shall not be able to find it. Gentlemen, you will find what I have told you to be true." (HC 6:565-66, CHC 2:256-57, 270-73 records the fulfillment of this prophecy.)

3:48 P.M. Joseph hears that the apostates have said "that there was nothing against these men; the law could not reach them but powder and ball would, and they should not go out of Carthage alive." He, Hyrum, and thirteen others are taken before Robert F. Smith, a justice of the peace and captain of the Carthage Greys. H.T. Reid and James W. Woods defend the Mormons and argue that this should be a civil, not a criminal, case. (HC 6:566-68.)

5:00 P.M. Bail is set at $500 each ($7,500 total). The Saints claim that the judge is trying to set bail at a higher amount than they can afford, but the amount is paid, and the defendants are freed.

6:00 P.M. Captain Dan Jones says he has overheard Wilson Law say that after so much work to get Joseph here alive, they will arrest him on one charge after another and will not allow him to leave. Jones tells Joseph that he witnessed Joseph H. Jackson touch his pistol and say, "the balls are in there that will decide his case." (HC 6:568-69.)

7:30 P.M. Most of the brethren leave for Nauvoo. Joseph and Hyrum go to Gov. Ford for an interview.

8:00 P.M. Constable Bettisworth arrives with a mittimus, a warrant committing Joseph and Hyrum to jail on a charge of treason (a different charge from the one for which they had paid bail). Joseph's lawyers, Reid and Woods, argue that such an order without a preliminary investigation or a possibility of paying bail is illegal. Woods requests that he be given time to appeal the order to Gov. Ford. Bettisworth says he will wait five minutes.

9:00 P.M. Woods returns from Gov. Ford, saying that Ford has told him that an executive cannot interfere in a civil judicial process; therefore he will not intervene. Robert F. Smith, who issued the illegal mittimus, is also a captain of the Carthage Greys, and this makes the Mormons highly suspicious of the fairness and legality of these proceedings. Governor Ford has told John Taylor that although he is sorry the order has been issued, "he thought that the best thing to be done in the premises was to let the law take its course. . . . It was a matter over which he had no control, as it belonged to the judiciary; that he, as the executive could not interfere with their proceedings, and that he had no doubt but that they would be immediately dismissed." Justice Robert F. Smith later says he committed Joseph to jail because he did not think the hotel was safe. Captain Dunn and 20 men escort Joseph and Hyrum together with Willard Richards, John Taylor, John P. Greene, Stephen Markham, and four others to jail. As they march through town, they fight off several drunks with their walking sticks. The jailor, George W. Stigall, puts them in the small criminal's cell, but later moves them to the large, more comfortable debtor's apartment, where the ten men spend the night. (This room, however, has several windows and a door that cannot be locked, and is therefore less secure.) (HC 6:570-74.)

June 26, 1844   *Wednesday*

7:00 A.M. The prisoners eat breakfast.

7:30 A.M. Joseph sends several messages to Gov. Ford, requesting a change of venue to Quincy, Adams County.

239

8:00 A.M. The jailor tells Joseph that Carthage citizens expected 9,000 people to attack Nauvoo, but only 200 show up.

8:10 A.M. Joseph again sends a messenger to Ford requesting an interview.

8:30 A.M. Messengers return to Joseph stating that Gov. Ford has apologized and will come for an interview very soon.

8:50 A.M. Mr. Reid arrives, gives Joseph some legal advice, and lists the witnesses he plans to call in the trial.

9:27 A.M. Gov. Ford arrives at the jail. For over an hour Joseph and Ford discuss the recent problems, each giving his point of view. Joseph says, "If it is deemed that we did a wrong in destroying that press, we refuse not to pay for it. We are desirous to fulfill the law in every particular, and are responsible for our acts." He says he had not wanted to come to Carthage, the most dangerous of all places, for trial. Gov. Ford doubts if Joseph is in any danger in Carthage or anywhere else, but promises that if he goes to Nauvoo tomorrow, he will take Joseph with him. (HC 6:576-85. For the actual legality of Joseph's action against the *Nauvoo Expositor,* see ULR 862-903.)

10:15 A.M. Gov. Ford leaves, after again promising the protection of Joseph.

12:00 noon Joseph remarks, "I have had a good deal of anxiety about my safety since I left Nauvoo, which I never had before when I was under arrest. I could not help those feelings, and they have depressed me." Joseph and the others take turns preaching to the guards, many of whom become so impressed with Joseph's innocence that they feel guilty guarding him, so they leave. Joseph also comments, "Could my brother, Hyrum, but be liberated, it would not matter so much about me. Poor Rigdon, I am glad he has gone to Pittsburg out of the way; were he to preside he would lead the Church to destruction in less than five years." Joseph's lawyer argues for his release but is turned down. (They cannot be freed until bail is set, and bail for treason, a capital crime, can only be set by a circuit judge. The nearest is at least a day's ride away.) (HC 6:592-93.)

12:30 P.M. Dr. Bernhisel arrives at the jail.

1:00 P.M. Several threats—"If the law will not reach them, powder and ball must"—are circulated in the presence of Gov. Ford during lunch. (HC 6:594.)

2:30 P.M. Constable Bettisworth demands that the jailor, Stigall, release the prisoners to him. Stigall refuses on the grounds that by law the justice of the peace can only imprison people, not free them. Threats are made to enforce Justice Robert F. Smith's orders by bringing out his troops, the Carthage Greys. Joseph sends a message to Gov. Ford.

2:40 P.M. Dr. Bernhisel returns from Ford and says that the governor is doing all he can.

3:00 P.M. Joseph writes his lawyers concerning Bettisworth's recent attempt to take the prisoners.

3:40 P.M. The constable arrives with the Carthage Greys and demands with threats that Joseph be turned over to him. He is. They march Joseph and Hyrum to the courthouse. Joseph, expecting to be shot momentarily, locks arms with the worst mobocrat he can find, and marches with him.

4:45 P.M. After almost an hour of debate about legalities, it is determined that court will be postponed until noon the next day. Subpoenas are granted to get witnesses from Nauvoo (20 miles away).

5:30 P.M. Joseph and Hyrum return to jail with others. Patriarch John Smith, Joseph's uncle, having traveled through several threatening mobs, visits Joseph.

6:00 P.M. Joseph receives several letters.

7:45 P.M. They eat supper.

8:00 P.M.	Lawyers Woods and Reid and John P. Greene visit the jail and say that the governor has decided to leave for Nauvoo at 8 o'clock the next morning with all his troops except his 50 most trustworthy. The trial is therefore postponed until June 29. During this time Dan Jones and Stephen Markham try to repair the door latch so it can be shut securely in case of attack.
9:00 P.M.	Woods, Reid, and Greene return to Hamilton's hotel.
9:15 P.M.	John Taylor prays. Willard Richards, Stephen Markham, Dan Jones, John S. Fullmer, and John Taylor stay with Joseph and Hyrum. Hyrum reads from the Book of Mormon about imprisoned prophets, and Joseph bears his testimony to the guards about the Book of Mormon, the restoration of the gospel, the administration of angels, and the reestablishment of the kingdom of God on earth. He claims these are the real reasons for which he is imprisoned, not because he has broken any law. Willard Richards, to whom Joseph has been dictating during the day, continues to write until the last candle goes out. When a gun fires later in the night, Joseph leaves his bed and lies on the floor between Dan Jones and John Fullmer. During the next few minutes he makes such comments as, "Lay your head on my arm for a pillow, Brother John. . . . I would like to see my family again. . . . I would to God that I could preach to the Saints in Nauvoo once more." Fullmer tries to cheer him up. Willard Richards takes Joseph's place on the one bed and falls asleep. Joseph asks Dan Jones, "Are you afraid to die?" Dan replies, "Has that time come, think you? Engaged in such a cause I do not think that death would have many terrors." Joseph replies, "You will yet see Wales, and fulfill the mission appointed you before you die." (HC 6:600-601.)

June 27, 1844   *Thursday*

5:00 A.M.   John P. Greene and W.W. Phelps visit the jail on their way to Nauvoo.

5:30 A.M.   The prisoners arise. Joseph asks Dan Jones to find out about the gunshot last night. Jones talks with Frank Worrel, one of the Carthage Greys. Worrel says, "We have had too much trouble to bring Old Joe here to let him ever escape alive, and unless you want to die with him you had better leave before sundown. . . . You'll see that I can prophesy better than Old Joe, for neither he nor his brother, nor anyone who will remain with them will see the sun set today." Joseph sends Dan Jones to report what he has heard to Gov. Ford. On the way, Jones hears others plotting to kill Joseph. Ford tells him he is "unnecessarily alarmed" and claims that "the people are not that cruel." Jones also records that he demanded that Ford protect Joseph because Joseph was a Master Mason, and promised that if Joseph was killed, he would testify to the world that Ford knew about it beforehand. Gov. Ford also refuses to give passes to Jones and others, so they cannot pass in and out of the prison. (HC 6:602-4.)

7:00 A.M.   Joseph and four others eat breakfast.

8:00 A.M.   Cyrus H. Wheelock receives a pass from Gov. Ford.

8:20 A.M.   Joseph writes to Emma. He tells her that he will not be going to Nauvoo with Gov. Ford as he had previously assumed. He adds a postscript, "I am very much resigned to my lot, knowing I am justified, and have done the best that could be done. Give my love to the children and all my friends." (HC 6:605.)

9:40 A.M.   Mr. Woods and Mr. Reid come to the jail. Dr. Southwick reports that he was in a meeting in which delegates from almost every state had met to discuss the best way to stop Joseph Smith's political career, saying, "If he did not

243

get into the Presidential chair this election, he would be sure to the next time." Captain Dunn and his men are ordered to accompany Gov. Ford to Nauvoo. The Carthage Greys are selected by Ford to guard the prisoners in the jail. Ford disbands over 1200 other men at Carthage and a couple of thousand camped eight miles away. Ford tells Cyrus H. Wheelock, "I was never in such a dilemma in my life; but your friends shall be protected. . . . In this *pledge* I am not alone; I have obtained the *pledge* of the whole of the army. . . ." Wheelock visits the prison and slips a pepper box revolver into Joseph's pocket. Joseph gives a single-barrel pistol to his brother Hyrum and says, "You may have use for this." Hyrum answers, "I hate to use such things or to see them used." Joseph replies, "So do I, but we may have to, to defend ourselves." Hyrum takes the pistol. Joseph then says that even Jesus did not at times think it wise to reveal all he knew because of physical danger. "So it is with the Church. . . . We have the revelation of Jesus, and the knowledge within us is sufficient to organize a righteous government upon the earth, and to give universal peace to all mankind . . . but we lack the physical strength, as did our Savior when a child, to defend our principles, and we have of necessity to be afflicted, persecuted and smitten, and to bear it patiently until Jacob is of age, then he will take care of himself." A list of proposed witnesses is read, but Alpheus Cutler and Reynolds Cahoon are crossed off. Dr. Richards records notes dictated by Joseph and Hyrum and addressed to their families. Joseph relates a dream he had in Kirtland in which his enemies tried to destroy him but ended up destroying themselves. Both Joseph and Hyrum bear their testimonies of the divinity of the work. Joseph writes a postscript to Emma, telling her that the troups have been disbanded and Governor

Ford will come to Nauvoo to give a speech. He then sends his letter off. John P. Greene tells Gov. Ford that there is a conspiracy to take the lives of Joseph and Hyrum. Ford replies, "Marshal Greene, you are too enthusiastic." One journal records that Joseph also sent a note to Jonathan Dunham requesting that the Nauvoo troups come to Joseph's rescue. Dunham, however, either never received or never acted upon the request. (HC 6:605-11.)

10:30 A.M. Gov. Ford and his troops leave for Nauvoo. Joseph sends Dan Jones to request a pass for Willard Richards.

11:00 A.M. John S. Fullmer leaves for Nauvoo to help Cyrus Wheelock gather witnesses for the upcoming trial. James W. Woods, Joseph's lawyer, leaves Carthage for Nauvoo.

11:20 A.M. Dan Jones returns with the pass for Willard Richards, but cannot get one for himself.

11:30 A.M. Almon W. Babbitt comes to the jail and reads a letter from Oliver Cowdery. Joseph and others try to get Dan Jones past the guards but cannot.

12:20 P.M. Joseph sends a letter to a lawyer named Browning asking him to be Joseph's attorney in the upcoming trial. Babbitt gives the letter to Jones and directs him to take it to Quincy, Ill. The guard thinks it is a letter for Nauvoo and claims that "Old Joe" has sent orders to raise the Nauvoo Legion. Dozens of men try to ambush Jones to get the letter, but he accidentally goes the wrong way and eludes them.

1:15 P.M. Joseph, Hyrum, Willard Richards, John Taylor, and Stephen Markham eat lunch.

1:30 P.M. Willard Richards gets an upset stomach. When Stephen Markham is sent out for medicine, the Carthage Greys throw him on a horse and run him out of town at bayonet point.

3:15 P.M. The guards become "more severe" and argue among themselves. John Taylor sings the full seven verses of "A Poor Wayfaring Man of Grief." Joseph asks him to sing it again, but John does not feel like doing so. Hyrum tells him, "Oh, never mind: commence singing and you will get the spirit of it." He sings. Hyrum reads extracts of Josephus. (HC 6:614-15; CHC 2:284.)

4:00 P.M. The guard is changed. Only eight guards remain at the jail, while the remainder camp a quarter mile away. (Some later testified that by this time the jailers' guns were only loaded with blanks.) Gov. Ford arrives in Nauvoo. The Saints assemble and he speaks to them. Among other things he says, "A great crime has been done by destroying the *Expositor* press and placing the city under martial law, and a severe atonement must be made, so prepare your minds for the emergency. . . . I know there is a great prejudice against you on account of your peculiar religion, but you ought to be praying Saints, not military Saints. Depend upon it, a little more misbehavior from the citizens, and the torch, which is already lighted, will be applied, the city may be reduced to ashes, and extermination would inevitably follow." At the end of his speech he asks for a show of hands as to who would obey the law even in opposition to the Prophet, and the Saints vote unanimously that they would sustain the law. (CHC 2:278-79; HC 6:623.)

4:15 P.M. Joseph talks to the guards about Joseph H. Jackson, William Law, Wilson Law, and others.

5:00 P.M. Jailor Stigall returns to the jail and tells the prisoners that Stephen Markham has been run out of town. Stigall suggests that the prisoners would be safer in the cell, and Joseph says that they will go in after supper. About this time a mob of about 150, made up of the disbanded militia and others, begins to march to Carthage chanting:

"Where now is the Prophet Joseph?
Where now is the Prophet Joseph?
Where now is the Prophet Joseph?
Safe in Carthage Jail!" (CHC 2:281.)
Joseph asks Willard Richards if he wants to go into the cell with him, and Richards answers, "Brother Joseph, you did not ask me to cross the river with you—you did not ask me to come to Carthage—you did not ask me to come to jail with you—and do you think I would forsake you now? But I will tell you what I will do; if you are condemned to be hung for treason, I will be hung in your stead, and you shall go free." Joseph says, "You cannot." Richards answers, "I will." The jailer's son brings in some water. The guard sends him for some wine. Soon afterwards, the guard brings in some wine and pipes. Joseph, John Taylor, and Willard Richards taste it and give the bottle back to the guard. (HC 6:616.)

5:16 P.M. The guard is called downstairs, where there is a sudden noise and a cry of surrender, followed by two or three gunshots. Willard Richards looks out the window and sees a hundred men with painted faces. The guards fire at the mob (some say they fired above the mob; others say their guns had blanks). The mob runs up the stairs, opens the door, and begins firing. At the same time shots come through the window. The four prisoners push the door shut, and try to knock down the guns sticking through the door. John Taylor uses Markham's large hickory cane, called "the rascal-beater," and Willard Richards uses Taylor's cane. Joseph grabs his six-shooter, and Hyrum grabs his single barrel. A bullet goes through the door and hits Hyrum on the left side of the nose. He falls back saying, "I am a dead man!" Another ball coming through the window hits him in the back almost simultaneously. Two other balls also hit

247

him as he falls dead. Joseph cries "Oh dear, brother Hyrum!" He fires his six-shooter down the stairway; two or three shots misfire. The mobbers retreat momentarily and then come back up the stairs and open fire again. John Taylor tries to fight off the rifles and bayonets with his cane, but he is hit time after time. He eventually falls and rolls under a bed for safety, but not until he is hit with five balls. One pierces his stopwatch, stopping it at 5:16. Joseph is also hit with one or two balls. He jumps to the window, pauses for a moment, and cries, "Oh Lord, my God!" and falls. Some reports state that he was still alive when he hit the ground, that he lifted himself up and was shot again. Others state that a man tried to cut off his head but his arm was paralyzed. The cry goes up that "he's leaped the window!"

The mob runs down the stairs to see him. During this time, Willard Richards pulls John Taylor's body into the next cell and hides him under a mattress. In all of the shooting, Richards has only been nicked in the ear, which, it is said, fulfills a prophecy given by Joseph over a year previously that "balls would fly around him like hail, and he should see his friends fall on the right and left, but . . . there should not be a hole in his garment." (HC 6:616-22. Several have argued that Joseph's final words were a Masonic distress signal. See CHC 2:287; BYS, W '68, 213-14; CEM 15-30.)

Some go back up into the room but cannot find Willard Richards or John Taylor. The cry goes up that "the Mormons are coming!" and the mob flees to the woods. Most of the town joins them before dawn. Eventually Richards carries Joseph's body back into jail. Ten of the twelve apostles at this time were in various cities in the East. Several of them record that they had definite feelings of depression at a certain time, and later found it to be the same time Joseph had been shot.

6:30 P.M. In Nauvoo, Gov. Ford and his men leave town after a great show of military discipline. Orrin Porter Rockwell later testified that he had overheard one of Ford's men telling him, "The deed is done before this time." Two or three miles from Nauvoo Ford meets two men riding to Nauvoo with the news. Ford holds them until he can get farther away from Nauvoo in case there is a fanatic reaction against him. (HC 6:623-24; HS 135.)

8:05 P.M. Willard Richards sends a notice to Nauvoo bearing the news of Joseph and Hyrum's death. On Elder Taylor's request he says that Taylor is wounded "not very badly." He also says that he believes it was a band of Missourians, and the citizens have left for fear of Mormon reprisals. "I promised them no!" At midnight Richards sends a second notice, once again urging the Saints not to take any vengeance. (HC 6:621-24.)

June 28, 1844

Willard Richards and Samuel H. Smith, Joseph's brother, take the bodies of Hyrum and Joseph back to Nauvoo in two wagons. They are taken to the Nauvoo Mansion, where the doors are closed and the thousands of mourners are told they will be able to see the bodies the next day. Dimick B. Huntington, William Marks, and William D. Huntington wash the bodies and dress them in white. Emma (four months pregnant) and Mary Fielding Smith and children are then admitted to see the bodies. Emma screams and falls back, and is caught by Dimick B. Huntington. She then falls forward onto Joseph's face and kisses him, calling him by name and begging him to speak to her once more. Mary Fielding Smith holds back her grief and keeps her composure. During this time Willard Richards and several others speak to eight or ten thousand Saints who have gathered, telling them to keep the peace and trust in the law to punish the assassins of Joseph and Hyrum.

June 29, 1844

Ten thousand people view the bodies throughout the day. The bodies are then removed from the caskets in private, bags of sand are put in their places, and the caskets are closed. A public funeral is held, with W.W. Phelps preaching the sermon. The caskets are buried in a prominent place. Around midnight the coffins containing the real bodies are buried in the basement of the unfinished Nauvoo House. The ground is smoothed over to hide the actual place, and a rainstorm that night helps eradicate the footprints completely. This is all done to prevent the desecration of the bodies by enemies. (In the fall, the bodies were moved and buried side by side near the Mansion. The bodies of Joseph's and Hyrum's deceased children were soon moved to be next to them.)

Epilogue

Thus ended the life of the Prophet Joseph Smith. But his death did not bring the demise of the Church his detractors had predicted. In many ways it further strengthened the unity of his followers. As the Church moved from the leadership of its founder to that of Brigham Young, a convert, Church members doubtless came to understand as never before that Jesus Christ is the leader of the Church, working through men He calls.

In the month and a half that followed the death of the Prophet, the Twelve gradually returned to Nauvoo. On August 8, 1844, a special meeting of the Church was held to determine who the new leader of the Church should be. Sidney Rigdon, who had returned to Nauvoo from Pittsburgh, preached for an hour and a half, presenting his claims to leadership. Then Brigham Young spoke, and, for many, became transfigured with the appearance and voice of Joseph Smith. Following the speeches a vote was taken, and the Saints unanimously voted to follow Brigham and the Twelve. A month later Sidney, still rebellious against the Twelve, was cut off from the Church.

But he was not alone in his apostasy. In the next few years, apostles William Smith, John E. Page, and Lyman Wight were among those who fell away and were excommunicated.

While the internal changes were taking place in the Church, persecution continued. Brigham Young had to go into hiding for a time to protect his life; the Nauvoo Charter was repealed on January 27, 1845; mobs burned 175 houses at Morley Settlement near Nauvoo in September 1845. Eventually the mobs drove the Saints from the area, taking over the town and the recently dedicated temple, but not before many of the Saints were able to receive their endowments.

Just a month after Joseph was killed, his younger brother Samuel died from overexertion and exposure suffered on the night of the martyrdom. On November 17, 1844, Emma bore Joseph's last son, David Hyrum Smith. In April 1845, at a general conference of the Church, Brigham Young proposed that Nauvoo be renamed "The City of Joseph." The motion was passed unanimously.

Perhaps the best final comment on the life of Joseph Smith was made by John Taylor:

"Joseph Smith, the Prophet and Seer of the Lord, has done more, save Jesus only, for the salvation of men in this world, than any other man that ever lived in it. In the short space of twenty years, he has brought forth the Book of Mormon, which he translated by the gift and power of God, and has been the means of publishing it on two continents; has sent the fulness of the everlasting gospel, which it contained, to the four quarters of the earth; has brought forth the revelations and commandments which compose this book of Doctrine and Covenants, and many other wise documents and instructions for the benefit of the children of men; gathered many thousands of the Latter-day Saints, founded a great city, and left a fame and name that cannot be slain. He lived great, and he died great in the eyes of God and his people; and like most of the Lord's anointed in ancient times, has sealed his mission and his works with his own blood." (D&C 135:3.)

Bibliography

Books

Allen, James B., and Alexander, Thomas G. *Manchester Mormons: The Journal of William Clayton, 1840-1842.* Santa Barbara: Peregrine Smith, 1974.

Allen, James B., and Leonard, Glen M. *The Story of the Latter-day Saints.* Salt Lake City: Deseret Book, 1976.

Anderson, Richard Lloyd. *Joseph Smith's New England Heritage.* Salt Lake City: Deseret Book, 1971.

Andrus, Hyrum L. *Joseph Smith and World Government.* Salt Lake City: Deseret Book, 1963.

———. *Joseph Smith: The Man and the Seer.* Salt Lake City: Deseret Book, 1976.

Andrus, Hyrum L., and Andrus, Helen Mae, comps. *They Knew the Prophet.* Salt Lake City: Bookcraft, 1976.

Arrington, Leonard J. *Charles C. Rich: Mormon General and Western Frontiersman.* Provo, Utah: Brigham Young University Press, 1974.

———. *From Quaker to Latter-day Saint: Bishop Edwin D. Woolley.* Salt Lake City: Deseret Book, 1976.

———. *Great Basin Kingdom: An Economic History of the Latter-day Saints, 1830-1900.* Cambridge, Massachusetts: Harvard University Press, 1958.

Arrington, Leonard J.; Fox, Feramorz Y.; May, Dean L. *Building the City of God: Community and Cooperation among the Mormons.* Salt Lake City: Deseret Book, 1976.

Backman, Milton V., Jr. *American Religions and the Rise of Mormonism.* Salt Lake City: Deseret Book, 1965.

Barrett, Ivan J. *Joseph Smith and the Restoration: A History of the Church to 1846.* Provo, Utah: Brigham Young University Press, 1973.

Barron, Howard H. *Orson Hyde: Missionary, Apostle, Colonizer.* Bountiful, Utah: Horizon Publishers, 1977.

Bennett, John C. *The History of the Saints: An Exposé of Joe Smith and Mormonism.* Boston: Leland & Whiting, 1842.

Berrett, William E. *The Restored Church.* Salt Lake City: Deseret Book, 1973.

Berrett, William E., and Burton, Alma P. *Readings in L.D.S. Church History; from Original Manuscripts.* 3 vols. Salt Lake City: Deseret Book, 1956.

Blake, Reed. *24 Hours to Martyrdom.* Salt Lake City: Bookcraft, 1973.

A Book of Commandments, for the Government of the Church of Christ, organized according to law, on the 6th of April, 1830. Zion (Independence, Mo.): W.W. Phelps & Co., 1833; reprint ed., Independence, Missouri: Herald House, 1972.

Brooks, Juanita. *John Doyle Lee: Zealot—Pioneer Builder—Scapegoat.* Glendale, California: Arthur H. Clark, 1973.

Burnett, Jerry, and Pope, Charles. *Nauvoo Classics: Mormon Collector Series Volume III.* Salt Lake City: Mormon Heritage Publishers, 1976.

Burton, Alma P., comp. *Discourses of the Prophet Joseph Smith.* Salt Lake City: Deseret Book, 1977.

Burton, Alma P. and Burton, Clea M. *Stories from Mormon History.* Salt Lake City: Deseret Book, 1976.

Cannon, George Q. *Life of Joseph Smith the Prophet.* Salt Lake City: Deseret Book, 1967.

Cheesman, Paul R. *The Keystone of Mormonism: Little Known Truths about the Book of Mormon.* Salt Lake City: Deseret Book, 1973.

A Collection of Sacred Hymns, for the Church of the Latter Day Saints, selected by Emma Smith. Kirtland, Ohio: F.G. Williams & Co. 1835; reprint ed., Independence, Missouri: Herald Heritage, 1973.

Corbett, Pearson H. *Hyrum Smith: Patriarch.* Salt Lake City: Deseret Book, 1976.

Crowther, Duane S. *The Prophecies of Joseph Smith.* Salt Lake City: Bookcraft, 1963.

Day, Robert B. *They Made Mormon History.* Salt Lake City: Deseret Book, 1973.

Doctrine and Covenants of the Church of the Latter Day Saints: carefully selected from the Revelations of God. Kirtland, Ohio: F.G. Williams & Co., 1835; reprint ed., Independence, Missouri: Herald House, 1971.

Evans, John Henry. *Joseph Smith: An American Prophet.* New York: Macmillan, 1943.

Faulkner, Harold Underwood. *American Economic History.* New York, Evanston, and London: Harper & Row, 1960.

Flake, Lawrence R. *Mighty Men of Zion: General Authorities of the Last Dispensation.* Salt Lake City: Karl D. Butler, 1974.

Flanders, Robert Bruce. *Nauvoo: Kingdom on the Mississippi.* Urbana: University of Illinois Press, 1966.

Ford, Thomas. *A History of Illinois from its Commencement as a State in 1818 to 1847.* Chicago: S.C. Griggs & Co., 1854.

Gibbons, Francis M. *Joseph Smith: Martyr, Prophet of God.* Salt Lake City: Deseret Book, 1977.

Gunn, Rodger S. *Mormonism: Challenge and Defense.* Salt Lake City: Hawkes Publications, 1973.

Hansen, Klaus J. *Quest for Empire: The Political Kingdom of God and the Council of Fifty in Mormon History.* Lincoln: University of Nebraska Press, 1974.

Hill, Donna. *Joseph Smith: The First Mormon.* Garden City, New York: Doubleday & Co., 1977.

Hirshson, Stanley P. *The Lion of the Lord: A Biography of Brigham Young.* New York: Alfred A. Knopf, 1969.

Jackson, Ronald Vern. *The Seer, Joseph Smith: His Education from the Most High.* Salt Lake City: Hawkes Publications, 1977.

Jenson, Andrew, comp. *Church Chronology: A Record of Important Events Pertaining to the History of the Church of Jesus Christ of Latter-day Saints.* Salt Lake City: 1914.

Journal of Discourses. 26 vols. Liverpool and London: F.D. Richards, 1855-1886; reprint ed., Salt Lake City, 1974.

Kirkham, Francis W. *A New Witness for Christ in America: The Book of Mormon.* 2 vols. Salt Lake City: Brigham Young University, 1960.

Lundwall, N.B., comp. *A Compilation Containing the Lectures on Faith.* Salt Lake City: N.B. Lundwall, n.d.

Madsen, Truman G. *Joseph Smith among the Prophets.* Salt Lake City: Deseret Book, 1966.

Matthews, Robert J. *"A Plainer Translation"; Joseph Smith's Translation of the Bible, A History and Commentary.* Provo, Utah: Brigham Young University Press, 1975.

McGavin, Cecil E. *Mormonism and Masonry.* Salt Lake City: Bookcraft, 1956.

_____. *Nauvoo the Beautiful.* Salt Lake City: Bookcraft, 1972.

McKiernan, F. Mark. *The Voice of One Crying in the Wilderness: Sidney Rigdon, Religious Reformer, 1793-1876.* Lawrence, Kansas: Coronado Press, 1971.

Miller, David E., and Miller, Della S. *Nauvoo: The City of Joseph.* Santa Barbara and Salt Lake City: Peregrine Smith, 1974.

Mulder, William, and Mortensen, Russell A., eds. *Among the Mormons.* Lincoln, Nebraska: University of Nebraska Press, 1973.

Nibley, Hugh. *Sounding Brass.* Salt Lake City: Bookcraft, 1963.

_____. *The Message of the Joseph Smith Papyri: An Egyptian Endowment.* Salt Lake City: Deseret Book, 1975.

_____. *The Myth Makers.* Salt Lake City: Bookcraft, 1961.

Nibley, Preston. *Brigham Young: The Man and His Work.* Salt Lake City: Deseret Book, 1960.

_____, comp. *The Witnesses of the Book of Mormon.* Salt Lake City: Deseret Book, 1973.

Oaks, Dallin H., and Hill, Marvin S. *Carthage Conspiracy.* Chicago, Illinois: University of Illinois Press, 1975.

O'Dea, Thomas F. *The Mormons.* Chicago, Illinois: The University of Chicago Press, 1957.

Pearl of Great Price Symposium. Provo, Utah; Brigham Young University Press, Nov. 22, 1975.

Pratt, Parley P. *Autobiography of Parley Parker Pratt.* Salt Lake City: Deseret Book, 1970.

The Relief Society General Board Association. *History of Relief Society, 1842-1966.* Salt Lake City: The General Board of Relief Society, 1966.

Roberts, Brigham H. *A Comprehensive History of the Church of Jesus Christ of Latter-day Saints,* 6 vols. Provo, Utah: Brigham Young University Press, 1965.

_____. *Joseph Smith, The Prophet-Teacher.* Salt Lake City:

The Deseret News, 1908; reprint ed., Princeton, New Jersey: The Deseret Club of Princeton University, 1967.

_____. *The Missouri Persecutions.* Salt Lake City: Bookcraft, 1965.

Schindler, Harold. *Orrin Porter Rockwell: Man of God, Son of Thunder.* Salt Lake City: University of Utah Press, 1966.

Smith, Hyrum M., and Sjodahl, Janne M. *The Doctrine and Covenants Commentary.* Salt Lake City: Deseret Book, 1951.

Smith, Joseph. *History of the Church of Jesus Christ of Latter-day Saints.* Edited by B.H. Roberts. 7 vols. Salt Lake City: The Church of Jesus Christ of Latter-day Saints, 1902-1932; reprint ed., Salt Lake City: Deseret Book, 1974, 1978.

Smith, Joseph Fielding. *Essentials in Church History.* Salt Lake City: Deseret Book, 1971.

_____, ed. *Teachings of the Prophet Joseph Smith.* Salt Lake City: Deseret Book, 1974.

_____. *Blood Atonement and the Origin of Plural Marriage.* Independence, Mo.: Press of Zion's Printing and Publishing Co., n.d.

Smith, Lucy Mack. *History of Joseph Smith by His Mother.* Salt Lake City: Bookcraft, 1958.

Stewart, F.L. *Exploding the Myth about Joseph Smith the Mormon Prophet.* New York: House of Stewart Publications, 1967.

Taylor, Samuel. *Nightfall at Nauvoo.* New York: Avon Publishers, 1973.

Todd, Jay M. *The Saga of the Book of Abraham.* Salt Lake City: Deseret Book, 1969.

Tullidge, Edward W. *Life of Joseph the Prophet.* New York: Tullidge & Crandall, 1878.

Watson, Elden J., ed. *The Orson Pratt Journals.* Salt Lake City: Elden Jay Watson, 1975.

West, Emerson Roy. *Profiles of the Presidents.* Salt Lake City: Deseret Book, 1972.

Whitney, Orson F. *Life of Heber C. Kimball.* Salt Lake City: Bookcraft, 1945.

Wood, Wilford C. *Joseph Smith Begins His Work, Vol. I: Book of Mormon 1830 First Edition.* U.S.A.: Wilford C. Wood, 1963.

_____. *Joseph Smith Begins His Work, Vol. II: The Book of Commandments, The Doctrine and Covenants, The Lectures on Faith, Fourteen Articles of Faith.* U.S.A.: Wilford C. Wood, 1962.

Youngreen, Buddy. *Joseph Smith, Sr. Family Reunion (souvenir program).* (Information based on the thesis "Joseph Smith, Sr., First Patriarch to the Church" by Earnest M. Skinner.) n.p.:n.d.

Zimmerman, Dean R. *I Knew the Prophets: An Analysis of the Letter of Benjamin F. Johnson to George F. Gibbs, Reporting Doctrinal Views of Joseph Smith and Brigham Young.* Bountiful, Utah: Horizon Publishers, 1976.

Dissertations and Theses

Bailey, Raymond T. "Emma Hale, Wife of the Prophet Joseph Smith." M.S. thesis, Brigham Young University, 1952.

Bowen, Walter D. "The Versatile W.W. Phelps: Mormon Writer, Educator, and Pioneer." M.S. thesis, Brigham Young University, 1958.

Godfrey, Kenneth W. "Causes of Mormon Non-Mormon Conflict in Hancock County, Illinois, 1839-1846." Ph.D. dissertation, Brigham Young University, 1967.

Van Alfen, Nicholas, "Porter Rockwell and the Mormon Frontier." M.A. thesis, Brigham Young University, 1938.

Periodicals

Abbott, John C. "Sources of Mormon History in Illinois, 1832-48; and a Bibliographic Note." *Dialogue: A Journal of Mormon Thought* 5 (Spring 1970):76-79.

Allen, James B., and Thorp, Malcolm R., "The Mission of the Twelve to England, 1840-41: Mormon Apostles and the Working Classes." *BYU Studies* 15 (Summer 1975):499-526.

Allen, James B. " 'We Had a Very Hard Voyage for the Season': John Moon's Account of the First Emigrant Company of British Saints." *BYU Studies* 17 (Spring 1977):339-40.

_____. "The Significance of Joseph Smith's First Vision, in Mormon Thought." *Dialogue: A Journal of Mormon Thought* 1 (Autumn 1966):29-46.

_____. "Eight Contemporary Accounts of Joseph Smith's

First Vision—What Do We Learn from Them?"
Improvement Era, April 1970, pp. 4-13.

Anderson, Richard L. "Circumstantial Confirmation of the
First Vision Through Reminiscences." *BYU Studies* 9
(Spring 1969):373-404.

──────. "Joseph Smith's New York Reputation Re-
appraised." *BYU Studies* 10 (Spring 1970):283-314.

──────. "The Impact of the First Preaching in Ohio." *BYU
Studies* 11 (Summer 1971):474-96.

──────. "New Data for Revising the Missouri 'Docu-
mentary History.' " *BYU Studies* 14 (Summer 1974):488-
501.

──────. "The Reliability of the Early History of Lucy and
Joseph Smith." *Dialogue: A Journal of Mormon Thought*
4 (Summer 1969): 13-28.

Andrus, Hyrum. " 'The Historical Joseph,' A Review of Joseph Smith the Mormon Prophet, by John J Stewart."
Dialogue: A Journal of Mormon Thought 1 (Winter
1966):123-25.

Arrington, Leonard J. "Religion and Economics in
Mormon History." *BYU Studies* 3 (Spring and Summer
1961):15-33.

──────. "James Gordon Bennett's 1831 Report on 'The
Mormonites.' " *BYU Studies* 10 (Spring 1970):353-64.

──────. "Church Leaders in Liberty Jail." *BYU Studies* 13
(Autumn 1972):20-26.

──────. "Oliver Cowdery's Kirtland, Ohio, 'Sketch Book.' "
BYU Studies 12 (Summer 1972):410-26.

Backman, Milton V., Jr. "Awakenings in the Burned-over
District: New Light on the Historical Setting of the First
Vision." *BYU Studies* 9 (Spring 1969):301-20.

──────. "A Non-Mormon View of the Birth of Mormonism
in Ohio." *BYU Studies* 13 (Spring 1972):306-11.

──────. "The Quest for a Restoration: The Birth of Mormonism in Ohio." *BYU Studies* 12 (Summer 1972):346-
64.

──────. "Truman Coe's 1836 Description of Mormonism."
BYU Studies 17 (Spring 1977): 347-54.

Baer, Klaus. "The Breathing Permit of Hor, A Translation
of the Apparent Source of the Book of Abraham."
Dialogue: A Journal of Mormon Thought 3 (Autumn
1968):109-34.

Berrett, LaMar C. "An Impressive Letter from the Pen of Joseph Smith." *BYU Studies* 11 (Summer 1971):517-23.

Birch, Debbie. "July 22, 1839: A Day of God's Power." *New Era,* March 1971, pp. 16-18.

Bitton, Davis. "Kirtland as a Center of Missionary Activity, 1830-1838." *BYU Studies* 11 (Summer 1971):497-516.

_____. "The Waning of Mormon Kirtland." *BYU Studies* 12 (Summer 1972):455-64.

Blair, Alma. "The Haun's Mill Massacre." *BYU Studies* 13 (Autumn 1972):62-67.

Bush, Lester E., Jr. "Mormonism's Negro Doctrine: An Historical Overview." *Dialogue: A Journal of Mormon Thought* 8 (Spring 1973):11-68.

_____. "The Spaulding Theory Then and Now." *Dialogue: A Journal of Mormon Thought* 10 (Autumn 1977):40-69.

Bushman, Richard L. "The Character of Joseph Smith: Insights from His Holographs." *Ensign,* April 1977, pp. 11-13.

_____. "The First Vision Story Revived." *Dialogue: A Journal of Mormon Thought* 4 (Spring 1969):82-93.

_____. "The Historians and Mormon Nauvoo." *Dialogue: A Journal of Mormon Thought* 5 (Spring 1970):51-62.

Cannon, Donald Q. "The King Follett Discourse: Joseph Smith's Greatest Sermon in Historical Perspective." *BYU Studies* 18 (Winter 1978):179-92.

Clark, James. "Joseph Smith and the Lebolo Egyptian Papyri." *BYU Studies* 8 (Winter 1968):195-203.

Crawley, Peter. "A Bibliography of the Church of Jesus Christ of Latter-day Saints in New York, Ohio, and Missouri." *BYU Studies* 12 (Summer 1972):465-537.

_____. "A Comment on Joseph Smith's Account of His First Vision and the 1820 Revival." *Dialogue: A Journal of Mormon Thought* 6 (Spring 1971):106-9.

_____. "Two Rare Missouri Documents." *BYU Studies* 14 (Summer 1974):502-27.

Crawley, Peter, and Anderson, Richard L. "The Political and Social Realities of Zion's Camp." *BYU Studies* 14 (Summer 1974):406-20.

Dunn, Richard J. "Dickens and the Mormons." *BYU Studies* 8 (Spring 1968):325-34.

Durham, Reed C., Jr. "Joseph Smith's Own Story of a Serious Childhood Illness." *BYU Studies* (Summer 1970):480-82.

———. "The Election Day Battle at Gallatin." *BYU Studies* 13 (Autumn 1972):36-61.

England, Eugene. "The Mormon Cross." *Dialogue: A Journal of Mormon Thought* 8 (Spring 1973):78-86.

Esplin, Ronald K. "Sickness and Faith, Nauvoo Letters." *BYU Studies* 15 (Summer 1975):425-34.

Evening and Morning Star, Independence, Missouri, June 1832 through September 1834, Kirtland, Ohio; reprint ed., West Germany, 1969.

Flake, Chad J. "The Newell K. Whitney Collection." *BYU Studies* 10 (Summer 1971):322-28.

Flanders, Robert Bruce. "The Kingdom of God in Illinois: Politics in Utopia." *Dialogue: A Journal of Mormon Thought* 5 (Spring 1970):26-36.

Foster, Lawrence. "A Little Known Defense of Polygamy from the Mormon Press in 1842." *Dialogue: A Journal of Mormon Thought* 14 (Winter 1974):21-34.

Gentry, Leland H. "Adam-ondi-Ahman: A Brief Historical Survey." *BYU Studies* 13 (Summer 1973): 553-76.

———. "The Danite Band of 1838." *BYU Studies* (Summer 1974): 421-50.

Godfrey, Kenneth W. "A New Look at the Alleged Little Known Discourse by Joseph Smith." *BYU Studies* 9 (Autumn 1968): 49-53.

———. "The Road to Carthage Led West." *BYU Studies* 8 (Winter 1968): 204-5.

———. "A Note on the Nauvoo Library and Literary Society." *BYU Studies* 14 (Spring 1974): 386-88.

———. "Some Thoughts Regarding an Unwritten History of Nauvoo." *BYU Studies* 15 (Summer 1975): 417-24.

Hale, Van. "The Doctrinal Impact of the King Follett Discourse." *BYU Studies* 18 (Winter 1978): 209-25.

Hartley, William G. "Ordained and Acting Teachers in the Lesser Priesthood, 1851-1883." *BYU Studies* 16 (Spring 1976): 375-98.

Hickman, Martin B. "The Political Legacy of Joseph Smith." *Dialogue: A Journal of Mormon Thought* 3 (Autumn 1968): 22-27.

Hill, Marvin S. "The Shaping of the Mormon Mind in New England and New York." *BYU Studies* 9 (Spring 1969): 351-72.

———. "Joseph Smith and the 1826 Trial: New Evidence

and New Difficulties." *BYU Studies* 12 (Winter 1972): 223-33.

_____. " 'The Manipulation of History,' A Review of 'Can We Manipulate the Past?' by Fawn Brodie." *Dialogue: A Journal of Mormon Thought* 5 (Autumn 1970): 96-99.

Hill, Marvin S.; Rooker, Keith C.; and Wimmer, Larry T. "The Kirtland Economy Revisited: A Market Critique of Sectarian Economics." *BYU Studies* 17 (Summer 1977): 391-476.

Howard, Grant S., and Tanner, Jerald. "The Source of the Book of Abraham Identified." *Dialogue: A Journal of Mormon Thought* 3 (Summer 1968): 92-98.

Howard, Richard P. "A Tentative Approach to the Book of Abraham." *Dialogue: A Journal of Mormon Thought* 3 (Summer 1968): 88-92.

Huntress, Keith. "Governor Thomas Ford and the Murderers of Joseph Smith." *Dialogue: A Journal of Mormon Thought* 4 (Summer 1969): 41-52.

Irving, Gordon. "The Law of Adoption: One Phase of the Development of the Mormon Concept of Salvation, 1830-1900." *BYU Studies* 14 (Spring 1974): 291-314.

Jackson, Richard H. "The Mormon Village: Genesis and Antecedents of the City of Zion Plan." *BYU Studies* 17 (Winter 1977): 223-40.

Jennings, Warren A., ed. "Two Iowa Postmasters View Nauvoo: Anti-Mormon Letters to the Governor of Missouri." *BYU Studies* 11 (Spring 1971): 275-92.

Jessee, Dean C. "The Writings of Joseph Smith's History." *BYU Studies* 11 (Summer 1971): 439-73.

_____. "The Original Book of Mormon Manuscript." *BYU Studies* 10 (Spring 1970): 259-78.

_____. "The Kirtland Diary of Wilford Woodruff." *BYU Studies* 12 (Summer 1972): 365-99.

_____. "The Early Accounts of Joseph Smith's First Vision." *BYU Studies* 9 (Spring 1969): 275-94.

_____. "Joseph Knight's Recollection of Early Mormon History." *BYU Studies* 17 (Autumn 1976): 29-39.

_____. "Howard Coray's Recollections of Joseph Smith." *BYU Studies* 17 (Spring 1977): 341-46.

Jessee, Dean C., and Hartley, William G. "Joseph Smith's Missionary Journal." *New Era*, Feb. 1974, pp. 34-36.

Kimball, James L., Jr. "A Wall to Defend Zion: The

Nauvoo Charter." *BYU Studies* 15 (Summer 1975): 491-97.

Kimball, Stanley B. "Heber C. Kimball and Family: the Nauvoo Years." *BYU Studies* 15 (Summer 1975): 447-79.

―――. "Thomas L. Barnes: Coroner of Carthage." *BYU Studies* 11 (Winter 1971): 141-47.

―――. "The Anthon Transcript: People, Primary Sources, and Problems." *BYU Studies* 10 (Spring 1970): 325-52.

―――. "Discovery: 'Nauvoo' Found in Seven States." *Ensign*, April 1973, pp. 21-23.

―――. "Nauvoo West: The Mormons of the Iowa Shore." *BYU Studies* 18 (Winter 1978): 132-42.

Larson, Stan. "Textual Variants in Book of Mormon Manuscripts." *Dialogue: A Journal of Mormon Thought* 10 (Autumn 1977): 8-30.

―――. "The King Follett Discourse: A Newly Amalgamated Text." *BYU Studies* 18 (Winter 1978): 193-208.

Lyon, T. Edgar. "Doctrinal Development of the Church During the Nauvoo Sojourn, 1839-1846." *BYU Studies* 15 (Summer 1975): 435-46.

―――. "The Current Restoration of Nauvoo, Illinois." *Dialogue: A Journal of Mormon Thought* 5 (Spring 1970): 13-25.

―――. "Independence, Missouri, and the Mormons, 1827-1833." *BYU Studies* 13 (Autumn 1972): 10-19.

Matthews, Robert J. "Adam-ondi-Ahman." *BYU Studies* 13 (Autumn 1972): 27-35.

Maynard, Gregory. "Alexander William Doniphan: Man of Justice." *BYU Studies* 13 (Summer 1973): 462-72.

Moody, Thurmon Dean. "Nauvoo's Whistling and Whittling Brigade." *BYU Studies* 15 (Summer 1975): 480-90.

McKiernan, F. Mark. "Sidney Rigdon's Missouri Speeches." *BYU Studies* 11 (Autumn 1970): 90-92.

―――. "David H. Smith: A Son of the Prophet." *BYU Studies* 18 (Winter 1978): 233-45.

Nibley, Hugh. "The Meaning of the Kirtland Egyptian Papers." *BYU Studies* 11 (Summer 1971): 350-99.

―――. "Prolegomena to Any Study of the Book of Abraham." *BYU Studies* 8 (Winter 1968): 171-78.

―――. "The Best Possible Test." *Dialogue: A Journal of Mormon Thought* 8 (Spring 1973): 73-77.

―――. "Phase One." *Dialogue: A Journal of Mormon*

Thought 3 (Summer 1968): 99-105.

Oaks, Dallin H. "The Suppression of the Nauvoo Expositor." *Utah Law Review* 9 (Winter 1965): 862-903.

Olson, Earl E. "The Chronology of the Kirtland Revelations." *BYU Studies* 11 (Summer 1971): 329-49.

Ord, Gayle Goble. "The Book of Mormon Goes to Press." *Ensign,* December 1972, pp. 66-70.

Parker, Richard A. "The Joseph Smith Papyri: A Preliminary Report." *Dialogue: A Journal of Mormon Thought* 3 (Summer 1968): 86-88.

――――, (translator). "The Book of Breathings (Fragment 1, the 'Sensen' Text, with Restorations from Louvre Papyrus 3284)." *Dialogue: A Journal of Mormon Thought* 3 (Summer 1968): 98-99.

Parkin, Max H. "Mormon Political Involvement in Ohio." *BYU Studies* 9 (Summer 1969): 484-502.

Partridge, Scott H. "The Failure of the Kirtland Safety Society." *BYU Studies* 12 (Summer 1972): 437-54.

Payne, Jaynann Morgan. "Eliza R. Snow, First Lady of the Pioneers." *Ensign,* Sept. 1973, pp. 62-67.

Peterson, Lauritz G. "The Kirtland Temple." *BYU Studies* 12 (Summer 1972): 400-409.

Poll, Richard D. " 'A Kingdom to Come,' A Review of *Quest for Empire: The Political Kingdom of God and the Council of Fifty in Mormon History,* by Klaus J. Hansen." *Dialogue: A Journal of Mormon Thought* 2 (Autumn 1967): 135-39.

――――. "Joseph Smith and the Presidency, 1844." *Dialogue: A Journal of Mormon Thought* 3 (Autumn 1968): 17-21.

Porter, Larry C. "Solomon Chamberlain—Early Missionary." *BYU Studies* 12 (Spring 1972): 314-18.

――――. "The Colesville Branch and the Coming Forth of the Book of Mormon." *BYU Studies* 10 (Spring 1970): 365-85.

――――. "William E. McLellan's Testimony of the Book of Mormon." *BYU Studies* 10 (Summer 1970): 485-87.

――――. "Reverend George Lane—Good 'Gifts,' Much 'Grace,' and Marked 'Usefulness.' " *BYU Studies* 9 (Spring 1969): 321-40.

Quinn, Michael D. "The Mormon Succession Crisis of 1844." *BYU Studies* 16 (Winter 1976): 187-233.

_____. "The Practice of Rebaptism at Nauvoo." *BYU Studies* 18 (Winter 1978): 226-32.

Rhodes, Michael Dennis, "A Translation and Commentary of the Joseph Smith Hypocephalus." *BYU Studies* 17 (Spring 1977): 259-79.

Rich, Russell R. "The Dogberry Papers and the Book of Mormon." *BYU Studies* 10 (Spring 1970): 315-20.

Richards, Paul C. "Missouri Persecutions: Petitions for Redress." *BYU Studies* 13 (Summer 1973): 520-43.

Rigdon, John Wickliffe. (Edited by Karl Keller.) " 'I Never Knew a Time When I Did Not Know Joseph Smith': A Son's Record of the Life and Testimony of Sidney Rigdon." *Dialogue: A Journal of Mormon Thought* 1 (Winter 1966): 15-42.

Sampson, Paul D., and Wimmer, Larry T. "The Kirtland Safety Society: The Stock Ledger Book and the Bank Failure." *BYU Studies* 12 (Summer 1972): 427-36.

Smith, Joseph, Jr. "General Smith's Views of the Powers and Policy of the Government of the United States." *Dialogue: A Journal of Mormon Thought* 3 (Autumn 1968): 28-34.

Snow, Eliza R. "Eliza R. Snow Letter from Missouri." *BYU Studies* 13 (Summer 1973): 544-52.

Sorenson, John L. "The 'Brass Plates' and Biblical Scholarship." *Dialogue: A Journal of Mormon Thought* 10 (Autumn 1977): 31-39.

Taylor, J. Lewis. "Joseph Smith the Prophet: A Self-Portrayal." *Ensign,* June 1973, pp. 40-44.

Thomasson, Gordon C. "Lester Bush's Historical Overview: Other Perspectives." *Dialogue: A Journal of Mormon Thought* 3 (Sept. 1973): 69-72.

Times and Seasons, Commerce, Illinois, November 1839 through February 15, 1846, City of Nauvoo, Illinois, photographic reproduction, n.d.

Ursenbach, Maureen. "Eliza R. Snow's Nauvoo Journal." *BYU Studies* 15 (Summer 1975): 391-416.

Walters, Wesley P., Reverend. "New Light on Mormon Origins from the Palmyra Revival." *Dialogue: A Journal of Mormon Thought* 4 (Spring 1969): 59-81.

_____. "A Reply to Dr. Bushman." *Dialogue: A Journal of Mormon Thought* 4 (Spring 1969): 94-100.

Watt, Ronald G. "Sailing 'The Old Ship Zion': The Life of

George D. Watt." *BYU Studies* 18 (Fall 1977): 48-65.

Williams, Frederick G. "Frederick Granger Williams of the First Presidency of the Church." *BYU Studies* 12 (Spring 1972): 243-60.

Wilson, John A. "A Summary Report." *Dialogue: A Journal of Mormon Thought* 3 (Summer 1968): 67-85.

Wirthlin, LeRoy S. "Joseph Smith's Surgeon." *Ensign,* March 1978, pp. 58-60.

———. "Nathan Smith (1762-1828) Surgical Consultant to Joseph Smith." *BYU Studies* 17 (Spring 1977): 319-37.

Woodward, Robert J. "Jesse Gause, Counselor to the Prophet." *BYU Studies* 15 (Spring 1975): 362-64.

Youngreen, Buddy. "The Death Date of Lucy Mack Smith: 8 July 1775-14 May 1856." *BYU Studies* 12 (Spring 1972): 318.

———. "Joseph and Emma: A Slide-Film Presentation." *BYU Studies* 14 (Winter 1974): 199-226.

Yorgason, Laurence M. "Preview on a Study of the Social and Geographical Origins of Early Mormon Converts, 1830-1845." *BYU Studies* 10 (Spring 1970): 279-82.

Zucker, Louis C. "Joseph Smith as a Student of Hebrew." *Dialogue: A Journal of Mormon Thought* 3 (Summer 1968): 41-55.

Index

268

151; funds donated for, 163; floor and seats of, 175; Joseph envisions design of, 213

Negroes, 180

New Portage, Ohio, 67

New York *Sun,* 200

Newel, Grandison, 99

Northern Times, 70

Norton, Ohio, 56

Norwich, Vermont, 2

"Old Standard," apostate group, 103, 105-6

Olive Leaf revelation, 37

Onandagus, 61

Packard, Noah, 75

Page, Hiram, 18

Palmyra, New York, 3

Papyri, Egyptian, 73, 82

Parrish, Warren, 100

Partridge, Edward, 20; called as bishop, 22; purchases land for Church, 29; Joseph writes to, 52; tarring and feathering of, 43

Passions, prophets are subject to, 79

Patriarchal blessings, 68

Patten, David W., 97, 108, 122

Peniston, William, 115

Peter, James, and John, 12

Petitions: taken to governor of Missouri, 45; sent to president of United States, 55; presented to Missouri state legislature, 127; sent to Congress, 205, 207-8

Phelps, William W., 15, 65, 72; Joseph receives revelation for, 24; sees vision of destroyer on waters, 26; Joseph sends "Olive Leaf" revelation to, 38; sings in tongues, 45; helps arrange Egyptian grammar, 73-74; is accused of land speculation, 97; is rejected as member of stake presidency, 108; confesses sins, 144

Philadelphia, Pennsylvania, 139, 140-41, 143, 147

Phrenology, 169, 203

Piexotto, Dr., 78, 80, 83

Plagues, 144

Plates of gold, 4, 6

Platform, political, of Joseph Smith, 213-14

Plural marriage, 25, 153, 175-76

Political motto of Church, 108-9

"Poor Wayfaring Man of Grief," 245-46

Pottawatamie Indians, 192, 194

Pratt, Orson, 18, 170, 174; Joseph receives revelation for, 19; publishes pamphlet, 147; excommunication of, 171, 172; rebaptism of, 181

Pratt, Parley P., 18; wonders at unseemly spiritual manifestations, 23; in Liberty jail, 126; receives change of venue, 134; escapes from prison, 135; publishes history of Missouri persecutions, 137; presides over conference in England, 168

Printing presses, destruction of, 43, 228

Prisoners, Church leaders taken as, 123

Pulsipher, Zera, 50

Quincy, Illinois, 129, 239

Quincy, Josiah, 224

Quorums of Church, confusion among, 86-87

Rancliff, Thomas, 190

Rattlesnakes, 59, 60, 63

Record keeping, importance of, 71

Reflector, the, 12, 14, 16

Relief Society, 162-63, 168, 174

Religious revivals, 3

Retribution, God's law of, 44

Revelations: Joseph begins to arrange, 17; false, 21; elders are challenged to imitate, 28; Saints decide to publish, 28-29; pseudonyms used in, 32

Rewards offered for Joseph Smith and Orrin Porter Rockwell, 174